RAIDING THE HEARTLAND

RAIDING THE HEARTLAND

AN AMERICAN STORY OF DEPORTATION AND RESISTANCE

WILLIAM D. LOPEZ

Foreword by Nicole L. Novak

Johns Hopkins University Press
Baltimore

© 2025 Johns Hopkins University Press
All rights reserved. Published 2025
Printed in the United States of America on acid-free paper
2 4 6 8 9 7 5 3 1

Johns Hopkins University Press
2715 North Charles Street
Baltimore, Maryland 21218
www.press.jhu.edu

Library of Congress Cataloging-in-Publication Data is available.

ISBN 978-1-4214-5370-5 (hardcover)
ISBN 978-1-4214-5371-2 (ebook)

A catalog record for this book is available from the British Library.

Special discounts are available for bulk purchases of this book. For more information, please contact Special Sales at specialsales@jh.edu.

EU GPSR Authorized Representative
LOGOS EUROPE, 9 rue Nicolas Poussin, 17000, La Rochelle, France
Email: Contact@logoseurope.eu

For Mia and Migs.
For Vera and Hugo.
Tell stories of grief. Tell stories of love.

Contents

Foreword ix

	Prologue	1
Introduction	**Documenting Cruelty in the US Heartland**	5
Chapter 1	**Raid a Factory, Tell a Story**	25
Chapter 2	**Choreographed Chaos**	45
Chapter 3	***Para Uno Que Tiene Familia, Es Más Difícil***	81
Chapter 4	**The Multiplication of Loaves and Fishes**	109
Chapter 5	**Where Do You Stop Being a Teacher?**	145
Chapter 6	**A New Overground Railroad**	163
Chapter 7	**It Was the Bed Bugs That Broke Her**	199
Epilogue	**A Beautiful Morning in the Heartland of the US**	225

Acknowledgments 229
Notes 235
Index 269

Foreword
Nicole L. Novak

From 2018 to 2021, Bill Lopez and I spent hundreds of hours driving around the rural heartland visiting small communities that had been subjected to immigration raids—places many people do not realize have become home to recent immigrants at all. As we visited homes, churches, and schools, we recognized the markers of everyday rural life in newly multicultural communities—a corsage from a high school homecoming dance, a worn pair of work boots by a back door, a *taqueria* opened in a storefront that was once a classic American diner. Families shared stories from before the raids—of seeking a safe place to raise their family, of finding jobs in rural industries in need of workers, of finding meaning and community in a local church.

Unfortunately, we found ourselves in these particular towns because their relatively bucolic recent pasts had been disrupted when immigration agents targeted local worksites with raids resulting in mass arrests. Military helicopters were usually the first sign of the raid, followed by dozens—even hundreds—of armed agents descending on midsize worksites like greenhouses and packing plants, corralling and arresting workers who were almost uniformly the primary wage earners in their families. Over and over, people described this experience as singular, unexpected, and devastating—often using analogies for familiar disasters of chance in rural places, like lightning strikes, floods, or tornadoes. As we sat in church halls, living rooms, and school classrooms, people recounted the fear and devastation experienced by the workers, their loved ones, and the teachers, clergy, and neighbors who cared for them.

Bill and I built this project as public health researchers who had spent years studying the harms perpetuated by immigration enforcement; we had documented the ways coordinated immigration raids resulted in traumatic mental health symptoms and poor birth outcomes, and the ways the harms of raids extended beyond the arrested immigrants themselves to affect their family members, neighbors, and beyond. In the field of public health, it is important to document harm—what we literally describe as "morbidity and mortality." And in the case of militarized immigration enforcement, the harms are vast. Describing harms and correctly attributing their cause are vital functions of public health.

But public health is a field of action that also requires taking steps to prevent, mitigate, or ameliorate harms to health. Bill and I knew that the devastation after immigration raids was only part of the story, and we set out to listen to the whole story—including how people responded in the wake of raids and took steps toward healing. Remarkable new relationships formed across lines of class, race, and immigration status. Local residents drew on generational experience responding to disasters of all types, building responses to protect and sustain their neighbors. Churches staged emergency safe havens, advocates and attorneys conducted rapid legal responses, teachers checked on their students. Importantly, immigrant workers and their families were at the core of that response, adjusting roles of wage earning and childcare so that families could continue to survive and thrive. In these organic community responses, we saw the seeds of a better future and healthier communities.

The stories in this book are relevant beyond public health, as public conversations about immigration—and immigrants—loom larger than ever. Anti-immigrant rhetoric and policies capitalize on fear and myths that are largely divorced from the stories of real immigrants and the communities where they make their homes. These stories illustrate what happens when anti-immigrant myths and fears are allowed to spiral, triggering devastating harms almost entirely in rural places out of the public eye. It also recounts the unlikely new alliances and relationships that form in the wake of these harms.

When I think back to the time spent gathering these stories, I often think of driving, in all its monotony and openness. We cycled through playlists of cumbia, '90s country, reggaeton, and our beloved Dolly Parton, fueled by local barbeque, drive-thru hamburgers, tacos, and spaghetti dinners in school gyms. As we drove to these remote places, far from the primary arteries of American life, we had time to reflect and grapple with the pain and perseverance people shared with us. As I write this, the harms of the raids continue to reverberate—the backlog in our immigration courts means that immigration cases regularly drag on for years, and the personal trauma and, in some cases, family separations, leave generational impacts. At the same time, the country is bracing for a new wave of immigration enforcement that threatens to be more aggressive and formidable than the period described in this book. We're confident that the harms we witnessed are not the only thing to reverberate today and that they seeded powerful new relationships, and even new political and advocacy approaches, that will continue to strengthen communities today.

RAIDING THE HEARTLAND

Prologue

THE HOLIDAYS ARE OVER, so I'm picking up after the activity of the Christmas season and all the festivities and family it brings. It's January 8, 2025, and Donald Trump's inauguration for his second term as president of the US is only 12 days away. I'm shifting the quilts that lay on the guest room bed to the new shelf my wife and I just cleared to make the room, which also serves as the office in which I sit to write this book, a warmer and more welcoming place for visitors. The quilts were mostly made by hand—by my wife's grandmother, to be specific, who passed away on June 7, 2023, after a long and full life of 101 years.

My kids called her Great Grammie, and it wasn't long before my wife and I, and even my wife's mother, began calling her Great Grammie as well, to borrow a little of the awe and adoration my children bestowed on her name. Great Grammie was an avid quilter. Somewhere in our old photo albums we even have a faded, folded newspaper clipping of the time she spent her Christmas season sewing quilts for the unhoused folks who lived in her small town of Dunkirk and had to brave the frigid winter of upstate New York on the streets or in whatever shelter was available.

Every time I see these quilts, I think of Great Grammie, and if my wife is nearby, sometimes I'll get a story about her or a bit of inside information about how much work it took to sew the complicated geometric patterns I was clearly taking for granted. While I never actually saw Great Grammie quilting, I could imagine the hands of this woman of Polish descent guiding the sewing machine, putting her love into these heirlooms that she would pass down to her children and her children's children and that would, eventually, keep her Latino great grandchildren and their friends warm on the couch during the holidays.

But not all memories the quilts spark are joyful. As I look down on the purple edging of the largest quilt, I am taken back to a day in 2019, to a small town in rural Iowa during the third year of Trump's first term as president when an 83-year-old woman named Edith offered her quilts to me and the two Latino students who joined me to interview her that day. Edith, who was white, was a legend in her town. Not only was she boisterous, outgoing, politically active, and funny, but after Immigration and Customs Enforcement, or ICE, stormed the nearby concrete factory and deported its workers, Edith welcomed Edgar—whose father had been picked up in the raid and sent back to Guatemala—to live in her home, even though she spoke no Spanish and had never cooked any Guatemalan foods, and much to the chagrin of her family. Her daring Midwest hospitality was the talk of the town, the talk of a national newspaper, and an encapsulation of the immigration debate at the time. What happens in these small towns when ICE suddenly takes a significant portion of the town's immigrant workers? What happens to their children? Who responds to such large-scale removals? How? What happens to them? What fault lines—across race, class, language, and immigration status—are revealed? And who tells the story of these catastrophes?

PROLOGUE

When Edith offered her quilts to Juan, Bella, and me, I felt the meaning of the gesture deep in my bones and trusted that my students, Latinos who grew up in the Midwest as well, also knew the meaning of the quilts they were invited to wrap around their shoulders.

Then Edith told us that thievery was in Latino blood.

INTRODUCTION

Documenting Cruelty in the US Heartland

A Church in the Heartland

Our bellies were full with all the pasta, salad, and dessert we could imagine. Some of the food was homemade, fresh from the kitchens of the majority-white community in this everyday rural Midwestern town.[1] Other food was brought in from local restaurants, allowing us to sample a range of popular tastes from this particular slice of northern Ohio. The coffee, perhaps a little watered down, was served in those small Styrofoam cups by rushed church parishioners who see a line of people chitchatting and want only to make them chitchat more. At 10 dollars a person, this dinner made St. John's Church in Salem, Ohio, a respectable sum of money from our small research team visiting from Ann Arbor, Michigan, to learn more about what a nearby immigration raid on a major meat supplier about a year prior did to the town.

As we walked out of the church cafeteria and into the setting sun, we approached a T- intersection that was alternatingly cut by the blue and red lights of two police cars. Large crowds had amassed on the sidewalk, waiting for the officers to tell them how to proceed. So we waited too. To the people of Salem, Ohio, standing at that T-intersection, as well as to everyone in the church and to the police officers standing nearby, it was probably evident that we were not counted in Salem's population of 11,910, 96 percent of whom were white.[2] While our research team has been as large as about 12, that day 7 of us—2 Latinos, 1 Latina, 3 white women, 1 Arab woman, and me, a Latino man—enjoyed the pasta prior to encountering the police outside. Four of us have parents who are immigrants. Two of us are part of mixed-status families,[3] or families with members who are not US citizens. One of us had a father deported.

Our little multicultural huddle standing hesitantly between a large stone church and two police cars made for a curious analogy of what we were studying, as well as the political moment in which we were studying it. St. John's Church is not that different from other Catholic and Christian churches that pepper the Midwestern landscape throughout the interior of the US. These churches tend to have multiple masses a week in English for a majority-white population. The announcements and flyers covering the bulletin board at the back of the church will all be in English. The letter board that displays words, phrases, and references to Jesus using movable plastic letters will also be in English. But many of these churches will have that one singular Spanish service, often led by a pastor who is fluent enough, perhaps having learned parts of the service while studying abroad. The service might be at an odd time on Saturday or late in the day on Sunday.

These Spanish and English services are kept separate, like so many aspects of Latino and white dynamics in these small rural towns. There is nothing insipid about this separation. Each community generally prefers their ceremony in the language with which they are most familiar, led by the pastors who speak it most comfortably and followed by the food they are most accustomed to eating. Unfortunately, both on Sunday and the other six days a week, it often means the white and Latino communities rarely cross paths.

And when you don't know someone, you tend to fill in the blanks about them any way you can. Many white rural residents of these small towns understand Latino immigrants based either on fleeting encounters at gas stations, the Walmart self-checkout, or while picking kids up from school or, worse, from the stories they hear on the news that paint Latino immigrants as job stealers, resource leeches, or machete-wielding murderers. This means it's very easy for a white population that rarely crosses paths with a Latino population to conflate skin color, language, and immigration status and assume that most Latinos they see—or anyone speaking Spanish or accented English—are undocumented, and treat them differently.[4]

One poll found that Americans of all backgrounds believed the number of undocumented Latinos in the US to be significantly higher than it was in actuality.[5] White Americans believed 32 percent of Latinos were undocumented; Asian Americans, 30 percent; and Black Americans, 39 percent. Even other Latinos tended to make this projection, believing that 36 percent of Latinos were undocumented. The actual number was only 13 percent. White Americans also believed that only 34 percent of Latinos were US born, when in reality, 67 percent of Latinos were born in the US.

Latinos in these rural spaces experience what researchers call *hypervisibility*. Mara Maria Maldonado, a professor of sociology at Oregon State University, drew on ethnography and interviews in Perry, Iowa, from 2006 to 2008 to describe what she calls racialized hypervisibility, or a "sense of 'standing out' associated with their physical presence as Latino-looking and

Latino-sounding bodies moving in and through community spaces."[6] Latinos in Perry, Iowa, like towns throughout the US heartland, are always noticed and because of racial profiling are often assumed to be part of a gang, to be driving without a license, or to be in the US without permission. Put most simply, hypervisibility means that Latinos in rural towns are always noticed by everyone, from white residents, to shop owners, to police to Immigration and Customs Enforcement, also known as ICE.[7] When we gather in groups, when our food is present among the church sampling of Ohio cuisine, when we practice for a quinceañera in the pavilion, when someone reads the English church reading with an accent, or when we walk alone on a sidewalk, each of these is noticeable, and because of the associations with criminality, each becomes police-able.[8]

The odd thing about hypervisibility is that it goes hand in hand with efforts to make oneself invisible. Whether undocumented and fearful of removal or simply brown-skinned and avoiding racist interactions, invisibility is a matter of survival. Yet this invisibility makes it harder to combat dangerous stereotypes and nearly impossible to organize, fight for change, or gain political power. When you can't gather in a group, it becomes so much harder to be prepared for disasters, and when that disaster hits, it gets harder to get anyone to care.

With traffic stopped at the T-intersection, we paused, unsure of what would happen next. It wasn't immediately clear to us what could result in this much police presence in a town this small. Then we heard a sound—a few sounds, actually—that made the purpose of the police clear.

From the front of the line came the music of six trombones, the students playing them marching in time with the drum major's direction. The trombones were followed by trumpets, clarinets, saxophones, drums, and tubas, and joined by a team of three baton twirlers. As the band began to cross the intersection, the traffic lights that hung overhead changed from green to red as the band walked underneath them, but it didn't matter. Everybody on foot kept on walking, whether the lights were red or green. No one in the cars seemed to mind at all, watching and listening to the band pass by, now under the direction of the police.

When I realized that the police were there just to stop traffic and direct the band, I let out the breath I didn't know I was holding, unclenching my jaw and smiling in relief. Perhaps it's paranoia, perhaps it's the healthy, protective paternalism of a professor who cares about his students, but I am deeply aware of how they are perceived and treated whenever they are with me in community settings. This is especially the case for students of color when they join Nicole—the project's colead, who is white—and me in predominantly white communities like this one.

But in this case, all was fine. No one was paying any attention to us, least of all the police. We had a football game to watch. The rest was invisible. We shook ourselves from our stupor and followed the raising and lowering of the drum major's baton as he turned the corner toward the field behind St. John's.

Directing Traffic

On June 19, 2018, about a year and four months prior to our visit, ICE raided Fresh Mark,[9] the meat-processing plant 1.5 miles away from where we stood where many in the Salem Latino community and surrounding areas were employed. With the help of a number of law enforcement organizations, ICE ultimately detained 146 workers. That many workers hadn't been taken in a single raid since 2008, when the meat-processing plant in Postville, Iowa, was raided, sending ripples of anger throughout the country and changing the way Presidents George W. Bush, Barack Obama, and Joseph R. Biden enforced immigration law.

Arguably, it changed how President Donald J. Trump enforced—and enforces—immigration law too; whereas Bush, Obama, and Biden ran away from the politically disastrous enforcement strategy, Trump ran toward it, embraced it, and branded it his own.

To hungry meat eaters all over the US, Fresh Mark provided bacon, ham, hot dogs, pepperoni, salami, sliced meats, and other specialty meat items.[10] The large number of Latino immigrants working at Fresh Mark was typical of many of these Midwestern towns. In response to the growing globalized competition of the 1970s, US industries decreased overhead by lowering wages, eliminating union contracts, and compartmentalizing jobs so they required fewer and fewer skills. As meatpacking came to resemble an assembly line, the focus on efficiency also increased risk, making the job one of the most dangerous in the US.[11] When American-born workers refused the dangerous, exploitative industry jobs they were offered, immigrants began to fill the gap.[12]

For ICE, the industrialization of jobs such as meatpacking conveniently clustered large numbers of Latino immigrants in the same place at the same time, with weakened union protections and limited recourse to the Occupational Safety and Health Administration, in a facility with too few doors for any reasonable number of workers to attempt to flee. It also provided a highly visible enforcement action in a town where Latino strategic invisibility had stifled potential political or humanitarian pushback.

The 146 detainees taken from Fresh Mark in Salem was only one raid of a string of them that would happen that summer of 2018 and continue in the summer of 2019. After the 10-year hiatus following Postville, the first such raid happened at another meatpacking plant in Bean Station, Tennessee, in April 2018, resulting in 97 arrests right in the middle of statewide academic testing for elementary and middle schools.[13] Jonathan Blitzer, writing for *The New Yorker*, wrote that the raid "turned the lives of hundreds of Tennessee kids upside down," as classrooms sat empty in the days that followed.[14]

About a month later, ICE raided a concrete factory in Mount Pleasant, Iowa, arresting 32 workers and pushing the small town to split "along faith lines" depending on whether the highly Christian community believed in a Bible that welcomed immigrants or one that preached the sanctity of law.[15]

ICE then moved a few states over to Sandusky, Ohio, about two hours from Salem, Ohio, where agents posed as health inspectors and offered donuts to lure workers into the break room.[16] Once enough workers were present, they arrested 114 of them, all within the shadow of the famed Midwest rollercoaster haven, Cedar Point. ICE used zip ties to bind detainee hands, as zip ties are much cheaper to deploy en masse when arresting so many workers at one time. Two weeks later, they raided Fresh Mark.

Two months afterward, they went west to O'Neill, Nebraska, where they arrested 133 workers across a handful of businesses, including a tomato greenhouse, a potato farm and packing facility, and a cattle feedlot.[17] In Sandusky and O'Neill, many of the workers were women, some of whom were pregnant. Three weeks later, ICE traveled to North Texas, arresting 159 workers at a trailer manufacturing company in Sumner.[18]

ICE took a respite from conducting large-scale worksite raids in the fall and winter, but agents returned in force in the spring and summer of 2019. In April, ICE raided a technology repair company in Allen, Texas,[19] arresting 284 people, 60 percent of whom were women.[20] Then in August, ICE conducted the biggest statewide operation in history, raiding seven food-processing plants in Mississippi to arrest 680 people on the first day of school.[21]

News reports in the days after the raids abounded, describing them uniformly as terrifying and chaotic to the communities in which they occurred. The millions of dollars and hundreds of agents mobilized to descend on a particular location in a particular moment summarily separated families, collapsed local economies, kept hundreds of children out of school, and sowed distrust among immigrants and the social services designed to help them.

In short, the large-scale worksite raid as a tool of deportation had been on hiatus since 2008. But by the summer of 2019, one thing was clear: The immigration worksite raid was back. If St. John's was an everyday Midwestern church and Fresh Mark was an everyday Midwestern business, the raid on Fresh Mark had become an everyday Midwestern raid, providing insight into what was to come.

≈

The Salem Police Department worked with ICE to carry out the raid on Fresh Mark.[22] Pictures show ICE agents leading out lines of workers still clothed in the white smocks, latex gloves, aprons, and face masks they wore as they processed pork into ham and bacon. Eventually, the 146 detained workers were herded onto buses and taken away to process for deportation.

According to the Salem police chief, police officers were on the premises to control the flow of traffic and, later, to help identify the children of those detained.[23] The police chief stated sympathetically, "I didn't want to see news stories about kids that weren't taken care of. We did everything in our power to make sure kids were our top priority." It was likely challenging for immigrant families in and around Fresh Mark to distinguish between the police in their blue uniforms who wanted to take care of their children and the ICE agents—whose bulletproof vests often bear large patches that read "POLICE ICE"—taking them away from their children at that moment.[24]

After the raid, families huddled in St. Peter's to figure out who had been taken and whether they were likely to see them again, or at least see them on this side of the Rio Grande. Some of these family members slept in the pews, too scared to drive, too scared to go home, too scared that their dark skin would make it too easy to see them and pull them over and that they, too, would be arrested and taken away from their lives in Ohio.

As we stood at that crosswalk in front of St. John's in November of 2019, it was highly likely that some of the very same officers involved in the raid were still at the department, standing in front of the very church in which immigrant families sheltered, doing now what they did then, controlling traffic and protecting youth.

Mojado and *Marcado*

After writing my first book, *Separated*, I taught a public health class at the University of Michigan on the impacts of immigration and policing in communities of color. In the class, we would watch the music video for "Mojado," the song written and performed by Guatemalan singer Ricardo Arjona and released in 2005. A song from the year I graduated from college, I didn't expect my younger students to recognize it. But I was surprised that most didn't know what the word *mojado* meant, either literally or, as it tends to be used, pejoratively. Part of this, of course, was because at a predominantly white university in a predominantly white city in a predominantly white state, most students did not speak basic Spanish. I grew up in San Antonio, Texas, where most everyone knew some Spanish, and even if they couldn't speak it, they could probably understand it when their parents or grandparents spoke it. But there in Michigan, most folks simply didn't know that *mojado*, which literally means "wet," was used to disparage the undocumented immigrants swimming across the Rio Grande from Mexico into Texas and emerging with their clothes—and backs—soaked with river water. Nor did they know there was an entire operation, Operation Wetback,[25] that removed over a million people from our grandparents' generation.

God, I hated the word "wetback."

But this was more than just a language issue. Like so many Latino topics we write about in public health, misunderstandings arise not only from a basic lack of familiarity with the language and culture but also from a lack of understanding of the systems that oppress us. That is, even though it results in dozens to hundreds of deaths a year, border crossing is not something we uniformly study in our public health classes, and even though it fractures thousands of families a year, our family and community health classes spend little time on the mechanisms of the Department of Homeland Security, under which falls Customs and Border Protection, or CBP, ICE, and United States Citizenship and Immigration Services, or USCIS. And although immigration status fundamentally shapes access to medical resources, health care, and interactions with nearly all government institutions,[26] it rarely comes up outside of courses specifically focused on immigration.

In Michigan, like many of the Midwestern states from which University of Michigan students hail, the US–Mexico border wasn't something you thought about every day or read about in your history classes. It didn't define your state or its geography. It did not, in 1848, move,[27] causing your Mexican ancestors to become American overnight and change the land they got to call their own.[28] And it certainly wasn't something you swam across to illegally enter the US, leaving you "wet" when you stepped onto US soil for the first time.

DOCUMENTING CRUELTY IN THE US HEARTLAND

I lived in San Antonio until I was 18. I went to college at Notre Dame in Indiana, then returned to Texas and lived in Houston for three years, where I received my master of public health. In 2008 I moved to Ann Arbor, where I live now and where I worked for the University of Michigan before studying here and ultimately becoming a professor. All told, I have spent about half of my life in predominantly Latino spaces in Texas and the other half of my life in predominantly white spaces in the Midwest. My life, split between these areas, has deeply informed my understanding of what it means to be Latino, what it means to be an immigrant, and how the general public understands the functions of what historian Adam Goodman calls "the deportation machine."[29]

In Texas we knew what the Border Patrol, or La Migra, was (the organization's actual name is Customs and Border Protection, or CBP, but no one calls it that). Some of us knew folks who worked for the Border Patrol or even went on to work for Border Patrol ourselves.[30] We didn't necessarily know much about the Border Patrol, but we knew they were generally the people who took people, usually Mexicans, away. I remember one Latino student in my high school class dressing up as a Border Patrol agent for Halloween and approaching an Asian American student while pointing to his CBP cap and loudly calling out "Border Patrol! Border Patrol!" This was ironic, for sure, as Border Patrol deports far more Latino immigrants than Asian immigrants. Another student, who was also Latino, actually corrected the faux-CBP agent, reminding him that an ocean lay between Asia and Texas, not a border. While Border Patrol would arrest Asian immigrants crossing the Atlantic if they made it to a port of entry, it would be the Coast Guard performing the arrests if they were stopped before making it to land. His point was well-taken: Don't be stupid; Border Patrol was much more likely to take someone Latino like us than someone like our Asian American friend. The student dressed as a CBP agent could have been, perhaps, making a larger sociological argument that Border Patrol exists as a shifting tool of social control that operates differently based on the needs of those in power. When we wanted to deport Asian immigrants, we told stories about opium dens and leprosy. When we wanted to deport the Irish, we told stories about alcoholism and Irish fever. And when we wanted to deport Mexican immigrants, we said—say—that they steal jobs, steal resources, are dirty and dangerous, and, as always, bring disease.

But I highly doubt my classmate was making any sort of sociological commentary. I think he was just bullying our racially different classmate by pretending to be among the most powerful people in Texas: Border Patrol agents.

As young Texans, whether Latinos or not, we knew that the border was where it happened. It's where you tried to cross for a better life. It's where the Border Patrol tried to catch you and send you back. The border was a cruel desert at some points, a plain crisscrossed with barbed wire at others. It was where white people who owned the land at the border would yell "Migra, Migra!" and laugh at Mexican workers diving in bushes to hide. And for many, it was where you died, drowning in the Rio Grande.

I realized how much I internalized this perspective—that immigration was about working, hiding from La Migra, or drowning—when I saw the Disney film *Coco* in 2017 and found myself choked up during one particular scene. Early in the film, Héctor, a comical skeleton who lives in the Land of the Dead, tries to sneak across a bridge made of marigolds into the Land of the Living. Héctor is denied passage by a uniformed agent who scans his face with a computer at the base of the bridge. But, jumping the turnstile, Héctor sprints onto the bridge before any of the agents can catch him.

When he first steps onto the bridge, it appears to be solid and able to support his weight. But as Héctor continues to run across it, the bridge begins to dissolve under his feet, marigolds shifting and rearranging with every step. Soon he's up to his knees in marigolds, then up to his waist, then up to his shoulders. Héctor begins to move his arms in a freestyle swimming motion, but the bridge he thought would take him to a better life in the Land of the Living is now transforming into a river of flowers in which he is about to drown. This was clearly a metaphor for surreptitious border crossing, right? The skeletal friend obviously represents the undocumented immigrant, the marigold river the Rio Grande. The Land of the Living is the "land of opportunity," and Héctor's near-drowning in an attempt to pursue it is just commentary on the immigrant experience, right? I suppose I would have to ask the film's writers to know for sure.

But the deportation machine in Michigan—for those who even know it exists—looks quite different than it does in Texas. In fact, it's actually very difficult to identify. There's no desert. No barbed wire. No wall. No drowning. And very little Migra. In *Separated*, I wrote about an immigration raid on my friend Guadalupe's apartment conducted by ICE and the police that occurred five miles from my home, a little over eight miles from where I taught my class to majority-white students. One of our good friends, Alejandro, was arrested by ICE at the Wendy's drive-through by the mall in the center of the city, just a few blocks from where the Wolverines play football. Our campus was shaken up when ICE agents sat down at the table at Sava's, a popular restaurant near downtown Ann Arbor, ordered breakfast, ate their breakfast, and then arrested the people who had made their breakfast, all less than two blocks from the University of Michigan multicultural center, less than three blocks from our student union, and a five-minute walk from the middle of our campus.[31] When I volunteered with the Washtenaw Interfaith Coalition for Immigrant Rights, we would frequently get calls to our urgent response line that ICE or the police were parked right outside the mobile home park, waiting to arrest residents as they drove to pick up their kids from school.[32]

As I learned more about the deportation machine in Michigan and throughout the Midwest, I came to understand that it's strikingly different from that of the southern border. It is often the police, not La Migra, who take people away, or at least catch them first before turning them over to the jail, which then turns them over to ICE. And when it is ICE doing the enforcement, people are taken out of their cars while driving kids to school or waiting for their order of french fries after a day of painting. They are removed from their homes as they warm up dinner for their families.[33] They are forced out of their bathrooms where they fled to protect their children.[34] Or they are taken from the kitchen of the restaurant moments after they finish scrambling the eggs. There are often witnesses, who sit by confused, powerless, or both. And those witnesses are often children. Those left behind after the deportation of a loved one draw their blinds, close their doors, and leave their cars in the driveway, fearing that they, too, could be taken away from their families. They stop taking their children to school, stop going to the doctor for anything from a regular check in to a prenatal appointment, stop being part of the community.[35] Invisibility for the sake of survival.

Fabián, a 21-year-old Colombian immigrant I interviewed after Guadalupe's apartment was raided, described this phenomenon as a feeling of being *marcado*, or "marked," for removal.

When ICE wants to get you and take you out of the country, you become hypervigilant, constantly looking over your shoulder for agents or deputies or the police or anyone in a uniform to pull up behind you. You start to feel safe in fewer and fewer places, having heard from a neighbor about the day their dad was snatched from his apartment.

If I had to describe it, I understood deportation along the southern border to be sweltering and sweaty, dusty and dirty, physically grueling, and bodily violent. In the Midwest, it was quiet, then violating and climactic, traumatizing, then utterly, bitterly, lonely and cold.

The problem was that the students in my class, although they lived in and often came from the Midwest and other rural areas throughout the country, not only had no idea what *mojado* meant but didn't necessarily know what *marcado* meant either. And they certainly were not alone in this. In a country whose population is about 60 percent white and 85 percent US born,[36] many Americans do not understand the harm of the deportation system simply through life experience. By the time they come to find out just how damaging and harmful the system is, they have already begun to justify it as a necessary tool in our country's war against invasion, infection, and violence from those with criminality in their DNA.

This book unpacks what I call large-scale immigration worksite raids, a particularly violent method of immigration enforcement, and considers the creative, collaborative responses and acts of resistance of immigrant communities that follow these raids. I define a large-scale worksite raid as an immigration enforcement action in which (1) ICE agents enter a commercial space, (2) in a single enforcement action, (3) on a single day, (4) in a single community. To conduct this study, I worked with Dr. Nicole Novak, a community health researcher, Iowan, mother of two, and longtime immigrant advocate who published "Change in Birth Outcomes Among Infants Born to Latina Mothers After a Major Immigration Raid,"[37] in the *International Journal of Epidemiology,* a groundbreaking manuscript showing that the stress caused by the raid of the meatpacking plant in Postville, Iowa, put Latino infants at increased risk of low-birth weight. It has been cited nearly 400 times. Along with a handful of public health students from the University of Michigan and University of Iowa, Nicole and I decided to use our public health training and relationships with immigrant advocates throughout the country to tell the story of these events in a way that would illustrate their causes and consequences, which most know very little about. But we also dedicated our work to expanding the story and bringing to the fore the strength, creativity, collaboration, and perseverance of those harmed by these raids, about which even less is known.

We worked with community partners to arrange visits in each of the six communities hit by large-scale worksite raids in 2018.[38] Through a network of immigration advocates, students, colleagues, and friends, we were generally within one or two people of someone who lived or worked in the town in which a worksite raid happened. In each community we visited, we went to the sites of the raids; the churches in which community members sought refuge after each raid; and as many local restaurants, symbolic spaces, and community homes as we were invited to and able. Collaborators became friends, friends became collaborators, and, as they do in the best applied-research projects, the lines between researchers and community members blurred.[39] We formally interviewed 77 individuals,[40] most in person, though a few were arranged and conducted later over video or the phone.

Conversing with those who have experienced or responded to disaster and loss is challenging in the best of circumstances for both the interviewer and interviewee. And while I have always worked in teams, I took on a different role this time, as one of the coleads of the project whose job it was to teach and mentor students, some of whom were Latino, Spanish speaking, and part of immigrant families. While these students provided an additional layer of insight, I frequently wrestled with what it meant to bring students into spaces where they would be hypervisible, seen as "the other," and possibly forced to confront the racism of the portion of the rural, white population who may see their parents (or them) as the problem.

In documenting these raids and their aftermath, I hope to accomplish at least three goals. First, much of our understanding of immigration enforcement and deportation comes from public discourse about the US–Mexico border. In many ways, this makes sense. The most common nationality among undocumented immigrants—37 percent—is Mexican,[41] and many non-Mexicans cross the US–Mexico border after making the trip northward from Central America. But border enforcement isn't the full story of immigration and deportation. This book will show you what it looks like to live in the shadow of deportation in quiet, predominantly white, rural areas throughout the interior of the US, highlighting both the harm of deportation and the agency, creativity, and organizing prowess inherent in efforts to resist it.

Second, violent immigration enforcement methods require public consent, or at least a lack of public opposition. This book will demonstrate how politicians carefully craft and recycle their stories of immigrants—often as genetically inferior pests and criminals—to suit their political goals and justify enforcement methods that would, in any other circumstance, cause public outcry. These stories, when repeated in news cycles without opposition, can be so ingrained in the public mindset that even those who materially support immigrants may continue to hold them.

And lastly, immigration worksite raids are selected as a tool of immigration enforcement *because* they are cruel and chaotic, not *despite* their cruelty and the chaos they create. The threats of violence and family separation are used to maintain a class of exploitable workers and discourage advocates from supporting immigrant communities, lest they be mired in the concentrated human suffering that mass deportation entails.

Is this book about President Trump? Does it only teach us about worksite raids? The answer to those questions is both yes and no. The immigration enforcement I document here all occurred during the first Trump administration, from January 2017 to January 2021. That large-scale worksite raids were essentially abandoned in 2008 only to be brought back in force in 2017 is certainly a critique of his administration's immigration enforcement strategy, specifically. And yes, this book is about worksite raids, as I imagine this specific tactic will be used again during Trump's second term or by future presidents. But President Trump took deportation tools already developed, relied on presidential powers granted through the Constitution, and stirred fear about non-white immigrants using stories as old as the US itself. He is not the first president to want to remove undocumented immigrants en masse, and I do not believe he will be the last. An analysis of the cruelty, chaos and violence of worksite raids provides an opportunity to understand what deportation looks like on a daily basis, especially in the rural US, even if on a different scale or under a different president.

I changed the names of interviewees, schools, and school districts to pseudonyms. Where necessary, descriptions of people were altered to hide their identities. The names of some organizations and churches were altered if they were small enough to be identified, political tensions remained, or they had not been speaking out in the media. When these organizations and churches were largely part of the public discussion—that is, when their role in the response was a matter of public record—I often preserved their names to honor their efforts. The names of public figures, like politicians or reporters, are retained. Translations are my own. When I needed assistance with translation, I relied on bilingual friends and colleagues who supported translation in my first book, including my mother. Some quotations were edited for clarity.

Scenes are drawn from a combination of audio and written field notes, recorded interviews, various media and historical records, media reports, follow-up discussions with team members and collaborators, and my memory and those of others on the team. I take responsibility for details presented in scenes throughout the book. Many immigrant communities with roots in Mexico, Central America, South America, or parts of the Caribbean use the word "Latino" or reference a country of origin, such as "Honduran community," when they identify themselves. I retain this language when talking about communities with which we worked. I use "Latina" or "Latinas" when discussing individual women or a group of women. More gender-inclusive alternatives, such as Latinx or Latine, are becoming more common and supported in public health.[42] When I reference articles, I retain the language in the article, such as "Hispanic." Demographic data come from the US Census unless otherwise noted.

≈

We followed the drum major and his band around the church and saw the bright green of football field turf surrounded by the red of the classic high school polyurethane track. The stadium lights were turned on to illuminate the field as the sun began to set. Two white field goal posts kept watch over each end of the field. The teams were warming up. And the aluminum bleachers were starting to fill with fans.

The parishioners were serving food. The police were there to help. The church that just a year ago had been filled with Latino immigrants whose families and friends had been taken was beginning to empty out. Even though the police officers were just there to protect the children, I couldn't imagine that many Latinos would be willing to walk past them to sit in the well-lit bleachers. I wondered if their absence would be noticed at all.

Their story—of hiding in the church, of being targeted for removal, of being exploited for their labor, of being pawns for politicians needing to garner votes, and of actively rebelling—is both set in stone in the grounds of our country and completely invisible if you don't know where to look. May this book show you where to look. And may you share what you find.

It was a typical night in the heartland of the US.

CHAPTER 1

Raid a Factory, Tell a Story

Disaster Is the Point

The worksite raid that happened a few miles away from that pasta dinner was not unique in 2018 nor in the history of the US. In fact, raiding worksites to detain and deport undocumented immigrants is as much a part of the American landscape as the sun setting over a high school football field on a Friday night. Immigration worksite raids have been occurring in the US throughout at least the last century,[1] with upticks in the 1970s and 1980s before peaking in frequency and growing in scale during the first Trump administration.[2] The general public may be familiar with some of these raids, having made their way into newspapers and onto the evening news. For example, Operation Wagon Train culminated in the arrest of 1,297 undocumented workers at six Swift & Company meatpacking plants in different states in 2006.[3] A raid on military contractor Michael Bianco Inc. in New Bedford, Massachusetts, resulted in the arrest of 361 undocumented workers in 2007. And perhaps best known to the general public, a raid on Agriprocessors Inc. in Postville, Iowa, in 2008 resulted in the record-setting arrest of 389 workers.[4]

Yet the general public knows very little about these raids: about how they work, what happens after, and how useful they are politically.

Worksite raids are generally organized and conducted by Immigration and Customs Enforcement (ICE), a branch of the Department of Homeland Security (DHS). DHS is led by the secretary of Homeland Security, who, as a member of the presidential cabinet, serves at the pleasure of the US president. No one elects the person in charge of DHS. They are not beholden to the US public in any way. Their only job is to enforce immigration law in a way that aligns with the president's preferences. If they fail to do so, the president can simply remove them from their position. Secretary of Homeland Security Kirstjen Nielsen serves as an example. Nielsen refused Trump's directive to close the ports of entry along the US border and quickly found herself being asked to resign.[5]

Put simply, if the president wants more deportations, the secretary of Homeland Security is apt to provide more deportations if she wants to keep her job. And if the president wants to use immigration raids to get these deportations, the secretary is apt to comply.

President Bush utilized large-scale immigration worksite raids, presiding over the biggest single-site raid in US history, in Postville, Iowa. President Obama, on the other hand, abandoned worksite raids,[6] opting instead for less visible methods of deportation. Obama's successor, President Trump, embraced immigration raids with the zealous fervor of a child who has just discovered an unguarded stash of candy. When President Biden was elected, one of his first acts in office was to send a memo to the secretary of Homeland Security to halt the use of large-scale immigration worksite raids.[7] Imagine, for a moment, what it might feel like to live in a community upon which a military operation could descend on your community and remove you depending on the will of the president. And imagine this could simply change every four years. It's hard to plan for your future, raise a family, or invest in your community under those circumstances.

So what is it that makes a president embrace—or abandon—worksite raids? What do these raids mean? To whom? And why can they be so useful in getting your voters to support you?

Simply put, immigration worksite raids tell a story. They are enormous spectacles that cost hundreds of thousands of dollars and require immense coordination across multiple government agencies. They draw news cameras and reporters from all around the country and, at least in the days that follow, often dominate the airwaves. They are heavily militarized and full of law enforcement, with people in uniform and bulletproof vests and cargo pants and sidearms and extendable batons and US flags and eagle logos and press conferences. They are talked about, written about, blogged about, and photographed. And they usually result in large numbers of brown-skinned people being taken away, heads bowed and hands zip-tied behind their backs.

With so many bystanders, there's usually someone willing to talk when a microphone is pushed in their face. Since raids often happen in everyday rural towns like Salem, Ohio, they remind the public that Latino immigrants—and hence the need to control them—exist all over the country, not just in states with border walls.

And because the public is so often unaware of what these raids entail, the story they tell is highly mutable, able to be twisted and turned to highlight the exact characteristics a politician needs to reveal to voters. Does your constituency want you to protect jobs for the American worker? Are they fearful that immigrants are taking their Social Security numbers and stealing their identities? Do they want to see how serious you are about law and order? Are they terrified of Salvadoran machete-wielding gang members? Do they need a president who isn't scared to use some military muscle, especially if we are in between wars? Highly visible worksite raids can address all these constituent concerns at once.

President George W. Bush's use of immigration worksite raids illustrates his attempt to address these points. First elected in 2000, Bush was reelected in 2004 when he defeated his Democratic opponent, John Kerry, in a bitter and expensive race. Bush's win over Kerry was decisive. But his popularity, along with that of the Republican Party, waned. So when the midterm elections came around in 2006, the Republican Party lost control of Congress, as Democrats took the majority in both the House and the Senate for the first time in 12 years.

With his presidency scarred by the invasion of Iraq and his response to Hurricane Katrina, Bush hoped to protect what was left of his legacy by passing comprehensive immigration reform during his last two years in office. The Comprehensive Immigration Reform Act of 2007, written by a bipartisan group of senators with the participation of the Bush administration, proposed a legalization program for undocumented immigrants that included a path to citizenship, a guest worker program, and a reform of the green-card application process to include a point-based "merit" system.

The Bush administration needed careful political maneuvers to please both Democrats and Republicans. For Democrats, Bush needed to show that he cared about immigrants and their families and wasn't just trying to deport everyone en masse. For Republicans who thought this measured, progressive vision of immigration reform was akin to amnesty, Bush needed to show that he was serious about enforcement.

RAID A FACTORY, TELL A STORY

Enter the worksite raid. Bush believed these raids would showcase a compassionate focus on the employers of immigrants, not the immigrants themselves, while simultaneously demonstrating that he wasn't scared to enforce the law with the well-armed, firm hand of a hawk.

So on December 12, 2006, the feast of La Virgen de Guadalupe, when Mexicans commemorate the appearance of the mother of Jesus to Juan Diego on a hill in Tepeyac, ICE brought nine specially outfitted Greyhound buses, three helicopters, and hundreds of agents to raid six Swift meat-processing plants in Iowa, Minnesota, Nebraska, Texas, Colorado, and Utah and arrested 1,282 workers, virtually all of whom were Latino. As workers jumped into cattle pens or scrambled behind machinery to hide,[8] ICE corralled them into a central location and separated them into groups based on skin color. Agents then questioned them about their immigration status and loaded them on buses to be taken away and processed for deportation.[9]

As the Bush administration had hoped, the event was highly visible, letting everyone know how seriously it took immigration law. The public relations machine also worked to craft a narrative of the Bush administration as the protector of the American people, justifying the raids in part to bust a "large-scale identity theft scheme."[10]

The Bush administration wasn't done yet. And it geared up for what, at that time, would be the biggest single-site raid in US history, the raid that has received more media attention than any other before it and since, the raid that has been the subject of more documentaries and podcasts than any other, and the raid that had the most to teach us about those that would occur under President Trump in the summer of 2018: the raid on Agriprocessors Inc. in Postville, Iowa.

It All Goes Back to Postville

To immigrant communities throughout the rural US, but especially to those in the Midwest, mentioning Postville is like asking someone about the funeral of a loved one too soon after their death, or wondering aloud about the tornado that destroyed their home while they are still living in a motel. It's both a traumatic wound from the past and a specter of possibility, a day that once was and, if the stars align poorly again, a day that could be again. Everywhere we go, people still talk about Postville.

Postville, located in the northeast corner of Iowa, was home to about 2,200 people when the Bush administration hit it with the force of a well-militarized hurricane.[11] On May 12, 2008, 900 ICE agents descended upon Agriprocessors Inc., a slaughterhouse that processed meat from cattle, chicken, duck, and lamb. By the end of the day, they had arrested a total of 389 workers, 96 percent of whom were Latino, including 290 Guatemalans and 93 Mexicans.[12] While a Black Hawk helicopter circled overhead, about 20 percent of the population of Postville was zip-tied, forced into buses, and driven away to be processed for deportation. Nearly every Latino in the community had lost someone, knew another family who had lost someone, or wasn't quite sure whether they had lost anyone yet or not.

The detained women were taken to county jails, while the men were transported to the National Cattle Congress in Waterloo, Iowa, about 80 miles from their homes and families in Postville.[13] The National Cattle Congress provided exactly what ICE agents and the DHS needed logistically: the space to set up a somewhat quasi-legal courtroom to process dozens of immigrants at one time with as little organizational overhead as possible. It also provided what detractors needed: a metaphor so over the top and obvious that it allowed them to take control of the story being told.

Bush's hope of presenting himself as a firm yet compassionate supporter of both immigration law and immigrants themselves was undermined by the reality of the Postville raid and the immigrant-processing procedures they set up afterward. It was all simply too cruel. Raiding a meat-processing plant, herding immigrants to a central location, and processing them for deportation, all while housing them on an actual site where cattle were auctioned off, was a narrative of treating human beings like animals that basically wrote itself.

ICE created a makeshift courtroom in which judges could preside over multiple detainees at once.[14] Defense lawyers were assigned up to a dozen clients and had less than 30 minutes to meet and educate each client, decide whether the client was fit to stand trial, determine whether the client had experienced any violations of their constitutional rights, and learn any personal information that might mitigate the client's sentence.[15] Erik Camayd-Freixas, one of the Spanish interpreters at the hearing, found the entire process so abhorrent that he broke his interpreter code of silence and wrote about the session in an essay to *The New York Times*.[16] He described the holding facility at the National Cattle Congress as "a 60-acre cattle fairground that had been transformed into a sort of concentration camp or detention center." Referencing the constrained and streamlined legal process, he began a trend that would only accelerate as descriptions of the day emerged, again leveraging the meatpacking metaphor to write, "Thus far the work had oddly resembled a judicial assembly line where the meat packers were mass processed."

To "process" that many detainees at the same time, ICE needed simple and straightforward cases. So, first, the government charged everyone they could with "aggravated identity theft," which made it a crime "to knowingly transfer, possess, or use, without lawful authority, a means of identification of another person, during and in relation to any felony violation of certain enumerated Federal felony offenses."[17] Going to trial for aggravated identity theft meant that you would wait in jail for six to eight months without bail before the trial began. You would then remain in jail during the trial. If you won the trial, you would be deported. If you lost the trial, you would spend no less than two years behind bars and then be deported. Those arrested were mostly men, often the financial providers for their families. So much time away from work was catastrophic for the wives and children depending on them for economic support. It was highly unlikely that their two-parent households functioned with just one, and if their wives—possibly undocumented themselves—began working and driving, the risk of both parents winding up in detention and being deported increased, an obvious catastrophe for the children left behind.

If you pleaded guilty to "knowingly using a false Social Security number," however, the heavier charge of aggravated identity theft would be withdrawn, you would serve only five months in jail, and then you would be deported.[18] While families would still be left without their financial providers, they wouldn't be in the same dire economic straits for quite as long. In other words, if the undocumented workers admitted to a crime they probably didn't commit, they could get deported faster—a terrible fate, yes, but one that allowed them to, at a minimum, get back to work in their countries of birth and send money to their families in the US.

Could the government have actually convicted anyone of aggravated identity theft? This was unlikely. Detainees were, after all, using stolen Social Security numbers, which many only understood to be part of the application process, to do the dirty work few other Americans wanted to do, not to plan and commit felonies. But that didn't matter. ICE had found the bargaining chip most important to the working-class immigrants sleeping on cots in the National Cattle Congress: Their families needed them. Even though the felony charge was bogus, proving its bogusness would have required them to stay away from their families for even longer, leaving them without the income generated by sawing the thighs off dead, defeathered chickens.

The aggravated identity charge represented the government's effort to reassert control over the story. Bush signed aggravated identity theft into law four years before the raid in Postville. When he did, he warned those in attendance that "last year alone, nearly 10 million Americans had their identities stolen by criminals who rob them and the nation's businesses of nearly $50 billion through fraudulent transactions."[19] The raid was protecting not only the American worker and American business but the everyday average American whose hard-earned income was ripe to be stolen by criminals. Those undocumented immigrants dismantling your cattle were just biding their time until they could do the same to your financial security.

On the ground, immigrant families fled Postville as quickly as they could gather their belongings. About a third of the population was gone just a few weeks after the raid.[20] With workers detained and potential workers fleeing out of fear, the plant had no one to staff its disassembly line and closed just a few weeks later after filing for bankruptcy. Bush and team may have hoped that the story was one of a compassionate yet protective leader, but as the details of the raid kept piling up, a different story began to emerge.

A month and 12 days after the raid, a hearing took place before the Subcommittee on Immigration, Citizenship, Refugees, Border Security, and International Law.[21] The session, chaired by Zoe Lofgren, a Democratic representative of the 19th District of California and a former immigration attorney and immigration law professor, began on a fiery note. Lofgren shifted the story away from the identity-stealing immigrant caricature that ICE had carefully crafted. Again using the obvious comparison to cattle processing, she said:

> It seems to me one of the hallmarks of our great country is that we do not treat people like livestock. . . . The information suggests that the people charged were rounded up, herded into a cattle arena, prodded down a cattle chute, coerced into guilty pleas and then to Federal prison. This looks and feels like a cattle auction, not a criminal prosecution in the United States of America.

Despite a valiant effort, the Bush administration was unable to control the story as it had hoped. It seemed that Bush had overplayed his hand, either by assuming that news cameras would not linger on the large numbers of immigrants being herded like cattle or that the public would not be offended by such treatment of immigrants if it meant more opportunities to work and remain free from identity theft.

After Postville, Bush distanced himself from large-scale worksite raids in the final moments of his presidency to avoid the public backlash that had clearly fomented. But Bush, Obama, and, later, Biden, wanted something fundamentally different than did President Trump. Bush, Obama, and Biden had to appeal to Democrats and Republicans if they wanted any sort of immigration reform that wasn't simply by executive order. Trump, on the other hand, had no desire to appease those in the political middle and embraced the executive order with force. He didn't reach out for Democratic support. He was barely even concerned with moderate Republicans.

The very element of worksite raids that eventually made them politically untenable for the Bush and Obama administrations—their dehumanizing cruelty—was precisely what made them so useful to Trump. The humanitarian disaster was not something to be figured out, hidden, or avoided. The humanitarian disaster, in fact, was not simply the fallout of an otherwise useful strategy. The humanitarian disaster *was* the strategy, and exactly the story he wanted to tell.

The Ascendency of President Trump

It is June 16, 2015, as Donald Trump descends a golden escalator to the atrium of his eponymous hotel. When he arrives at the bottom of the escalator, he passes his daughter, Ivanka, kisses her on the cheek, and walks to a podium on a makeshift rectangular stage while Neil Young's "Keep on Rockin' in the Free World" blares on the speakers. The stage is covered in a rich blue fabric, and a curtain of the same fabric covers the marble wall, polished to a shine, that peeks over the top of the curtain. In the middle of the stage stands an oaken podium with a small sign bearing the slogan that would slowly spread all across the US: "TRUMP: Make America Great Again!" The slogan would evolve to "Keep America Great" when Trump lost his reelection bid to Biden in 2020 and return to "Make America Great Again" when he defeated Kamala Harris in 2024.

Directly behind the podium are eight American flags, outlined with gold fringe and topped with silver eagles.[22] When he finally arrives, Trump plants his feet on the ground behind the podium and, like a mayor on a parade float, begins to wave his hand, basking in the audience's attention. He looks out toward the flashes of cameras and cell phones held overhead to record the moment. He lifts the microphone until it's even with his mouth: "Wow. Woah. That is some group of people. Thousands!," he declares. "This is beyond anybody's expectations. There's been no crowd like this."

About a third of the way through his speech, he declares something that will shake up the nation for years to come: "So ladies and gentlemen, I am officially running for president of the United States, and we are going to make our country great again."[23]

Even at the time, the event was bizarre. The "thousands" of people in the audience were reported to be only a few dozen. Some of those audience members had responded to a casting call for $50, while others had come down from their living quarters in the hotel out of curiosity. Still others walked in off the street to see what was going on.[24] The speech was meandering, which, for someone who had just revealed his desire to be a politician, was atypical. Trump brazenly described a dystopian America, took personal jabs at other politicians, and embraced nearly every racist trope imaginable, most of which other politicians would tie themselves in knots to avoid. And he did this while announcing his presidential run.

Trump jumped back and forth rapidly throughout the speech, sometimes from one policy issue to another, other times from one topic to an entirely separate topic, and still other times from policy to an ad hominem attack on a political enemy, often with a little braggadocio in between. For example, immediately after arguing that the Second Amendment was necessary to protect people from violent prisoners on the loose, he began to discuss the Common Core State Standards Initiative, an educational initiative from 2010 that details what K–12 students should know at the conclusion of each school grade:

> End—end Common Core. Common Core should—it is a disaster. Bush is totally in favor of Common Core. I don't see how he can possibly get the nomination. He's weak on immigration. He's in favor of Common Core. How the hell can you vote for this guy? You just can't do it. We have to end, education has to be local.

Rebuild the country's infrastructure. Nobody can do that like me. Believe me. It will be done on time, on budget, way below cost, way below what anyone ever thought.

Trump had no problem painting a picture of a US on the brink of collapse if not for his intervention, as was evident in the close of his speech: "Sadly, the American dream is dead. But if I get elected president, I will bring it back bigger and better and stronger than ever before, and we will make America great again."

In hindsight, the meandering speech, the corporate setting, the nonsensical fabrication of data—like the size of the crowd—and the dystopian worldview of an America that only Trump could save characterized well what we were about to see when Trump ascended to the presidency one year, seven months, and four days after the golden escalator ride. At the time of the speech, many Democrats, along with some of the Republicans running against him for the Republican presidential nomination, did not see Trump's presidential run as a legitimate threat, as everything he did flew in the face of the traditional, electable politician. But we later found out how much a significant portion of America didn't want a traditional politician. They wanted a story, a story Trump was willing to pitch, political norms be damned.

Initially, Trump's ascendency to his first presidency was attributed to economic anxiety among low- and middle-income whites. "Donald J. Trump won the presidency by riding an enormous wave of support among white working-class voters," *The New York Times* professed on November 9, 2016, the day after Trump was elected president of the US.[25] *The Washington Post* published a similar article on the same day titled "How Trump Won: The Revenge of Working-Class Whites."[26] According to Jim Tankersley, author of the piece,

For the past 40 years, America's economy has raked blue-collar white men over the coals. It whittled their paychecks. It devalued the type of work they did best. It shuttered factories and mines and shops in their communities. New industries sprouted in cities where they didn't live, powered by workers with college degrees they didn't hold.... On Tuesday, their frustrations helped elect Donald Trump, the first major-party nominee of the modern era to speak directly and relentlessly to their economic and cultural fears.

But the frail US economy allegedly shrinking in the face of globalization didn't quite capture the full story, nor explain why, if the economy affected everyone, white, Christian, male voters were flocking to Trump, while those of other communities, regardless of income, gender, and education, were not.

A study published in the *Proceedings of the National Academy of Sciences* offered an explanation.[27] It wasn't that Trump supporters felt left behind by a changing economy. Instead, they feared that the changing economy was, for the first time in their lives, going to benefit someone else. In the study, Diana Mutz considered the "left behind" hypothesis, or the theory that those whose wages stagnated or who had lost their jobs voted for Trump to punish the Democrats for their situation.

But concern about their financial future did not predict support for Trump. Instead, Mutz found that whites and men were more likely to support Trump, that feeling that "the American way of life is threatened" was a strong predictor of support for Trump, and that those who supported Trump were more likely to perceive discrimination against dominant social groups than lower-status groups (for example, believing that men, Christians, or whites experienced greater discrimination than Blacks, Muslims, women, or Latinos). Put simply, Mutz argued that white Trump supporters did not elect him because of a specific worry about money but because of anxiety about their own loss of status in society, possibly accompanied by a loss of income. If Trump didn't win in 2016, the first Black president would be followed by the first woman president. What did this mean for the white male demographic of the US who saw themselves in every president elected so far? Who was going to be in control? Diversity hiring initiatives, which had yet to become the political touchpoint they are today, were showing up in business, Hollywood, government, and education. Was the white man's time as uncontested leader over?

A well-known series of essays in *The Atlantic* by writer Adam Serwer described Trump's support by his white voting base in much more straightforward terms.[28] While Mutz talked about the white voter's perception of threat to their "dominant group status," Serwer said Trump's supporters simply loved him because he was cruel. Or, more precisely, they loved him because he was cruel to certain people, the people they believed to be primed to take what was rightfully theirs.

Plus, according to Serwer, rooting for Trump's cruelty became a sport of sorts, a team-building exercise in which those with power could bully those without and not have to worry about being sent to Human Resources. Serwer describes the camaraderie brought on by Trump's cruelty in his famous essay, "The Cruelty Is the Point."[29] Serwer begins by reflecting on the many artifacts of cruelty—such as child-size slave shackles or Ku Klux Klan robes—housed at the Museum of African American History and Culture. But, Serwer argues, it is not those artifacts that impacted him most when he viewed them in the museum. Rather,

> [t]he artifacts that persist in my memory, the way a bright flash does when you close your eyes, are the photographs of the lynchings. But it's not the burned, mutilated bodies that stick with me. It's the

faces of the white men in the crowd. . . . They were human beings, people who took immense pleasure in the utter cruelty of torturing others to death—and were so proud of doing so that they posed for photographs with their handiwork, jostling to ensure they caught the eye of the lens, so that the world would know they'd been there. Their cruelty made them feel good, it made them feel proud, it made them feel happy. And it made them feel closer to one another.

Trump's voting base didn't need him to present clear policy plans, and making up numbers was inconsequential in the face of what he really did: articulate the racist, sexist, nationalist fears of those anxious about their own replacement. They saw in him a man who not only looked like them but who confirmed that they were indeed victims and that certain pockets of American society were strategizing for the extinction of their way of life. Stoking this fear of extinction became a path to victory for Trump. And what could be better at stoking fears of white extinction than reminding people of the terrifying immigrants to the south?

Protecting Angel Moms

Throughout history, immigrant communities have always served as scapegoats for national problems.[30] Whether it's an uptick in crime, rising unemployment, or a sudden spread of infectious disease, immigrants serve as a Rorschach test of the nation's fears, a convenient answer to what is usually a complicated, multifaceted problem shaped by macro social and economic factors. Savvy politicians are well aware of this and strategically cast immigrants as particular types of villains that tap into the national angst while positioning themselves as the only remedy.

Trump had no problem blaming immigrants for any number of social ills. Take, for example, the oft-referenced portion of his golden escalator speech in which he talks about immigrants from Mexico:

> The US has become a dumping ground for everybody else's problems. Thank you. It's true, and these are the best and the finest. When Mexico sends its people, they're not sending their best. They're not sending you. They're not sending you. They're sending people that have lots of problems, and they're bringing those problems with us. They're bringing drugs. They're bringing crime. They're rapists. And some, I assume, are good people. . . .
>
> It's coming from more than Mexico. It's coming from all over South and Latin America, and it's coming probably—probably—from the Middle East. But we don't know. Because we have no protection and we have no competence, we don't know what's happening. And it's got to stop and it's got to stop fast.
>
> Islamic terrorism is eating up large portions of the Middle East. They've become rich. I'm in competition with them.

In just a few sentences, Trump casts the US as a postapocalyptic "dumping ground" of the villainous Mexican drug mules and rapists with ties to Islamic terrorism. Trump had found the perfect villain, and next he would find the perfect victim.

In an immigration speech given during a rally in Phoenix, Arizona, on August 31, 2016,[31] Trump begins by sharing that he just returned from a meeting with the president of Mexico. "We agree," Trump tells the audience, "on the importance of ending the illegal flow of drugs, cash, guns, and people across our border, and to put the cartels out of business." While he takes a quick diversion to mention his "love for the people of Mexico," he then immediately describes the multiple problems with the immigration system. The main issue, he shares, is the failure of politicians to secure the border, leading to "many people, so many, many people," whose children have been killed by undocumented immigrants.

Trump details the murders of five US citizens by undocumented immigrants, a 21-year-old college woman with a 4.0 grade point average, a 64-year-old veteran, and a 90-year-old man among them. Some of these descriptions are quite grizzly, such as the description of the killing of Marilyn Pharis: "[A] 64-year-old Air Force veteran, a great woman, according to everybody that knew her, was sexually assaulted and beaten to death with a hammer. Her killer had been arrested on multiple occasions but was never, ever deported, despite the fact that everybody wanted him out."

After clearly painting a picture of these immigrants as violent murderers, thriving in a system that fails to remove them, he reminds the audience that "most illegal immigrants are lower-skilled workers with less education, who compete directly against vulnerable American workers, and that these illegal workers draw much more out from the system than they can ever possibly pay back. And they're hurting a lot of our people that cannot get jobs under any circumstances." Threats to life, threats to the economy, threats to jobs. Immigrants can do it all.

As the speech nears its close, Trump invites all the "Angel Moms" to join him onstage. He doesn't describe what makes one an Angel Mom, but given the content of the speech, it is safe to assume that everyone understood an Angel Mom to be someone whose child had been killed by an undocumented immigrant. Whether "killing" meant murder or could extend to incidents like car accidents isn't clear. But it doesn't matter. Slowly, Trump is surrounded on stage by Angel Moms, each of whom wears a white shirt printed with the phrase "A Stolen Life" on the front. Beneath these words is a photo of the face of the family member they lost, along with their age. Chants of "USA!" slowly overtake the arena.

While the demographics of the Angel Moms Trump would foreground in his talks would change, this initial group looked a lot like him, with white skin and blond or light-brown hair. So it is a bit surprising when the first mother he invites up, a brunette, begins to speak with an accent. She discusses her son, Ronald da Silva, who was murdered by "an illegal alien who had been previously deported." Before she walks away, she says, "What makes me so outrageous is, we came here legally."

Each parent then goes up in turn, says the name of their child (or husband, or cousin), and describes when and sometimes how they were killed by "illegals" or "illegal aliens."[32] A white woman a little shorter than Trump with blond hair to the bottom of her shoulder blades remembers her son, Eric Zepeda, who was killed when his motorcycle was struck by a car driven by an undocumented immigrant. Judging purely from the color of her hair and skin, it's safe to assume the audience notices that this blonde white woman has a Latino-sounding last name, Zepeda. They have only a brief moment to wonder about her name, though, because she quickly explains that Eric Zepeda "was raised by a *legal* immigrant from Honduras." She emphasizes the word "legal" before she continues, "only to be murdered by an illegal."[33]

In truth, each family member onstage experienced pain that no person, especially a parent, ever should. No one is arguing that their grief was inappropriate or unjustified. The issue, then, is how their rage and grief was packaged by a president with his own anti-immigrant agenda. Trump provided a master class in fearmongering, using gritty details and individual instances of violence to propose the failure of an entire system, a system only he could fix. Near the end of the talk, he even created an immigrant hierarchy on which he would later depend: the good versus the bad immigrants, those who did it the "right way" and those who had no respect for wrong or right, those who were legal and virtuous, and those who were illegal and killed.

These Angel Moms (whether moms or not), who had lost their loved ones to the violence of undocumented immigrants, were largely white and mostly women and put a face on the stakes of the immigration debate, just as Trump had intended. What mother wouldn't do anything in her power, no matter how cruel, to defend her children? And what kind of husband would fail to protect his wife from the sadness of a child's death?

Foregrounding Angel Moms provided another advantage to Trump, one that is fundamental to the country's embrace of immigration raids. Trump could talk about Angel Moms and the immigrants streaming across the border who killed their children without ever having to specifically mention *Latinos*. He could discuss Mexico, Central America, and Latin America as much as he wanted while easily countering any accusations of racism: This isn't about race; it's about immigration status. That Angel Parents even included Latino and Black parents only helped the narrative. It couldn't be about race, then, could it?

Trump was quite skilled at telling stories that preyed on white America's deepest fears of violence. He also expertly leveraged these fears to propose solutions that were themselves wrought with violence and convinced the public to accept them. Whereas Bush wanted to be seen as firm yet compassionate in order to appeal to both sides of the political aisle, Trump had no desire to walk such a fine line. He didn't want to appease both political parties. He wanted instead to embolden those nowhere near the political middle, to confirm and stir their fears that someone was taking what was rightfully theirs and attempting to make Angel Moms of us all. The worksite raid in Postville was a cruel humanitarian disaster. It was also exactly what Trump wanted.

CHAPTER 2

Choreographed Chaos

Tornadoes, War, and Triage

But what does this humanitarian disaster look like from the inside? Everywhere we went, those who jumped into action after a worksite raid found it hard to explain what exactly a worksite raid was like. Many times, interviewees would search for something with which to compare the raid, share the analogy with us, reflect on the analogy to see if it made sense, conclude that the analogy lacked some defining aspect of the raid experience, and then refine their analogy or throw it away altogether. It often seemed as if they were working through their memories of the raid for the very first time in front of us and had to unpack the emotions and confront their belief systems in a way they hadn't before. For many in the rural US, a natural disaster analogy was a useful starting point.

Sarah, who taught English-language learners (ELL) from kindergarten through fifth grade in Morristown, Tennessee, compared the raid response in Morristown to the emergency response after Hurricane Katrina in 2005. Hurricane Katrina was one of the most catastrophic and costly hurricanes in US history. It battered the Gulf Coast, moving through Tennessee en route to Louisiana, where most of the damage took place.[1] When Sarah saw families huddled together in the school after the raid in nearby Bean Station, she said "[It] was the most tragic thing I'd ever seen. The only thing I've compared it to before was, after Katrina in Knoxville, they had a Red Cross center set up, and that was the only thing that was kind of similar to it."

But the emergency center set up in Bean Station was different from that set up after Katrina:

> This [the raid in Bean Station] felt way more devastating to me and I think maybe because it was way closer to home. Or I think it was also the not knowing anything that was so devastating, because with the Katrina shelter, there had obviously been a long time between the hurricane and by the time the shelter was set up, but [the raid] was just like, nobody knew any information. Everybody was just gathered there, everybody was terrified, nobody knew what was going on.

After Katrina, that is, those who sought shelter knew the hurricane was over. After the raid in Bean Station, it was unclear whether the disaster had ended.

Stacy, who also responded after the raid in Bean Station, began with a disaster analogy as well, saying "I've never been part of a natural disaster response team, but that's what it felt like. It just felt like we were scrambling to get basic resources, that it had been like a tornado or an earthquake or something."

But just like Sarah, Stacy found the comparison inadequate.

> It's hard to imagine any other kind of event that would trigger 600 kids to miss school in a small town, that the governor wouldn't be out there immediately. If it had been a tornado or something?

So there was something also really hard for all of us, when it felt like we knew how intense the pain and everything was, but it wasn't being seen or named by people.

For Stacy, while the raid was like a natural disaster, at least the government would respond after a natural disaster. The government wouldn't respond after a raid, however, as it conducted the raid in the first place. Al, who Nicole interviewed in Mount Pleasant, also began his explanation of the raid by comparing it to a tornado: "Now, I take this, as a community member, as very analogous to a tornado coming down and taking out 30 houses on the edge of town. How do we respond to that? . . . Same thing's happened out at that fire out in California."

Like the others, something about the tornado and wildfire comparison just didn't sit right with him, so Al continued to refine his analogy: "I really want to make that analogy stick. So, now, again, if the whole town had been taken out, we couldn't have done anything. So, if you had 30 houses taken out, 30 families, okay? Then, the rest of the town could help those folks. And we have those storms come through all the time."

Sometimes disaster comparisons, even after careful refinement to capture the chaos and public indifference that followed, were still unsatisfactory. Leah, who taught ELL for 15 years and was a band teacher for 7 years before that, compared the raid in Mount Pleasant to the terrorist attacks that occurred on September 11, 2001. While 9/11 was certainly a salient memory for everyone in the US, it was perhaps uniquely impactful for teachers, who had to decide what to do with the students in front of them.

Naomi, a Latina global health studies major working with us at the time, asked Leah if she remembered the day of the raid well enough to walk her through how it unfolded:

NAOMI: Let's go back to the raid. Do you remember the day and how you found out everything that happened on May 9th?

LEAH: Yeah, it's weird; it's one of those defining moments. It was like, I remember what happened when 9/11 happened. I remember stuff like that, like when the Challenger blew up, the space shuttle. This is one of those things. Except that I don't remember the date of the Challenger blowing up. But I do remember May 9th, for right now. May 9th is the day of the raid, and I won't forget that. At least I won't for another year probably. It was just bizarre.

Sylvia, the principal of an elementary school in Morristown, Tennessee, found out about the raid in the middle of the school day and wrestled with whether to tell her students that the parents who had dropped them off might not be there to pick them up. It occurred to her that she had been in a similar situation before, and she made the same comparison as Leah: "Yeah, it's like 9/11. I was still teaching when that happened. Some schools turned it on and watched it. At the school where I was, we were actually on a field trip when that happened, and we didn't tell the children. We didn't tell them when they got back."

These comparisons were helpful, but to many interviewees, something was still missing. Raids weren't just acts of nature like tornadoes. And while they stick in the collective memory of a community like planes crashing into buildings in the middle of a school day, there was something much more personal about them. Raids were performed by people on other people. People in body armor arrested people in meat frocks. People with zip ties bound the hands of people panicking over the fate of their families. And these people looked each other in the eyes. The interpersonal violence—or at least the threat of it—was face-to-face. Kind of like war.

≈

When I drove up to Southeastern Provision, a slaughterhouse in Bean Station, Tennessee, I was surprised to see dried cow intestines on the gravel drive in front. *Rolling Stone* magazine described Southeastern Provision as a slaughterhouse built of "multicolored sheets of corrugated metal [that] had been built haphazardly, with its various wings and outbuildings jutting out at odd angles."[2] But it wasn't the metal (nor the intestines) that really caught my attention. It was the wood. The building was some sort of slaughterhouse Tetris made of rusty metal, but there was also wood everywhere, wooden planks of uneven height that almost made it to the ceiling but left a foot or so gap, wooden boards placed horizontally to make up for the wooden planks that didn't quite reach the ground. While the intestines at my feet were dried out and crackly—and therefore odorless—I couldn't fathom the smell of the animal waste, blood, and gases that lingered in the deteriorating wood.

The slaughterhouse was already on the radar of the Tennessee Department of Environment and Conservation due to the pollution of multiple wells in the area,[3] including, supposedly, a culvert that had filled with blood. At one point the remains of slaughtered cattle seeped into the groundwater of the surrounding area after a septic failure, causing a boil-water alert for nearby residents.[4] Along with its poor environmental record, the owners of Southeastern Provision were accused of avoiding $2.5 million in taxes by hiring undocumented immigrants and paying them in cash.[5] Workers reported dangerous conditions, including the use of chemicals without protective equipment. It was clear that the workers at Southeastern Provision were working in an environment that was dangerous, poorly regulated, exploitative, and gory.

Given the evidence, the largest raid in Tennessee history occurred on April 5, 2018, when ICE, the Internal Revenue Service (IRS), and the Tennessee Highway Patrol raided Southeastern Provision, detaining 97 workers. Detained workers were sent to a National Guard armory in a neighboring county for processing,[6] while their families congregated in a school gymnasium next door before being moved to St. Peter's Catholic Church.

The night of the raid of Southeastern Provision, Larry rushed over to St. Peter's to set up cots for families who needed a safe place to sleep as they figured out who had been taken away. An older white man in approximately his mid-50s, Larry had a rich life of experience that he had no problem sharing with Nicole in a small room in the basement of Saint Peter's during a typically busy Sunday afternoon. Larry did not look particularly different from other white men in their 50s we had met in the rural US. But when he opened his mouth, you noticed that he had an accent you couldn't quite place. It wasn't Spanish. It wasn't British. His unique accent was one of many interesting things about him.

Larry was the son of a military father who fought in the Pacific Theater during World War II. He later got a job in New York and was sent to work in Suriname, a small country in the northeast of South America populated by the ancestors of enslaved people from Africa and Asia. Larry was one of seven children and one of three born in Suriname. Because his parents were US citizens, Larry was a US citizen as well, despite being born abroad. He spent his childhood first in Suriname, then in Trinidad, and learned English as his "second or third language, depends."

His experience growing up in another country, seeing other cultures, learning other languages, easily getting a job in a country in which he was not a citizen, and freely moving from country to country gave Larry "this outside view of America . . . When I see things happen, I have these other perspectives than most

Americans. And I struggle to communicate with Americans." In short, Larry's experience as an immigrant was pretty easy. And he knew this.

When he began talking about the raid, his confident and jovial tone gave way to sighs and stutters, and he frequently had to pause and compose himself.

"I was there. The Thursday night," he told Nicole in a room in the church basement. "I watched 160 children lose their parent.[7] Okay? . . . I mean, I watched these people walk around with that blank stare in their face, and I've seen it once before in my life."

He then recalled a military coup in Suriname to overthrow the government that took place in February of 1980. A brutal civil war between the Suriname Army and the Maroons—the descendants of the enslaved people who had gained their freedom—ensued. Eventually, the people revolted against what had then become a militarized government. Larry described the rebellion: "On the night of December 8, 1982, when people started revolting against [the government, they lined up] 60 of the most influential people in the country, up against a wall and shot 50, basically took over [in] two days. . . . And the following March, I was in that country. And I saw a whole country walk with that gaze."

According to Larry, those walking around the church looking for family members and food after the raid on Southeastern Provision had the same gaze, the same stare into the distance, as those who had just survived a military coup followed by a massive public execution.

But even this comparison fell short for Larry.

As he reached the end of an interview that seemed to both drain and energize him, you could hear him trip over his words, pausing, as if he were trying to decide whether he wanted to say aloud what clearly occurred in his head. Eventually, he steeled himself and continued through a knot in his throat: "In December 20th, my 15-year-old granddaughter died. I saw her in a cheerleading outfit in her coffin. She died in a car accident in California. And this raid here is right up there with watching my granddaughter in her funeral. One hundred and sixty children, in one day, in America, lost a parent, and yet half the country justifying it."

≈

Larry's time in Suriname had exposed him to life in a conflict zone. But he had never worn the military uniform himself. Father Jim, on the other hand, had been wearing the fatigues and combat boots of a soldier for 13 years when we met him in the same church as Larry that Sunday in July of 2018. A proud member of the Army National Guard—with service very well-documented on the Internet—Father Jim was stationed in Iraq during Operation Desert Storm, where he served in a field artillery unit guarding 25,000 Iraqi detainees in what was, at the time, the world's largest detention facility.

Father Jim's military uniform looked a bit different from that of his fellow soldiers, however. In one photo of him I found online, you can see him dressed in full desert camo, standing with his arms crossed on his chest in front of a line of about half a dozen tan Hummers. His head is razor-blade bald, his face clean and freshly shaven. Everything in the picture is the color of sand and dirt and dust except for the deep purple stole Father Jim has draped around his neck. In the Catholic tradition, purple is worn twice a year, during the liturgical periods known as Lent and Advent. The Catholic Bible recalls Roman soldiers draping a purple robe on Jesus's shoulders and placing a crown of thorns on his head to mock his supposed royalty before crucifying him. So while purple represents royalty, it calls to mind a specific type of royalty, one that includes sacrifice and penance and preparation for what is to come.

Father Jim had likely worn his purple stole many times throughout the years he served in the National Guard. As a Catholic chaplain, he was one of very few. When he first began, in fact, the Catholic Chaplain Corps was at 5 percent, meaning that for every 100 Catholic chaplains needed, there were only 5. His rarity kept him busy.

While stationed in Iraq, he was flown or driven to military outposts throughout northern Iraq to celebrate mass with small pockets of Catholic soldiers who would otherwise miss out on the service or attend the services of another faith tradition that contributes more chaplains to the military than Catholicism. On one memorable Easter Sunday, Father Jim was delivered to five separate locations across Iraq to celebrate Easter Mass, which Catholics consider their most important celebration (in that case, Father Jim would have been in a bright-pink stole, not a purple one). One of the many articles published about him also noted that his service in hostile territory earned him a Bronze Star for meritorious service in a combat zone, a fact he was too humble to mention to us.

When Father Jim speaks, you get the feeling he knows what he's talking about. And when he speaks about war? Even more so.

Father Jim greets Nicole and me at the door to St. Peter's. We are joined by Julio, a friend and collaborator from Tennessee who attended St. Peter's Church when young and was kind enough to set up the interview for us. Father Jim walks the three of us to his office and invites us to have a seat on a set of gray couches arranged in a U-shape. His small brown dog jumps up on the couch next to us, excited to join the growing congregation preparing to hear his human's impromptu sermon. The image of Divine Mercy, showing rays of light representing blood and water pouring from Jesus's heart, hangs on the wall.

Nicole, Julio, and I had all grown up Catholic and are familiar and comfortable with the space we are in. Julio had, in fact, doubled my altar serving record, having been an altar server for 12 full years to my 6. So perhaps it is the aura of spirituality in the room, or perhaps it is sheer nostalgia and our internalized familiarity with what happens when a preacher preaches, but we turn on the recorder, ask a question, and then sort of switch to parishioner mode and listen raptly to Father Jim's unfolding homily.

Like any good homilist, Father Jim begins with a joke, admitting that he was mixing up Julio with his brother, José, as both their names "start with J."

JULIO: My parents did that on purpose.

FATHER JIM: I hope not!

JULIO: Yeah. It saves on monograms for the towels.

The reverie breaks for a hearty communal chuckle before he continues, having solidified us as his attentive, enthralled audience.

Father Jim's isolation from other Catholic priests in northern Iraq prepared him well for similar isolation in Tennessee. If he wanted to care for his congregations, he learned, sometimes he needed to find someone else to share the load. Never was this more true than when it came time to respond to the raid that might have taken a significant number of his parishioners out of his pews. He shares:

> I can tell you what day it was that the raids occurred because I had a lunch appointment with an Episcopal preacher. He approached me and said, "Hey, would you be interested in meeting?"

I thought, well, I've gotta look, because sometimes Catholic priests, especially in the South, especially if they're sort of by themselves, we can have this loner mentality because there aren't many other Catholic priests. . . . And I thought this might be nice because an Episcopal priest would share a lot of the same theological training and appreciation for liturgical things and so forth.

Father Jim's lunch with the Episcopal pastor is abruptly interrupted by a phone call from Cindy, Larry's wife and the director of religious education at St. Peter's. Cindy asks Father Jim if he is aware of what is going on at the meatpacking plant where some of their parishioners work. He recalls the phone call for us: "[Cindy is] much more media savvy than I am. I think her cell phone had been just on fire with all of the emails and text messages and so forth. . . . And she said that immigration had rounded up people, and they had taken them to the National Guard Armory."

Cindy, playing the role of the religious education director whose congregants need much more than baptismal certificate translation, takes it upon herself to go over to the National Guard Armory to see whether any of her fellow parishioners had been detained. But ICE agents refuse to let her in. She relays this to Father Jim over the phone. Angry and concerned for his parishioners, he leaves lunch early to change into his National Guard uniform and head over to the armory himself.

The armory—located about seven miles from the church—is a two-story brick building with an American flag and green Sherman tank in front. An elementary school, whose teachers educate some of the children of plant workers, sits next to the armory, separated only by a circular driveway and a small open field. This means that some of the teachers thinking about 9/11 could look out of their windows and watch as uniformed men and women brought in the parents of their students and sat them in chairs in a room in front of a tank and a waving American flag.

Perhaps it is his religious aura, perhaps it is the camouflage uniform, or perhaps it is the good old-fashioned sexism and boy's club of law enforcement, but when Father Jim arrives at the armory, to his surprise: "They let me in. I did my military stuff, and then I just happened to look through the little glass panes that look into the armory hall, the drill hall itself. And I could see rows and rows of metal chairs, and then I could see little stations set up all the way around. I just sort of peek. I didn't say nothing."

And while the armory isn't the cattle fairgrounds that held the workers after the raid in Postville, Iowa, from Father Jim's description what was going on inside certainly sounds similar:

> One of the guys said, "Oh, you want to come in and take a look at what we're doing?" And I said, "Oh, yeah, sure," you know. So I stood there, and I felt really strange because I was in a military uniform. And they were all in various khakis and with their black polo shirts and whatever they had.[8]
>
> But there were different agencies. I think the sheriff's department was there, and immigration was there and I don't know. There were people wearing different kinds of badges and lanyards and everything.

After noting the various agencies present, including local law enforcement, Father Jim scans the crowd of detainees in search of his parishioners.

> But most of [the people detained] were facing away from me. The rows of chairs were facing away from me. But I noticed that they were "interviewing." I guess that's the nicest way to put it. They were interviewing people in the hallway. . . .

So, I guess they were pulling people into various hallways and interview rooms and asking them questions about how they got paid, how often they got paid. Did they get paid in cash and did they have to clock in. Those were the kind of questions that I could hear that the interviewers were asking them. Where they came from and so forth . . .

[From] what I gathered at the time, they were trying to also build a case against the owner on violations, on not paying them, or underpaying them, or whatever. So they were asking questions about how they got paid, how often they got paid, and various other things.

The agents "interviewing" the detained workers eventually do make a case against the owner of the factory, James Brantley, filing a lawsuit for "tax fraud, wire fraud, and employment of unauthorized illegal aliens."[9] He was charged with multiple state and federal crimes, resulting in an 18-month prison sentence, a $1.3 million payment to the IRS, and $1.42 million in restitution.[10] ICE agents thanked the workers who provided them with evidence for the successful suit by detaining them based on race, hurling racial slurs at them,[11] and punching one worker in the face during the raid.[12]

When the families and friends of those who work at the factory hear that the detained workers are being held at the National Guard Armory, many drive over to the armory themselves and wait to see if their loved ones will be released. But awkwardly waiting on the side of the road becomes dangerous for these families, not only because of the risk of oncoming vehicles but also because of the angry racial slurs hurled their way by Tennesseans passing by. So the principal from the elementary school adjacent to the armory lets the waiting families into the school gymnasium, where a small loaves-and-fishes-type miracle begins to unfold as the portion of the town not wiped out by the tornado starts to feed the portion that was.

When he learns all he can from the inside of the processing center at the armory, Father Jim returns to the church. Together with his staff, he begins to prepare the church for anyone who might need somewhere to sleep, especially, he says, children whose parents might have been detained. Volunteers, Larry among them, help Father Jim set up cots.

Father Jim orders pizza for everyone, but the influx of families he was predicting does not materialize. At about 1:00 a.m., the volunteers decide that no one is going to come to the church after all, and they all go home.

The next day, Father Jim wakes up, dons his vestments, and performs a short, 30-minute mass at 8:30 a.m. When it concludes, according to Father Jim,

> I got out of my vestments, and I look out the window, and then there's all these cars. Evidently, somehow a decision was made that St. Peter's would be the headquarters. I guess that made sense because it was a school day, and Friday morning you've got kids at [the] elementary school, and so you can't be there. And it is a natural place because most of the victims I would say would identify with being Catholic.
>
> So, I'm a person of routine. So, I had my breakfast. I had my coffee, and I walked down there. And it was just triage. And that I know because I'm in the military.
>
> And so, we prepare for mass casualties and everything else, and we have different stations and people run their different stations and do different things. And chaplains, which I am, we have to do our thing as well. So, we have to help tend to the dying and so forth.
>
> It was triage.

¿Un Helicóptero? ¿En Mount Pleasant?

Hurricanes. Earthquakes. Wildfires. Terrorist attacks. Coups. Triage.

Interviewees used these analogies to explain what it was like in the moments after a worksite raid, cumulatively describing the chaos, destruction, violence, trauma, and massive human need that unfolded. Even after all their careful revisions, however, these comparisons—mostly made by white US citizens exposed to immigration raids for the first time—still lacked something critical. So intense and climactic were these analogies that they made it seem as if a raid happens at a specific, decisive moment, and everyone is instantly aware of it. But this is far from the case. In fact, unless you are inside a building as it's being raided, it's hard to figure out where a raid is happening, when it started, when it ends, how far it will extend from that site, and who is conducting it. Instead, there's a haunting buildup, a graying of the sky and a darkening of the clouds as you wait to see how bad things are going to get. For many Latino families, the trauma came not only from the climactic moment of the raid but from the unrelenting feeling that it wasn't over and they might be next.

Diego came to the US in the mid-2000s on an H1B visa, generally referred to as a "work visa." He worked as a newspaper editor for nine years in Iowa and was constantly in contact with the Latino community throughout the state. He later took a job at a credit union, continuing to build on these relationships to offer financial security to the Latino families who trusted him. When ICE raided Midwest Precast Concrete on May 9, 2018, Diego's phone began to ping with the phone calls and text messages of desperate Latino families contacting one of the most knowledgeable Latinos they knew to find out what's going on.

Also using a comparison to a military invasion, Diego described the growing misgivings throughout the Latino community that something significant was about to happen:

> Because of all the closeness I have with community organizations and community leaders, when the raid happened, the first thing a community leader did was call me.
>
> He said, "Don Diego, something's happening here. Hay muchos carros de policía. / There are so many police cars. The people are nervous."
>
> They even told me there was a helicopter. A helicopter!? In Mount Pleasant!? Eso es, rarísimo. / This is extremely rare/unnatural/strange.... It didn't seem like a police intervention or anything; it seemed like a military thing, like an invasion. Y por la cantidad de policías ... / And because there were so many police and so much movement, and they closed a street, well, it was something that caused so much terror in the community.

Speaking in Spanish, Diego does not distinguish which bodies of law enforcement are slowly convening in their small town, numbering enough to shut down a street. Instead, he simply says *carros de policía*, not taking the time to decipher who exactly makes up *la cantidad de policías*. He also notes the helicopter, a rare site in a town with a population of about 9,000.

John, a 72-year-old volunteer who responded to the raid of Midwest Precast Concrete, described it to Nicole in much the same terms as Diego, noting the *cantidad de policías* who were not ICE and expressing the same shock at the sight of the helicopter circling overhead.

JOHN: The morning of the raid, I just was going out to take my normal morning walk, and of course, we go right past the courthouse, and here's all these police and the sheriff—[laughs]—in full body gear and this kind of thing.

And I said, "Well, let's see, who do we have? An armed shooter in the courthouse or something!?". Because it was amazing how many vehicles and police were out there. And later their story was, "Well, all we were doing was [standing] out there directing traffic."

NICOLE: That's a little overkill, directing traffic in full body armor!?

JOHN: With a helicopter above!

Diego's and John's reports were just two of the multiple times community members shared their chilling, frightening, or unsettling memories of the helicopters that showed up on the day their communities were raided. Helicopters were also a focal point of the raid in Postville, Iowa, with nearly every book, blog, study, and news report on the raid referencing the presence of the Black Hawk that hovered above Agriprocessors Inc. In fact, the cover image of the 2011 documentary *Abused: The Postville Raid* depicts a blue sky peppered with a few clouds over a rolling field of green grass, the Postville water tower, and two Black Hawk helicopters.[13]

It is no surprise that helicopters stand out in people's memories and make their way onto the covers of documentaries. Helicopters don't usually show up in these small, rural towns. And when they do, they are usually the much smaller civilian models proudly painted in the colors of the hospital that pays for them—like the civilian A-Star painted in the Hawkeye gold and black of the University of Iowa Hospital[14]—not the coal black of the military Black Hawk or the dark green of President Trump's Sikorsky. In towns like Mount Pleasant or Bean Station or Sandusky or Postville, they are simply out-of-place, loud, raucous, and exorbitantly expensive machinery that is *rarísimo* and prescient of the well-funded chaos to come.

Helicopters and law enforcement officers amassing outside of courthouses are not the only incongruities that put community members on edge. In Grand Island, Nebraska, a housekeeper notices a block of 100 reservations made for ICE agents in the hotel she cleans. In Sandusky, Ohio, a mother takes her daughter to the ice cream parlor and sees buses pulling in and out of the parking lot in the Border Patrol station across the street.

And when ICE has no cattle auction facilities or National Guard Armories to process those it detains, it builds its processing facilities itself, fueling the speculation of those nearby.

Yvonne was a Latina organizer born and raised in Grand Island, Nebraska, where she worked as an elementary school principal and volunteered with nonprofits dedicated to supporting immigrants. She had also worked for a private attorney, providing help with immigration cases. "Education and immigration have always been things that I've been involved with and had a passion for," she shared with the team.

One day on her normal morning commute to work, she saw what looked like the construction of some sort of staging area. Over the course of the next few weeks, Yvonne watched as the staging area grew. If it was going to be used, it was probably going to be used soon. But for what?

At the same time, Yvonne and others started noticing the presence of ICE officers in the area:

> We started seeing more ICE officials, immigration officials. People were calling and saying "Immigration's in town," "They're all staying out at the hotel out here," "They are over here," "We saw them at Buffalo Wings," whatever . . .

So people would call me and tell me to go out. They needed me to see what was true. There was people panicking, rumors flying. And so then I would go out and check to see what was going on, and then I'd send out an email saying something [to others in Grand Island] so that people would know to be careful.

The emails that went out in and around Grand Island, like the emails that went flying throughout communities all over the country, were filled with projections. These were educated projections, but projections nonetheless, most of which would never and could never be clarified or confirmed. Families throughout Grand Island were then left to decide how they would change their daily routines to avoid something potentially catastrophic, something that might not happen at all.

Neither Yvonne nor anyone else in town knew exactly what the holding center was for, though experience suggested the worst. Grand Island, Nebraska, was one of the sites of the notorious 2006 Swift raids of six meatpacking plants that resulted in the detainment of about 1,300 workers.[15] Like the memories of the Agriprocessors raid in Postville, the memories of the Swift raid in Grand Island hovered around town like ghosts that refused to leave. For some, these memories provided the lens through which any law enforcement activity was interpreted. For others they provided flashbacks, brief adrenaline rushes, and pits in their stomachs whenever they saw a uniformed officer or ICE van.

The National Council of La Raza commissioned the Urban Institute to investigate the impacts of the Swift raids, among others, resulting in the groundbreaking report *Paying the Price: The Impact of Immigration Raids on America's Children*.[16] The cover of the report shows a young Latina girl with her black hair in two ponytails on the sides of her head, sobbing in the arms of her mother, who works to console her daughter in the moments after her father was detained in a raid. The report describes how agents in Grand Island didn't just conduct their work in the Swift plants but spilled out into the community: "In Grand Island, ICE's ongoing door-to-door operations and arrests of immigrants in their homes maintained a high level of fear in the community for weeks, and families there would not even go to church or open the door for community leaders who brought them food baskets." So maybe it was a holding center for a raid at a worksite. But maybe not. And maybe it was a holding center for a raid at a worksite that would continue on into the neighborhood.

But maybe not.

While Yvonne, like everyone in the community, couldn't be sure, she was probably the person in the best position to take an educated guess. Yvonne herself was involved in the response to the raids on the Swift plants in 2006. Describing the raids, she said, "I don't know if you guys have ever seen a raid, but they are very, very emotional, very, very terrifying. It's horrible." Of the women involved in the raid, she added, "These women were in such a depression and so badly traumatized that they were unable to function." Yvonne and the immigrant and advocacy communities throughout Grand Island wondered if the once-in-a-lifetime raid that had knocked their fellow Latinas into dysfunction in 2006 was about to happen again 12 years later.

But as it turns out, the emails Yvonne sent out to prepare the Latino community in Grand Island arrived in the wrong set of inboxes. The wrong projection, the wrong immigrants scared into hiding. Yvonne continued: "So we watched it all week, and we started to see more cars and vans and stuff pull in. Then the next week, they put up a huge tent. What the hell was going on? We thought it was for [us in] Grand Island!"

Like Cindy and Father Jim in Morristown, Tennessee, Yvonne took it upon herself to drive over to what was probably a makeshift detention site to learn more about what was happening:

> And then the next day, they put up Porta Potties. It's all outside, so just for the heck of it, [I] went over to see what's going on. They said that it was for a graduation ceremony. . . . And I thought, you know, when you're having a graduation ceremony, you don't put dignitaries out in all this heat for the ceremony, and you don't give them Porta Potties to use.

Yvonne was pretty sure that ICE was lying to her.

≈

Yvonne was indeed correct, at least about some things. ICE was certainly lying. The tents and Porta Potties were a holding center for a raid about to happen, not, as they said, for a graduation ceremony. But there was one thing about which Yvonne was definitely wrong. She explained:

> On the 8th [of August], they had the raid. So I started getting calls at eleven o'clock. But we expected it here in Grand Island! We were planning here in Grand Island. So the day of the raid, I started getting calls at eleven o'clock, saying "ICE is in O'Neill!"
> So I took off for O'Neill and on my way to O'Neill I passed about six buses full of people . . . all headed up to Grand Island.

To recap, Yvonne, who feared that a raid was going to happen in Grand Island as she observed in 2006, left Grand Island when she found out that multiple raids were happening not in Grand Island but in O'Neill, 112 miles away, on a tomato-growing plant, a potato-processing plant, a feedlot, and other locations in and around the town. On her way she passed buses and vans full of detained workers being taken from the raids in O'Neill to the processing camp in Grand Island.

Yvonne then called her people in Grand Island to tell them to be on watch for the influx of detained workers who were about to be processed for something other than graduation. Even Yvonne, a Latina with years of immigration advocacy experience, with connections all over the state, who had literally been involved in worksite raids before, made the most informed, educated guess possible and was still off by 100 miles.

Yvonne continued on to O'Neill. Not knowing exactly where to go, she did what families all over the country hit by raids did at that time and headed over to the church. When she arrived, the priest directed her instead to an elementary school nearby. Here, nearly step for step, the unfolding of the raid in O'Neill mirrored that in Bean Station 1,000 miles away.[17] And this pattern—of confusion, of lies, of *cosas rarísimas*, and then of churches and schools serving as the gathering sites for those searching for their families—would be mirrored throughout every town in which a raid occurred that summer. More often than not, the media and the public would miss the pattern and consequently miss the opportunities to support the immigrant families, faith communities, and educators entangled in these disasters. As we'll see later, the media and the public were caught up in a different immigration disaster: the separation of children at the US–Mexico border.

Tocando la Puerta de Fulano

Even when you have amassed enough clues and know with certainty that a raid is happening, you still have no idea when and how it is going to play out. Will it happen at one business, like the raid on Southeastern Provision in Bean Station? Will it happen at multiple businesses of the same chain, like the raids on two Corso's Flower and Garden Centers in Sandusky? Or will it happen in a string of ostensibly unrelated businesses, with agents spilling over into nearby homes and detainees dragged two hours away, as in O'Neill?

It's also nearly impossible to figure out the timing and location of raids because everyday average law enforcement—law enforcement that can result in your deportation—is happening at the same time. The police don't get the day off just because ICE is conducting a raid.[18] ICE, fully aware of how confusing this can be, is happy to exploit your confusion. This blurry line between ICE, whose job it is to remove you, and other law enforcement officers, who can remove you but might or might not, is why Spanish-speaking immigrant communities tend to use the word *policía* to describe anyone in uniform. The man is the man, and the man can cuff you and take you away.

I meet Pastor Isaac at one of the two Evangelical churches in northern Texas at which he serves as pastor. This church, located in Paris, Texas, resides in a simple storefront that sits below a large white water tower with "Paris" proudly written on it. The *I* in the word "Paris" is dotted with a star that I can only presume to be the "lone star" displayed on the Texas flag used to commemorate our temporary status as an independent republic after the state ceded from Mexico in 1836 and before it was annexed into the US in 1846. The storefront is just a few miles away from the 65-foot-tall Eiffel tower capped by a red cowboy hat that is one of the most famous roadside attractions Paris has to offer (yes, the hat is included in the tower's official height). The storefront is indistinguishable from the storefronts around it, and the church would be equally unnoticeable if not for the large sign in front providing the times of church services above the church's name and the image of a dove and a cross. This time, the dates and times are listed in Spanish.

Inside, the church is a large open space with a dropped ceiling and halogen lights. Pastor Isaac has built a couple of freestanding rooms in the back of the space, one that is used for storage and one that he uses as an office. Nicole and I are joined by Eileen, a Panamanian reporter and Olympic fencer who tagged along with us that day to make a podcast (you meet a wonderful mix of people doing fieldwork). When we are done making small talk in the back of the church, Pastor Isaac invites me into his office, where we begin to laugh and joke, my brain slowly switching over to Spanish so we can do the interview in his first language. Outside his office, I hear someone begin to play the guitar. Other instruments—a keyboard, a drum set, a bass guitar—are variously joining in, and it's clear that the church's band is about to begin rehearsing for the service tomorrow.

The churches over which Isaac presides are about 1 hour and 15 minutes apart, so Isaac spends many hours a week behind the wheel of his car. When I point out to Isaac that his Sundays must be full of driving, he responds, "*iy cada jueves!* / yes, and every Thursday too!". "*Sí, porque aquí [en Paris], tengo culto el domingo y miércoles,*" he goes on to explain. "Here, in Paris, I have service on Sunday and Wednesday. And there, I have service Sunday afternoon and Thursday afternoon. So two times there, and two times here." Isaac is not the only person in his family who traverses the rolling North Texas plains multiple times a week. His son, he explains, who plays the drums in the band in both churches and is in fact warming up outside the office right now, is also at both churches multiple times a week. In characterizing his role as a pastor, Isaac uses the word *culto* to describe the church services he performs for his congregants. I am not familiar with the term *culto*, so I invite Isaac to tell me a little more about what it means. He explains that *culto* comes from the Spanish word *cultivar*, the cognate for the English word "cultivate," meaning to plant, to grow, or to till the earth to create a fertile place for a seed to thrive.

When Isaac tells me how much driving he does every week, my heart tightens briefly in my chest, and my blood pressure picks up. I remain seated, take a breath to let the adrenaline surge dissipate, and try not to let the concern show on my face. This feeling of changes in my body related to anger, grief, or worry about interviewees, which I need to keep invisible during an interview, is one with which I am quite familiar. I don't want Pastor Isaac to see how worried I am about his driving, so I actively try not to move or shift in my chair. For one, it sounds like he doesn't have much of a choice, at least not if he wants to *cultivar* his Latino community, spread out as it is across North Texas. But I also don't want to divert the conversation. I don't want Pastor Isaac to talk about how risky it can be to drive in an area where his brown skin matches only about 10 percent of the Paris population.[19] I want him instead to talk about what it was like to respond to the raid in Sumner, Texas, just 10 miles away.

But my mind goes off on its own, doing some quick calculations of everything I study, everything I hear, and everything I've seen throughout the time I have been doing this work. And I can't help but think about what might, maybe, possibly, happen to Pastor Isaac if a police officer doesn't like Latinos, doesn't like immigrants, or simply needs to meet a quota or bring in some money to the county through an extra traffic ticket.

By now, most of the public is aware of racial profiling by law enforcement during traffic stops. Defined as the targeting of an individual based on phenotypic features associated with race, such as skin color, hair color and texture, and, in some instances, articles of clothing (such as a hijab or turban),[20] racial profiling is a violation of the Fourth Amendment that results in racial disparities in arrests, investigations, and law enforcement violence.

Activists and advocates throughout the country have further forced the issue of racial profiling into the public discussion after the killings of people of color, most of whom were men, most of whom were Black, such as Walter Scott, Daunte Wright, Philando Castile, Patrick Lyoya, Tyre Nichols, and Antonio Valenzuela, which resulted from traffic stops.[21]

Studies with tens of thousands or even millions of cases show that drivers of color—especially Black drivers—are pulled over at rates higher than our white peers. In a study published in *Nature and Human Behavior* that included nearly 100 million traffic stops, researchers found that Black drivers were more likely to be pulled over by police, with the annual per capita stop rate for Black drivers at 0.10 compared to 0.07 for their white peers.[22] Law enforcement agencies all over the country have acknowledged the disparity, with some making efforts to address the inequity.[23] This is the case both in big cities and in the rural countryside. In New York City, for example, about 60 percent of the people stopped by the New York Police Department were Black or Latinx, despite making up only about 49 percent of the city's population.[24] In Chicago a report found that Latino drivers were twice as likely and Black drivers six times as likely to be stopped as white drivers.[25] The American Civil Liberties Union of Nebraska found that Black, Latinx, and Native drivers were two to three times more likely to be pulled over than their white peers.[26]

Notably, for Latinos, the rates at which we are stopped when driving isn't always higher than that of white drivers. Depending on factors like how dark our skin is,[27] or whether police departments even bother to record data for Latinos at all,[28] sometimes we are pulled over at rates about equal to our white peers.[29] So maybe Isaac is more likely to be pulled over. Or maybe not.

I'm listening to Pastor Isaac talk, doing my best to concentrate on what he is saying, and I realize I don't even know for sure if he's undocumented, though I can take an educated guess based on what we've discussed. If he is undocumented, that would certainly change the risk calculations going on in my head.

Being pulled over is only one of the many issues at play. More important, perhaps, is what the officer does after he knocks on your car door and asks you to roll down your window. The evidence is clear that Latino and Black drivers are more likely to be searched after we pull over to the shoulder of the road than our white peers. A large-scale analysis of 100 million traffic stops across the US published in the journal *Nature* considered the search rate for eight state patrol agencies across the country. The researchers found that Black drivers were searched 4.3 percent of the time, Hispanic drivers 4.1 percent, and white drivers just 1.9 percent of the time. The authors found the same pattern for the six municipal police departments in the study.[30]

Is this search rate justifiable? Perhaps, the authors suggest, Black and Latino drivers are twice as likely to be searched because we are twice as likely to carry contraband, such as drugs and firearms, in our cars. This would mean that while we are searched at twice the rate of the white population, we would be searched at a rate proportionate to our odds of carrying contraband. But this is not the case. In fact, the authors show, Black drivers tend to have contraband at rates equal to white drivers, while Hispanic drivers have contraband less often than our white peers.

So maybe Isaac would be racially profiled and unjustly pulled over. And if so, maybe he would be unjustly questioned about what he had in his car.

But I have no reason to believe Isaac has drugs or guns in his car anyway. He is a pastor after all, driving across the state to give a sermon in one church while feeding those he sheltered after a raid in the other. So if Isaac were racially profiled and unjustly pulled over and then his car was unjustly searched, he probably wouldn't be unjustly taken to jail (though that certainly didn't mean he couldn't be unjustly killed).

But, truth be told, I am less worried about what Isaac has in his car and more worried about what he doesn't have in his wallet.

If Isaac is indeed undocumented, a single traffic stop could thrust him into the "traffic stop-to-deportation pipeline."[31] Undocumented immigrants in Texas, like undocumented immigrants in about 30 other states throughout the country, cannot get driver's licenses. So if Isaac is pulled over, it may not even matter whether his car is searched or not. When he is unable to hand the officer his license and insurance, what will the officer do?

We've seen cases in which the officer gives the licenseless driver a ticket, advises the driver to get a license (an impossibility of which both parties are aware), and sends the driver on his way. Maybe that is what would happen to Isaac, though the traffic ticket could come back to haunt him later, say, at a future traffic stop at which he will still not have a license and would now have a history of driving without one. If the officer prefers, he could take Isaac to jail then and there, even with no prior offense. If the jail has an agreement with ICE, which is up to the sheriff, he could end up being moved through the pipeline and deported.

I could just ask him whether he has a driver's license, but I don't dare. He doesn't need yet another person asking him for his papers.

≈

Pastor Isaac has moved on in the conversation, knocking me out of my reflective stupor. He drives a lot. So does his son. They have to. He preaches. His son plays the drums in the band. Their community is spread out. That's just life in rural Texas. I could calculate the odds forever in my head, or I could just say "It's risky," accept it, and move on. I move on, praying he's invisible when he's behind the wheel.

This spirit of risk and cultivation Isaac demonstrates in his weekly drives across the plains of North Texas came to a fore after the raid on Load Trail, when Latino families gathered at his church to figure out who was missing, where to get relief, and how to make do with the loss of a primary financial provider.

On August 28, ICE raided Load Trail, a family-owned business that manufactures trailers for hauling. Three hundred ICE agents, including some that landed on the property in helicopters, executed a criminal search warrant at the business. Businesses that hire undocumented workers like Load Trail, ICE shared in a press release, "create an atmosphere poised for exploiting their illegal workforce."[32] Ultimately, ICE did not make any criminal arrests, instead detaining 159 members of that exploitable workforce for working with false documentation.[33]

Pastor Isaac tells me that, in the days following the raid of Load Trail, many people started arriving at his church for simple everyday items like soap, shampoo, and diapers. I ask Pastor Isaac to explain why he thinks they were showing up to ask for these items.

> No querían ir a las tiendas porque, el gran problema era que, William, los primeros días, mire, nos daban información [como], "Ahorita llegaron a tocar la puerta de fulano de tal." "Ahorita llegó Migración a la a la Wal-Mart." "Ahorita llegó migración a la gasolinera." / No one wanted to go to the stores because, the big issue was, William, in the beginning, look, they gave us information like,

"Now they are knocking on the door of what's-his-name." "Now immigration is at Walmart." "Now they are at the gas station."

When Isaac walks me through this eerie sensation of ICE being everywhere and nowhere at the same time, he uses the phrase *tocando la puerta de fulano de tal,* a rich and illustrative word choice that deserves a moment of unpacking. *Tocar la puerta* simply means "to knock on the door." *Fulano de tal* is a colloquial phrase that can be translated to "so-and-so" or "whoever" or "what's-his-name." Isaac is saying that they—whom he calls *migración* but most likely means ICE—were "knocking on the door of so-and-so." He then contrasts the *puerta de fulano de tal* with Walmart and the gas station, which implies that ICE is going back and forth between homes and big and small businesses. It's noticeable how vague Isaac manages to be in one sentence. Whether ICE is knocking on the door to a home, a department store, or a corner store, and whether the people on the other side of the door are undocumented or not, fundamentally changes what the ICE agents on the other side of *la puerta* can do. But folks in the community can't always make these distinctions,[34] and, arguably, none of it matters all that much anyway. There's just a *toc toc toc* of someone who, somehow, some way, might manage to get inside and deport someone on the other side of the door. This lack of clarity is precisely what ICE wants. As a matter of fact, ICE trains to make it so.

Everyone in the US, regardless of immigration status, is protected by the US Constitution, including the Fourth Amendment's prohibition against unreasonable searches and seizures.[35] This means entering a home that is not your own without permission to do so requires a judicial warrant. Because immigration violations are civil infractions, ICE generally has administrative warrants, not judicial warrants, and thus must obtain consent before agents can enter a home based on these constitutionally protected rights.[36] Not everyone knows this, and when I explain it in class or during public presentations, audiences often pause as if they have misheard me, trying to wrap their heads around why anyone would ever invite ICE into their home. This confusion is reasonable. After all, if ICE agents were at your door and wanted to come in to detain you or someone with you, why would you ever let them in?

ICE is well aware of this conundrum, so agents use a few simple strategies to shift the situation in their favor. ICE calls these subtly manipulative techniques "ruses" and defines them as techniques meant to "control the time and location of a law enforcement encounter."[37] That is, if a resident refuses to let you in because you are ICE and want to detain them, make them think you are not ICE and don't want to detain them. Among the simplest ruses ICE agents use to gain consent to enter a home is to identify themselves as local police. They do this by wearing the same colors as the local police, acting like the police, or, sometimes, even identifying themselves out loud as the police. Their vests often have "POLICE ICE" in capital letters across them or have "POLICE" next to an indecipherable ICE logo and above "IMMIGRATION AND CUSTOMS ENFORCEMENT" in font about one-quarter the size. Agents may say they are investigating a crime, or hold up a picture of someone and ask if they can come in so you can help identify them, or claim that a relative of yours is the victim of identity theft. When asked if they have a warrant, they may respond that they do, in fact, have a warrant.[38]

When they don't want to impersonate the police, they'll sometimes pretend to be someone from another business. They may put ladders on their vans to make them look like work vans, wear a fake uniform, or carry a clipboard. It's against ICE regulations to impersonate a specific business, like FedEx or UPS, but a random fake emblem of a nonexistent business on a shirt or business card is just fine.

These ruses demonstrate a particular brand of ICE deception. They are not outright lying, merely constructing the situation so that the logical assumption—that they want to read your electric meter, not deport your brother, for example—works in their favor. They are also cautious to make claims that are true in the way that the average person understands them, even if they are technically incorrect. Are they police? Certainly not. ICE is a branch of a federal agency and charged specifically with enforcing immigration law. The police represent local jurisdictions and look for violations of criminal law. But the average person, especially the average Latino immigrant, certainly uses *"policía"* as a catch-all word for anyone who investigates a crime, anyone in a uniform with a gun, and anyone who can detain them. So when ICE says they are the police or have an enormous patch on their uniforms that says "POLICE," they just mean it in the colloquial sense, not the legal sense. Does ICE really have a warrant? Well, yes, they have a piece of paper that is literally called a warrant. But it is not the kind of warrant that lets them enter a home, which was obviously the point of the question. Is ICE really investigating a crime? Not really. If they were investigating a "crime," they would likely have a judicial warrant that allows them to enter the home without consent specifically for the criminal infraction, not the administrative warrant for the civil infraction that they wave through the peephole in the door. But ICE never said they were investigating a crime by its official definition. They were investigating the idea of a crime.

Pastor Isaac continues. "The people were in a serious panic, even though nothing was certain. Some people confirmed that they had just arrested *fulano de tal* / what's-his-name. And I don't think that's what happened but that was the word on the street. There was just so much panic in the town, and it was so very, very sad."

The band is clearly done warming up, and as the instruments and singers start to coalesce, it's impossible not to be moved by the music. I tap my foot to the steady 4/4 time of the bass as we continue our interview.

Pastor Isaac tells me that as he was trying to make sense of exactly whose door was being knocked on, a mother came into the church to ask for his help. Rumors were spreading that ICE was at Rhino, a vehicle rental company in nearby Sherman. "I want you to go over there because my daughter is there, and they are *tocando la puerta*," she told the pastor. Pastor Isaac agreed and headed over to Rhino to see if the woman's daughter had been detained. When he got there, he was handed a photo of the people who were *tocando la puerta*.

Isaac didn't know who they were, nor were they wearing anything that could help him to identify them. So, as he often does, Isaac reached out to another Latino pastor, Pastor Cristián, for some guidance. Besides, Isaac says, the sheriff was a member of Pastor Cristián's congregation,[39] so perhaps Pastor Isaac could make a quick call to inquire whether Cristián could ask the sheriff if he knows what's going on.

Pastor Cristián, who happened to be with the sheriff at that moment, showed the sheriff the picture and asked him if he knew who the people *tocando la puerta* of *fulano de tal* were.

He recognized them.

"Yes, those are my workers," the sheriff told him.

Shocked and a little bit confused, Pastor Cristián asked the sheriff why they were going around town knocking on doors. Were they working with ICE, searching for immigrant workers who had fled the scene?

No, that's not it at all, the sheriff explained. The deputies in the picture weren't actually *tocando la puerta* and had nothing to do with the immigration raid at Load Trail. They were just knocking on doors in the area to investigate an unrelated case.

The choir is done practicing, so Juan's voice is the only thing audible in the room. I can feel his exasperation as he raises his voice to reply to me, angry about the absurdity of the situation *"¡No eran de ICE! Eran de sheriff!* / They weren't even ICE agents! They were from the sheriff's department!" Pastor Isaac asks me, clearly rhetorically, what I expect people to think, given that they were just walking around in civilian clothes with their vests on, not in sheriff's department uniforms.

In a local news report, the municipal chief of police addressed the rumors that local law enforcement officers were working with ICE, saying "That is absolutely false. . . . The police department has not been contacted by any federal authority to assist in the investigation or arrest of anyone who may be suspected of a violation of federal immigration law."[40] Other law enforcement departments in the area, including the sheriff's department, as Pastor Isaac had attested, also denied having anything to do with the raid. No one really claimed, however, that they weren't doing other types of police work, like going door-to-door in civilian clothes in the same area at the same time. Or that if anyone hopped in their car to drive over to the church, they wouldn't, maybe, possibly, be asked for their license.

It was the community's fault for confusing the police officers in civilian clothes who were knocking on the doors of people's homes with the ICE officers whose uniforms said "POLICE" who were knocking on the doors of people's workplaces.

≈

I finally give in to the foot tapping and ask Pastor Isaac what song the band is playing. I feel like I have heard it before, and Pastor Isaac has clearly heard it before, but neither of us can name it. We listen for a few more seconds, but nothing comes to mind, so I start to ask questions again.

But right as I open my mouth, the bass picks up and the lead singer jumps in:

¡El Poderoso de Israel!
¡El Poderoso de Israel!
¡Su voz se oirá, nadie lo detendrá!
¡Al poderoso de Israel!

Isaac interrupts, having heard the eponymous refrain. "*'El Poderoso de Israel,'* that's what it's called," he tells me.

The song continues. And rather than jump back into the conversation, Isaac and I pause again to listen, as if now that we have the title, we are listening to the song with new ears. Maybe the song is catchy to me not because I knew the drummer had to drive through the counties of three different Republican sheriffs to play it but because of its subject matter. Both the Bible and the Quran tell of the enslavement of the Israelites by the Egyptians, who forced them to build the Egyptian cities of their ever-expanding empire. After centuries of exploitation, their god finally sends the prophet, Moses, to march them out of Egypt and out of slavery, only to find his path blocked by the Red Sea. With the Egyptian army closing in, Moses raises his staff, and his god, el Poderoso de Israel, parts the waters of the Red Sea to reveal the earth below and provide the Israelites with a path to freedom. When the Egyptians follow the Israelites onto the fresh earth, Moses lowers his staff, closing the sea walls around the Egyptians, drowning them.

When the song's refrain is over, Isaac continues the interview, moving from one story of worker exploitation and persecution that ends in freedom to another whose ending is not quite as clear.

CHAPTER 3

Para Uno Que Tiene Familia, Es Más Difícil

¿Está Bien Tu Esposo?

Elisio is very, very quiet as the interview begins. In fact, it isn't even clear if he is going to speak at all. His wife, Juana, however, seems to be in her element, sitting with Elisio and me in the back room of the Trinity Presbyterian Church of Mount Pleasant. Juana speaks in rapid clips and long, extensive paragraphs that spill out over the folding table between us. Sometimes I am able to ask Juana an entire question. Other times, Juana will start speaking right in the middle of the question, answering the parts she wants and ignoring the rest. She clearly likes to take a bird's-eye view of things, providing context and background and recounting all the other people involved in response to almost every question. Judging by Juana's energy and enthusiasm, she clearly has a story to tell. But judging by the silence and building tension in Elisio's body, it seems like he does too.

Juana and Elisio are the parents of two young boys, aged seven and four. Juana doesn't work outside the home, spending most of her time caring for her house and her two children while

Elisio works at Midwest Precast Concrete with the many other Latino immigrants who live in and around Mount Pleasant, Iowa. At the concrete factory, Juana says, the workers "eran como una familia dentro de ahí. Se llevaban bien todos. . . . Pasaban la mayoría del tiempo ahí / were like a family in there. They all got along. They spent most of their time together there."

The congenial working environment contributes to Midwest Precast Concrete's success at creating cement columns, beams, and stadium risers by pouring concrete into molds, curing it on-site, and shipping the finished pieces to Iowa, Illinois, and Missouri.[1] The work, like much of the work done by immigrants, can be dangerous, both because precast concrete is caustic to skin and because of the general risks of moving large and heavy objects. Gloves, goggles, and helmets can all reduce these risks when they are available. People often work in close proximity, and restroom breaks can be hard to fit in, though workers do tend to enjoy their lunchtimes together.

Like many immigrant mothers throughout the rural US, Juana volunteers with her church while her husband works and her children are at school. She was part of the League of United Latin American Citizens, or LULAC, an organization that focuses on the civil rights of Latinos throughout the US, and later joined Iowa Bridge, a volunteer organization at Trinity Presbyterian, bringing a very different set of skills than the white, English-speaking volunteers who form the majority of the group.

But, Juana shares, only five people were volunteering with LULAC, and Juana didn't really do very much. It wasn't until officers surrounded Midwest Precast Concrete and detained her husband and 31 other workers that more people started volunteering, and the demographics of the church in which we sat shifted from completely white, to a little bit less white, with a few Latino families joining the congregation. In that church

Juana feels welcomed, loved, like she and her family are appreciated, immigrants or not, Latino or not, regardless of their immigration statuses.

Eventually, after Juana is done sharing her thoughts on the shifting demographics of the church, the interview arrives at the day of the raid. "If it's okay with you, can we think about the day the raid happened?" I ask Juana.

Juana agrees. Elisio continues to not say anything at all.

≈

It was Wednesday morning, sometime around 8:00 or 8:30 a.m., with the end of the school year around the corner. Juana had just done what she does every weekday morning and dropped her 7-year-old son off at school, conveniently located within sight distance of Midwest Precast Concrete. She then takes her niece to the dentist, about 35 minutes outside of town. An hour or so later, Juana receives a text message from a coworker of her husband. "¿Está bien tu esposo? / Is your husband okay?," the text message read.

The text surprises Juana, and she isn't quite sure why her husband might not be okay. Her brain jumps to a couple of worst-case scenarios: "Yo me imaginé un accidente . . . / I imagined that my husband was in an accident, or, maybe, the police had stopped him. But I never would have imagined what she told me next. . . . Immigration is at the plant."

Juana's head is spinning as she thinks through the many possible alternative scenarios that could follow. Had her husband somehow escaped before he was arrested? Was he detained? Had he been shot? Had he already been cuffed and shipped out to a jail or to a detention center out of state? Or was he still in Mount Pleasant, waiting for her, while she was at the dentist with her niece a dangerous drive away?

As Juana considers what to do next, her phone rings. It is her son's teacher, who, without missing a beat, asks Juana the exact same question: "¿Está bien tu esposo?" From her son's school about a block away from the raid site, the teacher can see the immigration cars piling up. "Veo muchas patrullas ... / I see so many patrol cars, so many cars from ICE," she tells Juana on the phone.

Juana's panic increases, so the teacher on the phone attempts to reassure her: "Okay, well try not to worry. I am going to figure out what is happening. We can't do anything now, but I can go to your house and see if your husband is there." The teacher, going out of her way to help the parents of one of her students, drives over to Juana's house, hoping that Juana's husband was somehow inside, somehow not being handcuffed by ICE a block away from his son, somehow not going to disappear at the end of the day.

But Elisio is not at home.

While it is feasible that Elisio escaped or was off the property for some reason when ICE arrived, the odds were increasing that Elisio wasn't going to make it home that night. Juana feels helpless, at the dentist with her niece while her husband is—possibly—detained.

Juana weaves her story together like she's weaving a tapestry, winding her way from person to person, from teacher to co-worker to parent to friend, an amalgamation of fear and apprehension, of foreboding and growing uneasiness. But the carefully woven tapestry of relationships and emotion is missing something, something that caused Elisio to sink lower in his seat, to coil like a snake about to strike.

I try to slow the conversation enough to give Elisio a chance to uncoil and take a breath, perhaps to tell a different story than the one Juana is telling. Does he think she is saying something wrong? Does she not know what actually happened?

I make eye contact with Elisio, shift my body to face him just a little more, and, in a measured tone, invite him into the conversation: "¿Y usted estaba trabajando cuando pasó todo? / And you were working when all this happened?"

Quiet descends for a moment, and I am not clear if he is going to speak.

But he does. "Si. Estaba en la hora de break cuando llegó./ Yes. I was on break when they got there."

Here, the tenor of the interview changes drastically, as Juana's expansive mosaic of the wide network of mothers and teachers outside the factory gives way to Elisio's laser-focused, second-by-second unpacking of the event from the inside, a retelling that seems to take literal physical energy out of him.

BILL: And do you know how many people from ICE were there?

ELISIO: I have no idea. I think, maybe, more than 100. . . . The police from town were there too. . . . There were so many. I think there were more than 100, because there was a helicopter too [breath].

BILL: So did they all come in the same door?

ELISIO: No, they surrounded the whole company. They surrounded every entrance of the company. Two or three people escaped because they hid.

BILL: God. That's horrible. And [the ICE agents] were armed and everything?

ELISIO: [Breath] Yes.

BILL: With guns or . . . [2]

ELISIO: Yes. They had handguns and rifles.

BILL: That's horrible. Being inside at that moment must have been . . .

ELISIO: [Breath] Ahorita es un poco más fácil hablar de eso, pero cuando acababa de pasar, era un poco difícil porque es duro. Para uno que tiene familia, es más difícil / Now it's a little easier to talk about, but when it had just happened, it was tough, because it's just so intense. For someone who has a family, it's even harder.

At this point in the interview, the mood in the room changes again, as if both Juana and Elisio just had a breakthrough, both arrived at the point in the story that they had always, at least subconsciously, intended, despite taking different paths to do so.

Elisio and Juana were not telling different stories; they were telling a single story from different vantage points. But that wasn't clear to any of us until the moment their stories overlapped. Juana's emotional and interpersonal tale had entwined with Elisio's visceral and physical retelling, their narratives coalescing around the human beings they cared about most in the world: their children. What would happen to their children? As Elisio said, for those with families it was the worst.

This fear for the fate of your children was a terror experienced by immigrant families throughout the country at that time. It was also a terror the Trump administration was happy to exploit.

≈

Juana and Elisio were right to worry about their children. A growing body of health research details what everyone essentially knows: The sudden removal of a parent is emotionally and psychologically harmful to children, reshapes the resources available to them, and impacts their health and life trajectories for years to come. To give just a handful of well-established examples, Rojas-Flores and colleagues considered post-traumatic stress disorder (PTSD) symptoms in 91 Latino citizen children with at least 1 parent at risk of detention or deportation.[3] PTSD symptoms—which can include anxiety, depression, hyperactivity, aggression, or overall dysfunction—were significantly higher for children of detained or deported parents than citizen children whose parents were either legal permanent residents or undocumented without prior contact with immigration enforcement. Children of deported parents were also more likely to display externalizing problems (like aggression and behavioral issues) and internalizing problems (like depression and anxiety) than children whose parents were not deported.[4] Many other studies show the same mental and emotional impacts on children,[5] such as increased vigilance and stress or symptoms of depression, anxiety, and trauma.[6]

Even if they were unable to articulate it clearly in mental health language from the *Diagnostic and Statistical Manual of Mental Disorders IV*, Juana and Elisio knew they had to do something to protect their children from what was to come. But what?

Many factors influence how children will fare after parental deportation. Notably, some families "stretch and strengthen," drawing support from aunts and uncles, grandparents, and friends to support the children of detained or deported parents.[7] This can mean that an uncle will make a car payment that the remaining parent can't make, an *abuela* will watch her *nietos* while Mom picks up an extra job, or a *compadre* will give you the name of a lawyer he heard was honest and inexpensive.

The child's age when the parent is detained can also be critical. Children with a parent arrested and deported before the age of 6 years tend to do better than older children because they may not remember the details of the deportation or are too young to ask follow-up questions after someone explains the situation. Similarly, those who experience parental deportation after age

14 are better equipped to handle its impacts as a young adult with more emotional maturity. It's that middle range, from ages 6 to 14, when kids are most vulnerable, and the impact of the deportation of a parent is most likely to follow them into adulthood. This distinction is important, of course, when calculating the societal impact of deportation and considering the health of the next generation of Latino adults whose parents were deported when they were kids. But I doubted Juana and Elisio would find any comfort knowing that Elisio's deportation would crumble their older son just a little bit less than their younger son because their younger son didn't know his father quite as well.[8]

To protect their children as best they can, Elisio and Juana need to prepare for Elisio's deportation, to reach out to the family and friends around them, hoping that they, too, might "stretch and strengthen" to ease the pain of Elisio's arrest and removal. But, realistically, when Elisio is one of 32 people arrested in an area with very few Latino families, was anyone left who was not already stretched beyond capacity? Would anyone have any strength—or resources—left to give?

Ya No Había Ni un Trabajador

As Elisio gets a little more comfortable talking to me, he and Juana find their flow with the conversation. They often begin by following my prompts, then build off each other's responses, Elisio starting with his first-person, visceral experience and Juana zooming out, just a bit, to remind us of the rippling impacts of the raid on others in their community. The rapport between the two of them is warm and friendly. It's clear that they care deeply about each other. There is love in the room, right alongside the grief.

BILL: Do you remember what you were thinking about the moment that it happened?

ELISIO: The only thing I thought about was her and my children. What is going to happen to them? Because it's harder for a woman to stay by herself with two kids, so [I asked myself], "What is going to happen?"

JUANA: My brother-in-law worked at the same place. So it was two families at the same time. Te quedas como en shock. . . . Perdí mi cabeza un momentito y dije, "Que vamos a hacer?"/ You just end up like in shock. . . . I lost my mind for a moment and just asked myself, "What are we going to do?"

Juana calls the factory and is able to confirm that indeed, a raid has taken place at the factory where Elisio worked. She decides to go over to Midwest Precast Concrete to pick up the belongings that Elisio had left behind.

Juana parks the car outside the factory and enters into the big warehouse space, crossing through one of the doors that ICE had blocked off only moments before.

Juana describes the scene upon her arrival. "Fue una desolación.[9] Fue algo como que . . . era increíble / The place was desolate. It was just . . . incredible/unbelievable." On the tables in front of her sit bowls of half-eaten soup and tortillas with bites taken out of them, food they had just purchased from a woman who makes it fresh. Helmets, which make the dangerous work of mixing, pouring, and moving concrete a little safer, are lying on the tables, having just been removed to make the lunchtime gathering a little more relaxed. Juana describes the scene again. "Era soledad ahí.[10] Era increíble / It was loneliness/emptiness. It was unbelievable." Yet another type of family broken apart.

Juana wasn't the only one impacted by the stillness in the once lively, bustling factory floor. The room, Juana describes, is laid out like many other precast concrete factories throughout the country, with a large space to mix and pour concrete into molds on one side and offices for supervisors to watch the workers through their office windows on the other. She describes the only people left in the factory: "Those in the offices were sobbing, just watching out of their windows.... Obviously, [the supervisors] knew that [the workers] had kids, had wives, and it was like, 'What's going to happen to them?' They were also in shock."

The invisible line in the middle of the factory floor dividing the heavy labor of making precast concrete from the intellectual space of the office also served as a line of racial demarcation. The supervisors, Juana shares, were white, while the workers, like Elisio, were mostly Latino. Juana, perhaps because she was projecting, assumes the white managers were also distraught at the thought of the broken Latino families before them. She even uses the same phrase to describe them—*en shock*—that she uses to describe her own reaction to the raid.

I am rattled by the scene Juana was describing: white managers sobbing, Latino workers disappearing, Latina wives picking up their husbands' belongings. At times like this, when an interviewee richly captures the social moment better than an outsider ever could, I usually try to remain quiet and use body language to invite the interviewee to elaborate on the moment as long as they are moved to do so. I repeat the scene back to the interviewee, simply and slowly, both to make sure I understand it correctly and to invite the interviewee to confirm, change, or emphasize certain details of the story.

BILL: So, it was the whites watching the Latinos pick up their things?[11]

I thought I had stated a simple enough summary, but Juana pauses. She does not confirm my summary. Nor does she expand it. I am confused and caught a little off guard. Clearly, I have missed something. Clearly, I have said something wrong. What did I miss?

Juana remains quiet for one more beat, as if thinking through the question, then replies, "Realmente, cuando yo llegué, ya no había ni un trabajador / Actually, when I got there, there wasn't a single worker still there," she tells me.

Juana is not really correcting me. She is instead working through an issue with language and gender that I had not noticed when I summarized the situation. No, *los Latinos* were not picking up the belongings. *Los Latinos*—the men, the husbands, the fathers, the workers—were all taken or had disappeared. *Las Latinas*—the women, the wives, the mothers—were picking up their belongings. *Los Latinos* were gone. It was just soup, half-eaten tortillas, overturned helmets, and *Latinas* left on the factory floor.

Desolación.

≈

A defining feature of worksite raids in the rural US is that these raids do not simply remove immigrants; they remove working, driving immigrants, many of whom are men and fathers. Rural communities with lower population densities, communities like that of Mount Pleasant, often have limited public transportation systems to move from one area of town to another. Going to work requires you to get behind the wheel of a car, whether or not you have a license. The jobs available to immigrants in these communities often involve physical, back-breaking labor like pouring concrete, welding metal, or dismantling cows—jobs traditionally done by men.

In families in which both parents are undocumented,[12] husbands and wives may choose to pool the risk of losing a family member to deportation by having fathers work and do most of the driving while mothers stay home and care for the children. This way, while it's possible a father may be detained at or on the way to work, the mother not working or driving makes it less likely that she will be asked for a driver's license she cannot get or a work authorization she does not have. But this means that when a father is detained, the family loses both a worker and a driver, leaving a mother behind to weigh the risks, costs, and consequences of working and driving herself.

Sociologist Joanna Dreby describes women whose husbands have been detained or deported as "suddenly single mothers,"[13] or the mothers who, because of the removal of their husbands from their lives, "[scramble] to be the sole providers of their US-born children with no preparation for single parenthood." Further, Dreby explains, whereas families in which a parent has lost a job often depend on US government aid, undocumented workers taken by ICE cannot access programs like unemployment or workers' compensation, which are specifically designed to keep families afloat when a parent cannot work.

But it is not only the food, water, diapers, school fees, and electricity bills that suddenly single mothers must struggle to pay without a breadwinner, nor the school drop-offs, doctors' appointments, and extracurricular activities they must navigate alone. Mothers like Juana now have to find the tens of thousands of dollars it costs when a loved one must prepare for a deportation trial.

In one exchange, Juana describes the situation of two other women whose husbands were detained alongside Elisio. Unlike Elisio, however, these husbands were still detained, 260 days after the raid.

Por ejemplo, hay dos mujeres. Esas dos mujeres, es increíble. / For example, there are two women, these two women, it's incredible. It makes me a little sad to talk about, but, see, some of us already have our husbands out. But those women have daughters [and] sons, and their husbands are still detained because of the raid. It's been eight months.[14] And [those mothers] are working so hard.

I know that they are working from Monday to Saturday, overtime, sometimes working other jobs, and aren't able to spend any time with their children. And it's not because they don't want to. They have to pay for the calls they make to their husbands [in detention], send them food to eat. They are going to visit them . . . Paying lawyers . . .

As Juana explains, the extra hours these mothers spend at work to make up for the financial loss of their husbands' detention means yet more time away from their children, who have now lost their fathers to a raid and their mothers to second or third jobs.

While Juana is thankful she does not have the extra costs of visits, phone calls, and commissary while Elisio is detained, her situation hasn't come cheap either. The reason Elisio was sitting in the church with Juana and me that day was because Juana had found a way to pay a $10,000 immigration bond so he could await his trial outside of detention. Not every detained immigrant is lucky enough to be offered bond. And not everyone who is offered a bond is able—or chooses—to pay it.

When an undocumented immigrant is detained, the DHS can choose to keep him in detention until his court hearing or offer him a bail bond, also referred to as an "immigration bond" or simply a "bond." Whether or not a detainee is offered a bond depends on a number of factors, including, for example, the detainee's previous immigration history, time in the US, family situation, and likelihood of fleeing. When a judge decides it's appropriate to offer a bond to a detainee, the judge decides on a specified amount that, once paid, allows ICE to release the detainee to await his court case outside of detention. The person who pays the bond will get her money back as long as the detainee attends all future ICE check-ins and court hearings and follows through with the final verdict of his case—even if that verdict is deportation.

It is unconditionally advantageous to one's immigration case to pay the bond and be released from detention, as this allows you to meet with your lawyer face-to-face as frequently as needed. Paying a bond also significantly delays one's immigration case, as the court prioritizes hearings for those who are detained, allowing you more time in the US. In addition to the practical advantages, detained parents often want to spend what could potentially be their last days in the US with their families, not in detention. So being offered a bond by a judge is generally seen as a win in immigrant communities.

Yet whether to request or pay a bond when offered is a complicated and painful decision for many immigrant families. For one, bonds can be prohibitively expensive. In 2018 the median bond amount in the US was between $7,000 and $10,000. Nearly 40 percent of detainees had a bond—like that of Elisio—of $10,000 or more. Five percent of detainees had bonds of a crippling $25,000 or more.[15]

But does the bond amount really matter if you are going to get the money back anyway?[16] At worst, isn't paying a bond just a short-term blow to one's financial standing? This may be true theoretically, but it's easy to imagine the challenge of finding $7,500 of accessible money overnight. For many low-income families (and plenty of middle-income families as well), this amount of expendable income simply isn't available. In fact, the median savings account balance for all families in the US is only $8,000, $2,000 less than Elisio's bond, meaning that, for the average family, paying an immigration bond would take everything and more out of their savings.[17] For many families, especially single-income, working-class families, whether or not they will get the money back is irrelevant, as the cash isn't there in the first place. When families decide to pay the bond, they often resort to borrowing money from relatives and neighbors, selling cars or houses, or taking on other jobs. But in towns like Mount Pleasant, when 32 working men are taken out of your community at the same time, there may not be enough money to go around.

While some families are able to scrape up the money to pay a bond, other families never try. When someone is unlikely to win an immigration case, paying a bond alongside the exorbitant costs of lawyer fees feels like a poor use of resources and a delay of the inevitable. Thus, some detainees will agree to "voluntarily depart," avoiding the expenditures of bonds and protracted relationships with lawyers and keeping their immigration record free from an order of removal (though families still have to come up with the money for their plane ticket out of the US).[18] Others choose to voluntarily depart simply because they cannot bear the thought of leaving their families without money and wish to hurry their removals along so they can get back to work, even from the other side of the border.

≈

When Juana tells me about the mothers who took extra jobs to cover for their husbands' absences, I can hear remorse in her voice. She clearly feels guilty that Elisio is here with us, in this church, while those detained alongside him remain behind bars. I have heard remorse like Juana's in interviews before.[19] When we think about the psychological impacts of deportation, we often focus on those who had a loved one removed, not those who *almost* had a loved one removed or whose loved one hasn't been removed *yet*. I know that when Juana looks at Elisio, she thanks God that he's there next to her. But I can also sense that into Juana and Elisio's relationship creeps a complicated feeling of fortune, luck, or privilege that Juana feels she doesn't deserve. This is one of the worst repercussions of the deportation machine, causing those who avoid its direct harms to feel an insipid sense of survivor's guilt because they are able to enjoy the most basic of human needs: togetherness.

Los Niños No Duermen Hasta Que los Padres Lleguen

It's not only the suddenly single mothers who must dramatically alter their daily lives to compensate for detained fathers. When old enough, the children of detained parents also join the workforce, even postponing or leaving school to do so. Ana, born in Mexico and living in Nebraska when the raids in O'Neill occurred, shared with Nicole a story of a student whose mother had been detained:

> There was one particular story from a girl, a high school senior.... Her mom was detained. She had a very small child—I don't think he was more than three years old—and another sibling, and she was the oldest one.
>
> When her mom was detained, she now had to take care of her siblings. She was about to graduate high school but instead of doing that and thinking about college, she had to think about, "How am I going to keep my two siblings here with me and how am I going to provide for them?"

Moving out of her home, the student moved in with another family to help her with childcare."[T]hat impact of having your parents or both parents gone, and then you have to grow up right then and there, and be there for your siblings, and be the one trying to hold your family together, and, again, that's a lot of stress."

Tanya Golash-Boza,[20] a sociologist at the University of California Merced, calls the situations these children and teenagers face "abrupt transitions to adulthood." As she describes, "The deportation of a wage-earner easily pushed the families over the edge into severe poverty. The families had to make difficult choices to survive, often relying on teenage children to make an abrupt transition to adulthood by joining the labor force and taking charge of younger siblings."

Of course, not every child whose parent is detained in a worksite raid is of working age. For young children, it isn't always clear what is going on, where their parents are, or if they are coming back. Often, their mothers, in addition to navigating financial catastrophe and counseling their older children during their abrupt transition to adulthood, have to decide how much of the confusing, traumatic, and convoluted stories they want to share with their young children about their fathers' sudden disappearances. Should they stretch the truth? Change the subject? Outright lie and hope the story resolves itself before the children ever know?

Like the impact of deportation itself, much of what parents tell their children depends on their children's age. Older children can often put the pieces together quickly, observing their mothers' changing moods, overhearing them cry, or noticing new phone calls from English speakers whose names they don't recognize. Sometimes older children—especially high schoolers—have their own cell phones and access to social media and seek out or happen upon the news of the detention independently, as Facebook live feeds and hashtags detail the raids at the places their fathers work.

But for younger children, like Juana and Elisio's 4- and 7-year-olds, it's up to the remaining parent to explain what is going on. Juana chose to delay telling her children as long as she could, a fact that Elisio interjects during the interview to explain:

> JUANA: Yes. Yes, I had to tell them [where Elisio was] because they kept saying, "Where's Dad?," "Where's Dad?"—
>
> ELISIO [INTERRUPTING]: Well, you didn't tell them that I was arrested.
>
> JUANA: No, no, not yet.
>
> ELISIO: You told them that I was working, and that—
>
> JUANA: —and that you were going to come back home when you were done.

Here, Juana, like so many mothers throughout the US, takes a gamble, hoping that Elisio will be home before she has to explain to her kids that they may never see their father again, at least not in the US.

Pastor Cristían, the pastor who helped Pastor Isaac identify the law enforcement agents who had been *tocando las puertas* of homes nearby, described to me how common it was for other parents to tell the exact same type of lie that Juana had told to her children:

> BILL: Thank you so much [for speaking with me. Before we end,] is there anything else you want to add?
>
> CRISTÍAN: A raid is not the solution at all. It's not the solution; it creates more problems, problems that it's going to take years to overcome. . . . It's not the solution, it's not. We need solutions, and that is not the solution. . . .
>
> For example, let's talk about the 7-year-old girl or boy [whose] dad did not come home. A lot of families have not [said]

to the children, "Dad is not coming home. He's in ICE detention, and in a little bit he is going to go back to Mexico, or to the place where he came from."

I know some families that have not [said] that to their children. They just say, "Hey Dad went to work. He went to work."

BILL: And they still don't know.

CRISTÍAN: Exactly.

In rare cases, a mother's gamble could pay off, at least in the short term. She could, for example, lie to her younger child about where Dad was, and in the meantime, Dad would be released from detention. Perhaps his release was due to humanitarian concerns, and he would never be called back in for deportation, or perhaps he paid his bond, and was released from detention. While it is possible that a young child would never have to know how close the family came to having a family member removed, most children would probably find out about the lie when they were teens or young adults and have to process the lie, the grief, the relief, and the betrayal all at the same time.

No matter the outcome of the detention, the sudden disappearance of a family member, coupled with the parents who, to use Juana's words, had *perdido sus cabezas*, leaves an indelible mark on children, impacting their willingness to be away from their parents even for their regular, everyday routines.

Joaquín, a Quiché interpreter who supported Indigenous Guatemalans after the raid in Salem, Ohio, told me:

> Hace un año, un año y medio, y hasta hoy en día, no hemos podido convencer a los niños que eso ya no pasa.... Porque ellos dicen, "mi papá yo sé que está trabajando, pero hasta que no regrese a la hora yo no puedo dormir." Hasta hoy los niños no duermen hasta que los padres lleguen. Si, antes no era así / Even after a year, a

year and half, up to today, we haven't been able to convince kids that [a raid] won't happen again. They say, "my dad, I know he's working, but until he gets back home I can't sleep." Even to this day, the children can't sleep until their parents come back home. It wasn't like this before.

In the summer of 2018, the rural US was filled with children who couldn't sleep until their parents came home. At about the same time, however, keeping children up at night was about to become a matter of policy. And while the public didn't pay much attention to Juana and Elisio's children, the sheer scale of family separation on the Texas–Mexico border was about to make the public sleepless too.

The Summer of Family Separation

Juana does not need any prompting to tell her story or expand upon Elisio's, but Elisio seems to need some encouragement, some sign that his trek into emotionally dangerous territory will be valued by everyone in the small side room of Trinity Presbyterian in Mount Pleasant. After Juana describes the desolate scene at the factory now absent of *trabajadores*, I invite Elisio to bring us back to the moment that ICE entered the facility.

> So when I saw that there was no way to exit, I figured it was better to just sit down and wait. I said to myself, if I try something, they could do something to me, even shoot me, or something like that. So when I sat down, they grabbed me, and they sent me to the area where they were getting all the people together.
>
> But many of the people who ran, who were so afraid, yeah, si los golpearon / they hit/struck/beat them. . . . They threw them to the floor and put their knees on their neck. [The workers ran] because they were scared.

Elisio isn't happy with his description of this chaotic violence, so he slightly corrects himself, realizing he made it sound like his coworkers were running because they were scared of being choked by the knees on their necks or beaten or shot or killed by the agents arresting them. But that isn't why they ran. That isn't why they were scared. Or at least not the main reason. Elisio continues: "Well, [they ran] not because they were scared . . . but because they could only think about their families. What was going to happen to them?"

Little did Elisio know that the decision-making process he articulated—I sat down, gave up, and let them arrest me, not because I was scared to be beaten, shot, or choked but because I was terrified of what would happen to my family—was about to be systematically exploited by the Trump administration the very next week.

≈

"If you cross this border unlawfully, then we will prosecute you. It's that simple. If you smuggle illegal aliens across our border, then we will prosecute you. If you are smuggling a child, then we will prosecute you, and that child will be separated from you as required by law."

On May 7, 2018, just two days before Elisio is arrested on his lunch break, US Attorney General Jeff Sessions stands on the beach in Border Field State Park in San Diego to announce the implementation of the administration's "zero-tolerance" immigration policy.[21] Flanked on his left by Tom Homan, who served as the director of ICE at the time and would be designated "border czar" during Trump's second term, and a Border Patrol agent on his right, Sessions speaks in his characteristic southern drawl as the waves of the Pacific Ocean lap at the rusted metal bars that separate San Diego from its counterpart in Mexico, Tijuana. Less than a minute into the speech, a protestor interrupts Sessions, yelling into a bullhorn: "Are you separating families? Is that why you're here? You're not welcome here. Do you have a soul? You are evil!"

Sessions pauses a moment, seemingly distracted by the protestor, but eventually looks back down at his script and continues. The administration, he explains, will now have "zero tolerance" for anyone who enters the US anywhere along the length of the southern border. All attempted entries will be referred to the Department of Justice (DOJ), which Sessions leads. While those cases are moving through the criminal courts, migrants will be held in prison. Not everyone understands the full repercussions of Session's announcement. Is he announcing a new policy or just telling us about an old one? Wasn't it already illegal to try to cross the border without permission? Weren't those who crossed the border illegally always prosecuted?

In fact, Sessions was not announcing a new policy. He was announcing a new way to enforce a policy that already existed. This technical difference—between a new policy and a new way to enforce an old policy—was irrelevant on the ground, like a *toc toc toc* on your *puerta* by an ICE agent who wasn't technically police. Soon enough, the American public was about to understand that the prescient protestor yelling into the bullhorn on the Border Field State Park beach that day was correct: Sessions was in fact there to separate families.

To explain it as simply as possible, immigration law is enforced by the DHS at the federal level. Immigration law infractions, like crossing the border illegally, are considered civil—not criminal—infractions. These civil infractions result in an "administrative" resolution, such as deportation, a stay of deportation, or the granting of a visa.[22] Detention is, according to DHS, not meant to be disciplinary or punitive but is a place to wait until your administrative case has closed.[23] Various types of detention facilities exist, including those in which families are detained together.

Administrative solutions may also take into consideration the conditions of the migrant's crossing. For example, are they fleeing violence or poverty, or are they sick, elderly, pregnant, or traveling with children? In these cases, the DHS may opt for what it considers more humane administrative solutions, such as releasing migrants with ankle monitors instead of detaining them away from their families. Civil cases do not guarantee the right to an attorney. The vast majority of border crossers, including those crossing with their children, are committing a civil infraction and thus have no lawyers to support their case unless they can find and pay for them themselves.

Sometimes, immigration law infractions result in criminal offenses. These cases are taken over by the DOJ. For example, if a migrant is arrested attempting a second border crossing, or is caught with drugs or firearms in his possession, the case will be referred to the DOJ, which will decide on the penalty. This penalty will likely include incarceration in prison. After serving the sentence in prison, the detained migrant is turned back over to the DHS, who will then administratively address its immigration charge, often through deportation. When awaiting a criminal trial, the migrant is sent to prison. In prison, there is no option to stay with your family.

The DHS can prosecute any border crosser criminally if it wishes, however. In fact, the DHS had already been criminally prosecuting border crossers for some time in places like Tucson, Arizona, where I sat in 2014 and watched as dozens of immigrants were chained together and brought before a judge under the Bush-era Operation Streamline, which continues to this day. But Sessions was not instituting strategic, localized clusters of criminal prosecutions in select cities across the southern border. Sessions was ordering the DOJ to criminally prosecute everyone, no matter where they crossed, no matter if it was their first or fifth time crossing, and no matter if they were alone, with a group, pleading asylum, or with their families. Sessions was, essentially, ordering the mass separation of parents from their children.

While not everyone understood the full repercussions of Sessions's announcement on May 7, it only took a few months—along with some diligent reporting of folks like Jacob Soboroff, Caitlin Dickerson, and Lomi Kriel—for the country to figure it out. On the afternoon of June 18, reporter Ginger Thomas published a news report containing audio of very young children sobbing after they were separated from their parents.[24] Cracking voices can be heard crying in Spanish, "Mami!," "Papi!," and "No quiero que paren a mi papá; no quiero que lo deporten / I don't want them to stop my dad; I don't want them to deport him." If the sound of wailing children didn't anger the public enough, about 57 seconds into the leaked audio the masculine baritone voice of a Border Patrol agent can be heard taunting the detained children. Translated from Spanish, the agent says, "Well, we have an orchestra here. What's missing is a conductor." The cover of *Time* magazine showed a crying Latina toddler with messy brown hair looking up at Donald Trump beneath the text "Welcome to America." The image of the toddler had been cropped out of a now-famous image taken by Getty photographer John Moore, in which a two-year-old Honduran child is standing a foot from her mother in the dirt in McAllen, Texas, after crossing the Rio Grande in a raft. While the toddler is the focal point of the photo, the gloved hand of a Border Patrol agent can be seen reaching into the front hip pocket of the child's mother.[25]

Soon, every news outlet shared their own images of the massive numbers of families with dark-brown skin and black hair sitting on concrete floors, shoulder to shoulder with other migrants, sometimes covering themselves with foil blankets. Jacob Soboroff, an NBC News correspondent and the author of *Separated: Inside an American Tragedy*,[26] wasn't allowed to record anything when he toured Casa Padre, the converted Walmart in Brownsville, Texas, that served as a shelter for 1,500 boys aged 10 to 17, so he took a notepad:[27] "kids everywhere, oreos, applesauce, smile at them," then, quoting Casa Padre's chief programs officer, he wrote, "They feel like animals in a cage being looked at."

Like the holding of detained immigrants in a cattle-processing center after the raid in Postville, Iowa, the constant media stream of visibly terrified children was too much for the public to bear. On June 17, just a month and a half after Sessions had stood on the beach at Border Field State Park, former First Lady Laura Bush (whose husband had developed Operation Streamline) wrote an op-ed stating that "zero-tolerance policy is cruel.[28] It is immoral. And it breaks my heart." Maggie Gyllenhaal and 30 Hollywood actors came together with the American Civil Liberties Union to read an affidavit from "Mirian," a mother separated from her son at the US–Mexico border.[29] Many national health organizations, including the American Academy of Pediatrics,[30] the American Psychological Association, the American Medical Association, the American College of Physicians, and the American Public Health Association released written statements denouncing family separation.[31] All these efforts, often spearheaded by breakthrough reporting, coalesced to force Trump to put an end to zero tolerance after only a few months.

Ultimately, between 2017 and 2021, the Trump administration separated at least 3,900 children from their parents along the US–Mexico border. Some of these children, like Constantin Mutu, four months old when he was taken from his parents, hadn't even celebrated their first birthdays. As it turns out, the logistic impossibility of tracking children separated from parents did nothing to dissuade the administration from zero tolerance in the first place, and the program was rolled out without a plan to track which children belonged to which parents.[32] Five years after the separations began, 1,000 children were still waiting for reunification,[33] with many arguing the number to be significantly higher.[34]

Forcing a swift end to zero tolerance was indeed a victory, brought on by the hard work, dedication, organizing, and rage of parents, media, and advocates across the country. The short reign of the policy served as an example of what was possible when so much energy coalesced to bring down something that a significant portion of the population agreed was unacceptable. It was a collaboration of people across all walks of life leveraging the full range of their influence.

It was a collaboration of which Elisio and Juana could only dream.

≈

As the interview climbs over an hour, Juana tells me that sometimes, when she is helping her son with his homework, they'll talk about his future. "Quiero ser un soldado para ir a la guerra y salvar el mundo! / I want to be a soldier so I can go to war and save the world!," her son tells her.

Other times, Juana's son tells her, "No mami, yo quiero que ese presidente se vaya porque no nos quiere a nadie! / No mami, I want this president to leave because he doesn't like any of us!"

In the latter cases, Juana responds to her son's statement with a question: "Well . . . is he *your* president?"

"No! NO!" Juana imitates her son's response empathetically.

And whether it's because Juana's impression of her son catches us off guard or because we appreciate the irony of a seven-year-old Latino boy, the son of immigrant parents, saying "Not my president!" just like the white citizens who marched in front of the Trump hotel to protest family separation, Elisio and I chuckle heartily, appreciating a moment of respite in the 64th minute of a challenging interview. Then Juana continues, recounting something else her son tells her. "Este presidente está loco. Él tiene divididas las familias / This president is crazy. He has families divided." No one laughs.

The three of us talk a little bit more about *el presidente loco*, and as the interview climbs to the 67th minute, I try to bring the conversation to some sort of conclusion. The air is thick with emotion, with sadness, ambition, guilt, shock, pain, even joy, and it all feels so real, so valid. I realize how badly I want to sit with Juana and Elisio in this small room in this small Midwestern church forever, unseen by a world that believes the range of humanity they just expressed doesn't exist, that sees them as animals who deserve their punishment and their children as acceptable collateral. But we can't stay here forever. As Juana says, if we want that world, we'll have to create it:

BILL: Muchas gracias por compartir tanto conmigo / Thank you for sharing so much with me.

JUANA: No, gracias a ustedes por venir /No, thank you all for coming. [The raid] impacted us, but we are moving forward, we are moving forward, staying positive, and I hope to God that sometime soon there is something, some change, and we can be at peace and be able just to do what we want to do [laughs], to keep teaching our children how to keep moving forward and struggle for what they want.

And as I tell [Elisio], I am here for as long as God wants me to be because I want to see my children grow up. I want to see my children graduate. I want to see my children say, "Mamá y papá lucharon por nosotros, por nuestros futuros, y por darnos algo major / Mamá y papá fought for us, for our futures, and to give us something better."

≈

Like so many immigrant parents during the summer of family separation, Juana decided to continue fighting, not for her own future, but for a future not her own: the future of her children. But unlike families separated by zero tolerance, the children separated from their parents by worksite raids would not benefit from the anger of protective parents throughout the country. Hollywood actors wouldn't read Juana's testimony and former first ladies wouldn't write op-eds in major papers. Medical organizations wouldn't release statements, government employees wouldn't rebel, and entire administrative offices wouldn't be formed to address the harm done to immigrant families in any of the coming administrations.

But that wouldn't stop Juana.

If she wanted to build a future for her children, a future beyond the safety of the church, a future where her children didn't have to be invisible, she'd do what she and other mothers like her had done from the day they arrived in the rural US. She'd work with the church she loved, with the teachers who loved her kids. She'd drive miles to meet lawyers who would work for free, and when she couldn't drive, she'd find someone with a license who could. And through it all, she'd make sure her kids did their homework and got to soccer practice.

Juana was ready.

It was time to organize.

CHAPTER 4

The Multiplication of Loaves and Fishes

Find a Church and Get Started

I met Destiny in September of 2017, back when the raid in Postville was the only worksite raid people ever thought about, if they thought about worksite raids at all. A proud Texan Latina, Destiny had come to Detroit to participate in a conference arranged by Justice for Our Neighbors, an organization that provides free legal advice and representation to low-income immigrants and that was Destiny's employer at the time.

Five feet tall with jet-black hair that reached the middle of her back, Destiny had more organizing energy than anyone I'd ever met. When I saw her in organizing spaces, she moved around frenetically, giving everyone she talked to her attention and sensing with some preternatural ability how their work, her work, and the work of everyone she had ever met would benefit from collaboration.

Destiny is very talkative, and when she tells you about something she deems unjust, you can feel her blood pressure rise and hear the tone and cadence of her voice change as she grows angry. She's so animated, and her emotion so contagious, that when she is mad at something you can't help but get mad too. There's one iconic picture of Destiny in which she's facing the camera, though she seems to be looking right past it. Her eyes are teary and her throat tight as she yells into the bullhorn she is holding to protest the separation of children from their parents in McAllen, Texas, in 2018. While any type of injustice seems to make Destiny angry, when the injustice affects Latino immigrants, especially those who, like her, had spent a portion of their lives undocumented, she gets *really* angry.

But what initially amazed me the most about Destiny's anger was that it provided only the starting point for what would come after. By the time you talked to her again, she would already have introduced someone she had met last month to someone she had met last year, and some cross-organizational collaboration would have blossomed into a program to address whatever had angered her in the first place. She had a way of seeing past categories, seeing past limits, and pursuing solutions to problems others had yet to identify.

When Nicole and I decided to visit Sumner, Texas, population 4,500, 90 percent of whom are white,[1] and the site of the raid on Load Trail, it was only natural to reach out to Destiny, whose hometown of Tyler, Texas, was about two hours away. After the raid on Load Trail on August 28, 2018, a raid that made Destiny very, very angry, she drove from Tyler to Sumner many times to do what she always does to turn her ire into a collaborative, communal solution. The raid response would probably not have happened—or at least happened as it did—if not for Destiny's efforts. It also would not have happened without a church.

≈

THE MULTIPLICATION OF LOAVES AND FISHES

Destiny hears about the raid in Sumner the way so many others heard about the raids that were taking their neighbors away at the time—through social media:

> I had a friend, Michael, he actually lives in Mount Pleasant, [Texas], and he inboxed me. He's like, "Destiny, there's a raid going on. You should do something about it. . . ."
>
> And I thought the raids were more things that didn't occur. I know my parents would talk about it at times, but back in the '70s when, in Tyler, those raids would go on. And so I thought it was a thing of the '70s . . .
>
> I sat on my couch, because I just got back from a meeting, and I hit the link. He sent me a live video or something, and I clicked on it, and I was like, "No, this can't be real! It can't be real."

Seeing the video, Destiny admits that the legendary worksite raids of her immigrant parents' youth have returned, so she begins to contact those she knows who may be able to do something, or who know someone who might be able to do something. She calls her friend Blanca, a reporter, and the women share what they have heard about the raid and brainstorm what they can do. They are unable to come up with a plan, especially since neither of them has ever been to Sumner or any of the towns around it, though they agree that a reporter will probably be useful. Blanca agrees to meet Destiny somewhere close to the raid site.

Destiny next calls her friend Melanie, a fellow Texan Latina and immigration attorney. Melanie doesn't know exactly what to do either, but she knows that her knowledge as an immigration lawyer will eventually be needed. She tells Destiny, "Well, if you can find us a church, I'll help you set it up." Destiny agrees. She relays the message to Blanca, and the three women agree to head to Paris, Texas, a larger town 10 miles southeast of Sumner, in whatever church Destiny can find.

So Bianca, the reporter, heads toward Paris to begin her reporting. Melanie, the lawyer, heads toward Paris to begin setting up her immigration legal services. And Destiny, the organizer, heads toward Paris to meet the two and anyone else she can gather. The three get in their cars, unsure of exactly where they are going but hoping they'll figure out the answer in the two hours before they arrive.

In the passenger seat of her Chevy Tahoe—complete with a Beto O'Rourke sticker on the rear windshield—Destiny has a box of the Know-Your-Rights materials she uses in her role with Justice for Our Neighbors. En route to Paris, she leaves a voicemail for a pastor to request to meet at his church. He declines.

Destiny recalls her frustration with the pastor who, she believes, doesn't understand the urgency—nor the religious significance—of the situation:

> [The first pastor] was like, "Well, you have to have approval of so-and-so" or this or that. But when people are in need, sometimes some things should be bypassed. When your people are suffering, do you just wait till you get approval or somebody's hungry? And the Bible gives us very strict instructions or very clear instructions: "For I was hungry, you fed me. You clothed me."

When Destiny explains her frustration with the pastor who denied her the use of his church, she references a story in which Jesus shared with his followers the requirements to be allowed to enter heaven (Matthew 25:35–40): "For I was hungry and you gave me something to eat, I was thirsty and you gave me something to drink, I was a stranger and you invited me in, I needed clothes and you clothed me, I was sick and you looked after me, I was in prison and you came to visit me."

Destiny's reasoning is notable. At this point in her story, she wasn't providing—or planning to provide—food, drink, shelter, health care, or visits to the detained specifically. In fact, it wasn't exactly clear what she was going to provide at all. She simply knew that her faith required her to find a need and address it, so she drove without hesitation to the most concentrated site of need she could imagine. But Destiny's motivation would turn out to be prophetic, as churches would later supply each of the provisions in the biblical verse or play a major role in their coordination.

The denial of one church was certainly not going to stop Destiny. In fact, neither would the denial of a second church. Destiny describes her belief that, no matter how many roadblocks she encounters, an answer eventually reveals itself if she keeps pushing forward. "I honestly believe God blessed me with a gift of talent because so many doors have opened up for me when people have told me, 'Oh, Destiny, that's never going to happen.' That's not true. Because God will always make a way, and God is leading me."

Unfortunately, religious leaders did not find the decision to welcome immigrants into their churches quite so straightforward, and pastors had to balance the dictates of their faith with the politics of the church. The race, wealth, and political affiliations of the church congregation—not the small Latino portion of it but the congregation as a whole—all played centrally into pastors' decisions about whether to allow their churches to house immigrant families.[2]

Pastor Cristián, the second pastor Destiny calls, knows it is politically unfeasible to let Destiny use his church, given the white, wealthy, Republican congregation that attends all the services except the Spanish one. But this doesn't mean he can't help in other ways.

Pastor Cristián and Destiny make a video about the raid of Load Trail, which they share on Facebook, and soon enough the video goes viral. More and more people in the community start to learn about the raid and realize that the needs of those involved extend far beyond reporting and legal services. Plus, reporting and legal services take a degree of specialization that limits who can provide them. Anyone can bring food, bedding, soap, or money. They just need to know where to go and how to get started. Pastor Cristián introduces Destiny to yet one more pastor. This pastor, Pastor Isaac, ultimately agrees to let Destiny use his church.

Destiny parks her Tahoe in front of Pastor Isaac's church, pulls out the box of Know-Your-Rights materials from the passenger seat, walks through the storefront doors, and begins unpacking the box's contents. Destiny's work as program administrator at Justice for Our Neighbors has prepared her for this kind of catastrophe, albeit not at this scale. She begins passing the orange-and-yellow Know-Your-Rights papers out to whoever enters the church, explaining that even as immigrants, even as undocumented immigrants, they, too, have rights. Don't sign anything. Wait until you talk to an attorney, she tells anyone who will listen.

For the first 12 hours she is there, Destiny says, she isn't sure exactly what is going to happen. She takes the lead when she has to, defers to others when she needs to, and does what she can to understand the emerging patterns of need from developing chaos.

Soon enough, the many seeds Destiny has planted start to bear fruit, with each phone call resulting in phone calls to one or two more people, before a whole network of lawyers, reporters, organizers, and other community members show up at the church doors. Because the raid on Load Trail was the sixth to take place during that summer, national organizations like the

Workers Defense Project, the Refugee and Immigrant Center for Education and Legal Services, and Movimiento Cosecha also converged on Pastor Isaac's storefront Evangelical church to support the small Latino community in North Texas. With the church identified, everyone knew where to go to get started.

But getting to the church was another issue altogether.

I-35

Nicole and I flew into the Dallas–Fort Worth (DFW) airport on December 7, 2018, less than four months since Load Trail had been raided and 159 people were detained and shipped to detention centers to process for removal. We planned to meet Destiny at Pastor Isaac's church, the same church where she, Melanie, and Blanca met after the raid, about a two-hour drive from DFW. By this point, flying into a major airport before making the long drive to churches and raid sites had become routine. I flew into Iowa City, for example, before we drove about an hour away to Mount Pleasant. We flew into Knoxville before the hour drive to Bean Station. Tellingly, while you couldn't find the churches into which everyone fled in the cities with major airports, you could find detention centers, ICE offices, courthouses, and the lawyers who were involved in the aftermath. Two of these big city lawyers, Melanie and Jay, agreed to meet with us before we left Dallas for Paris and Sumner.

I pick Nicole up in a rental car, and we drive to Melanie's office, stopping for coffee at a Starbucks just off I-35, then parking in front of the massive 15-story tower of offices. We enter the lobby, walk across the polished floor to one of the six silver elevators, and press the button to be taken to the sixth floor. The elevator dings and we walk through double doors into the waiting room in Melanie's suite. About eight people are in the waiting room when we get there, including two small infants no older than 4 months. Everyone appears to be Latino. I smile as I think of my own kiddos, 6 and 10, back in Michigan.

I take a moment to appreciate the view from Melanie's sixth-story window. The sky is mostly clear, the land flat, the trees short so that the limited water in the arid Texas soil doesn't need to be pulled too high up the trunk from the ground. I'm familiar with the wide-open skies of Texas, but it's not the sky that makes me nostalgic at that moment. It's the highways.

I learned to drive my 1998 red Dodge Shadow on San Antonio highways, including I-35. Then I spent countless hours on the highways in Houston. If you haven't lived in a city like San Antonio or Houston and instead have lived in rural communities, you may not be familiar with all the highway miles that criss-cross your state. But if you need to go from the pews of the church you are sleeping in to sit in front of Melanie's desk to tell her your immigration story or your husband's, you become familiar with a few hundred miles of them—and all the related opportunities to be pulled over—in a hurry.

Melanie had been practicing immigration law for 12 years, falling into it when other jobs were not available. She tells us: "[Immigration law] was not initially my plan. I actually was going to be a normal attorney, and then I needed a job, and it was for an immigration firm. And so, [I] definitely fell in love with doing it, because I think it kind of serves the same purpose in helping people."

Clearly, Melanie believes her work as an immigration lawyer is extremely important to the lives of immigrant families, likely the very families we met in her waiting room as we entered her suite. While she doesn't describe her motivation as religious, her desire to help those in need feels palpable and personal.

She explains the importance of immigration attorneys to the families of those detained in the raid of Load Trail:

> A greater need than anything for these people is legal counsel. Legal counsel. They just need legal counsel. They need information. They need to know what's going to happen next. They need to know that they're eligible for bond. They need to know that they can request whatever type of relief they're eligible [for]. They need to know what the steps are in the process.
>
> They need to know, "Oh. Well, he's in jail here. What's going to happen next?"
>
> Yeah, they have needs. They need to pay their bills. They need whatever. But I have found that [all needs besides legal relief are] always secondary.

Perhaps Melanie sees immigration attorneys as essential because she is one (it isn't hard to imagine a pastor saying the same thing about his church), but her argument stands to reason: You have to figure out who is missing, find out where they are being held, and then try to get them back. Lawyers made that final task—getting them back—much easier.

In immigration court, unlike criminal court, you do not have a right to legal counsel, so many detainees are left to decide whether they want to represent themselves against the well-paid DHS attorneys on their own, often in a language that is not their first. This can result in some absurdly unjust situations, like toddlers defending themselves in court alone.[3] The Vera Institute reports that 77 percent of immigration cases in 2019 didn't have legal representation at all.[4] Having a lawyer makes you much more likely to win your case. According to a study by the American Immigration Council,[5] immigrants in detention who had a bond hearing were four times more likely to be granted the bond and released from detention when they had legal representation. Immigrants with legal representation were also more likely to win their removal cases and avoid deportation altogether. Simply, if you want to get out of detention or avoid getting removed, it is best to get a lawyer.

While legal representation is essential, Melanie acknowledges that there aren't enough immigration lawyers to go around.

> The problem with immigration attorneys—and I can say this, because I am an immigration attorney—is that we are already overwhelmed, and we already provide a lot of service in this area. Obviously, most immigration attorneys who do this are doing it because they have a passion for it . . . and want to help people, and want to be available. But the problem is that our capacity is just not there. When you're dealing every day with people who are getting detained, or families who are about to be deported, or whatever. This is our life every day. The raid just makes it all happen at one time, but this is our life every day.

Melanie, like Destiny, responded to the raid by doing what she normally does, just on a much bigger scale. Most of the time, Melanie and Destiny, who are familiar with the harms of the immigration system, are able to handle the trauma they encounter. But many others, like teachers, social workers, and those who would later volunteer to drive potential deportees on the endless highway miles, are not familiar with the harms of immigration enforcement, and finding out about them through such a baptism by fire pushes many to a breaking point.

Thirty-five minutes into the interview, it's clear that Melanie wants to wrap up. We tell her how much we appreciate her work. We thank her assistant as we leave, and we hop in the car, on to I-35, and head over to visit with another lawyer while we are in town.

THE MULTIPLICATION OF LOAVES AND FISHES

≈

Jay Tucker's office is 17 miles away from the 15-story tower that housed Melanie's office. Jay, a white man with glasses, a slight southern accent, and a big silver mustache over his top lip, is on the leadership team of the North Texas Immigration Alliance, a nonprofit organization that provides legal services to refugees and immigrants who have suffered human rights abuses. Jay's office is one of many in the single-floor building, with a number of offices spread throughout to provide privacy and work space to a growing network of staff and an army of volunteers. A brownish carpet decorated with circles covers the floor, and bookshelves with children's books line the walls, making the building interior feel more like a school than a law office.

I snap a quick picture of a bumper sticker stuck on a filing cabinet that invites the reader to join the Dallas Volunteer Attorney Program. On the pink-and-green sticker is the image of a small child's hand holding the thumb of an adult hand. Above the image, black text on a pink background says, "Pro Bono: It's Like Billable Hours for Your Soul," with a small halo over the word "Soul." The space feels like a thriving, stable, growing nonprofit that has found a specific niche—filing asylum claims for immigrants who are victims of extreme violence—and fulfills that niche well.

Jay describes the organization:

> JAY: Our model is a pure pro bono model, so we are a pretty small organization. We're the largest we've ever been in our history, which is 14 staff. But we have about 250 volunteer lawyers that do the bulk of the legal work.
>
> BILL: And is that throughout Texas . . . Dallas?
>
> JAY: No, it's Dallas. It's really any place where the people are in immigration court in Dallas. And the Dallas immigration

[court] covers a large area, like all the way up into Oklahoma and out to West Texas and into East Texas. But all our volunteer lawyers are here, so the clients need to be able to meet with their lawyers [here].

Jay finds out about the raid on Load Trail when he sees coverage on the local news the Tuesday it occurs. Since his organization primarily focuses on asylum cases, and most of those detained in the Load Trail raid would not be pleading asylum, Jay continues to go about his work, figuring that other attorneys more suited to the type of relief the workers would request—lawyers like Melanie—will show up. Indeed, lawyers like Melanie do show up. But, as she described, the "capacity is just not there." More help needs to come from elsewhere: not from those who are perfect for the job but for those who are willing to try.

Jay gets a call from a colleague a few days later.

> So that Friday night, I got a call from [a lawyer with] a workplace rights organization here in Dallas. And [she] texted me and said "Can you send some lawyers to Paris? We're doing a clinic there tomorrow."
>
> It was a Friday night, and I'm like "All my lawyers are actually out of town this weekend, but I can go if you want me to."
>
> She's like "Yeah, we actually need people."
>
> So I went up, I drove up to Paris with her Saturday morning.

Jay gets in his car and drives two hours to meet up with his colleague at a small Evangelical church in Paris, a different church from the one at which Destiny, Melanie, and Blanca met. He works all day Saturday, wrapping up at about 10:00 p.m. Then he gets up and does it all again, this time ending his day a little earlier, at 5:00 p.m. A weekend full of work after a week full of work.

THE MULTIPLICATION OF LOAVES AND FISHES

But as Jay prepares to return to Dallas, his colleague tells him that there's another church, a small church led by a different Latino pastor, Pastor Isaac, nearby, with lawyers doing the exact same thing she and he are doing now. So Jay drives over to that church, joining Melanie and adding another lawyer to the growing multitude.

When he finishes, whenever that may be, he still has to drive 110 miles to Dallas if he wants to sleep in his own bed.

Jay and Melanie seem cut from a very similar visionary, compassionate, self-sacrificing cloth. While they may differ professionally and personally—Jay directing a nonprofit, Melanie a law firm, and Jay a white man to Melanie's Latina woman—some of the similarities between them and among other lawyers throughout the country who responded to the worksite raids of 2018 are remarkable.

Jay explains that he had actually seen this spontaneous legal organizing about a year and a half earlier, when Trump instituted Executive Order 13769 in his first term, which banned immigrants from Muslim-majority countries from entering the US. The order, known colloquially as the "Muslim ban," was rolled out as was the family separation policy in 2018: chaotically, opaquely, and with no real strategy to deal with the immense humanitarian needs that would come after. Many immigrants traveling on visas from countries such as Iraq and Afghanistan left their countries of birth legally able to enter the US, only to have that legal right of entry eliminated while their planes were in the air. In the first week, the Muslim ban forced about 2,000 people into Customs and Border Protection secondary inspection.[6] Reports showed that the DHS had to interpret the order after Trump had already signed it.[7]

Eleven of the thousands of those detained because of the Muslim ban were detained in the DFW airport, the same airport

Nicole and I had flown into a few days prior to meeting Jay. There, dozens of Muslim men and women gathered for prayer, kneeling in front of the baggage carousel in Terminal F while people of other faiths circled outside the airport to pray and chant for the release of those detained.[8] Lawyers found whatever floor space they could, propped open their laptops, and began to see what they could do. The International Refugee Assistance Project circulated a form sheet for lawyers to commit to sign up for "airport triage."[9] Jay was among the lawyers huddled on the floor of the DFW airport.

Jay recalls:

> When the Muslim ban rolled out here, it was a very organic response from lawyers at the airport. There were, I don't know, a couple hundred lawyers went out there, volunteered, set up a war room. . . .
>
> I've never seen anything like it. And people went, lawyers came, they put their own credit cards down to rent a room, they brought laptops in. We had observers down there talking to people. We were talking to baggage handlers who were leaking information about people that were still being held by Border Patrol back in the back, and we started getting out writs of habeas corpus there in that room and getting people released.

Writs of habeas corpus order the custodians of detainees to bring those detainees to court to determine if the detention is lawful. If a detainee cannot be brought to court, he is released. The influx of writs of habeas corpus forced the hand of the DHS, which was unable to mobilize its own army of lawyers to accompany detainees to court, especially for cases they were unlikely to win. The first iteration of the Muslim ban was eventually overturned because of a writ of habeas corpus filed by the American Civil Liberties Union, among others, on behalf of Mr. Darweesh and Mr. Alshawi,[10] both of whom had valid visas to enter the US. Darweesh worked for the US military, resulting in threats to his life in Iraq. Despite the Muslim ban being overturned, analysis shows that it resulted in the separation of siblings and spouses from each other and children from parents;[11] families delayed having children, funerals were missed, and weddings were postponed; and individuals targeted by the ban reported anxiety, depression, and emotional distress.

Jay contributed to the influx of writs filed at that time, even though, before that day, he wasn't familiar with them. He explains that he ended up in the airport on that random weekend in exactly the same way he ended up in a storefront church in Paris, Texas, on a random weekend the very next year: "I had a lawyer call me. He said, 'Hey Jay, you know anything about writs of habeas corpus?' I went, 'Nope.' He's like 'Well we're going out there. Can you help?' I went, 'Yeah.' And I just went out there on Sunday morning."

As Jay explains, the legal response to the raid of Load Trail, whether consciously or not, mirrored the response of many attorneys throughout the country to the Muslim ban: organic, word-of-mouth, learn-as-you-go, there-goes-my-weekend service, sparked by anger over injustice, and, in some cases, a religious calling, then focused with laser intensity into a solution. In the case of the Muslim ban, these lawyers were successful. As one *Slate* article put it, "The Lawyers Showed Up: And because we still live in a country where the law matters, they won."[12] It seemed the Trump administration had sparked an army of pop-up lawyers ready to take on whatever the administration could throw at them, even if they knew little about the type of law they were being asked to practice.

Jay shares,

The airport [after the Muslim ban] and this workplace raid, neither of those are really likely to produce a client that is the type of case we do. So that's really kind of outside of our mission.

People that showed up in Paris, people like the two, three organizing lawyers at the airport, none of them are immigration lawyers. You know, one's a plaintiff's lawyer, one was in a big law firm, the third is a former city councilman in Dallas. All of them just like community-oriented good people, and they just showed up. Actually, one of the guys showed up 'cause his friend said, "What, are you gonna go to church this morning and leave people stuck in detention?" and shamed him into going [laughs].

I'm not prone to make this kind of statement, but I think it's just a racist agenda, and it just permeates the whole thing because it's systematic. You name a type of immigration, it's under attack right now. And if those of us who care about this, it's way past like, "Oh that's not really my issue."

This is like yeah, they're coming after all of us; they're coming after all of our clients. We can either cooperate, collaborate, or just sit by and watch it happen.

Yet while the communities hit by worksite raids benefited from the army of conditioned, superhuman lawyers who had been trained by Trump's previous attacks on immigrants, the DHS had something working in its favor this time that it did not when these lawyers attempted to overturn the Muslim ban. In this case these lawyers couldn't flock to the airports near their homes. News crews couldn't drive from their downtown offices to short-term airport parking. Masses of supporters holding up posters and signs couldn't stage protests in the cell phone lot. Instead, these lawyers, reporters, and supporters had to drive away from those airports, away from their offices, away from their homes, and away from their own families, first to the isolated site of the raid or the churches nearby and then to the detention centers spread throughout the state and beyond, where detainees were being held. Just as the DHS does when it funnels immigrants into the Mexican desert to die, the DHS used the terrain to its advantage. As Jay states, "I don't know if that's [the DHS] strategy to put these detention centers in remote places where it's less likely they'll access counsel, but, whether they mean it or not, that's the impact. It's a dramatic decrease in the availability of legal services."

≈

Slowly, communities throughout the rural US would struggle to find the balance between the specialist and the generalist, the ideal and the sufficient, and wrestle with the pain and sacrifice of reactively cobbling together an ad hoc team to resist a racist system doing everything it could to undermine it. As Jay insinuates, the enemy was not only ICE, but exhaustion: the exhaustion of volunteering, the exhaustion of driving for hours, and the exhaustion of running on adrenaline, grief, and faith.

Nicole and I thank Jay profusely as the interview ends. We get back in the car, hopping on I-35 to get some Texas barbecue for dinner. There's a place that serves delicious food, we are told, a short 20 miles away.

The Marthas and the Marys

Trish Sanders is in her mid-60s, with circular, thin-rimmed glasses and short, grayish hair. She wears a Fitbit on her right wrist, changing the band every so often so its color matches her outfit. Graduating from college with a 4.0 grade point average, Trish later worked as a human resources (HR) manager in southeast Iowa before becoming the executive director of administration and HR for an advertising agency headquartered in a major city in California. Trish is engaging, dynamic, visionary, and articulate, and whether she has a natural knack for organizing people—or developed the skill through years of work in HR—her ability to think through the infrastructure needed to allow individuals to come-as-they-are and still engage in impactful, socially relevant work is evident in everything she does.

When Midwest Precast Concrete was raided in 2018, Trish was serving as the chair of Iowa Bridge, housed in Trinity Presbyterian Church of Mount Pleasant. The organization was well supported by the church pastor and benefited from a steady stream of dedicated volunteers, some of whom, mostly white like Trish, had been with Iowa Bridge since it was founded in 2015 and others of whom, Latina and Spanish-speaking like Juana, had only begun working with the organization after the raid took their husbands away.

Iowa Bridge was not designed with a raid response in mind. Instead, the vision of the organization was to support Syrian refugees fleeing violence and economic hardship following a civil war that began in 2015 and left a large portion of the population jobless, homeless, and hungry.[13] Iowans had welcomed refugees who fled Vietnam in the 1970s, helping them find homes, doctors, and schools for their children. Trish saw no reason she and her fellow Iowans couldn't repeat the welcome.[14]

Trish shares her memories of the news at the time:

> Every night you saw these boats, the survivors—or nonsurvivors—were coming to shore in Greece. And it was just very heartbreaking to think that you have these people who so desperately have to escape their home countries.
>
> And we just wanted to help.
>
> We wanted to say, "Hey, there's no reason we can't do that. We've done it before in our community; we can do that again."

THE MULTIPLICATION OF LOAVES AND FISHES

Not all Americans were as enthusiastic as Trish was to accept Syrian refugees, even as the death toll in Syria climbed into the thousands. But this hesitancy waned on September 2, 2015, when the photo of two-year-old Syrian Alan Kurdi, lying face-down on a Turkish beach after drowning in the Mediterranean Sea alongside his mother and brother, covered the front page of newspapers nationwide. The photo shifted the popular conception of refugees from adults huddled together in rubber boats aimed for your shores to innocent children falling into the sea.

Researchers published a paper in the *Proceedings of the National Academy of Sciences* about the photo, stating in surprisingly straightforward terms "that the world was basically asleep as the body count in the Syrian war rose steadily into the hundreds of thousands. The iconic image of a young Syrian child, lying face-down on a beach, woke the world for a brief time, bringing much-needed attention to the war and the plight of its many victims."[15]

After the photo of Alan Kurdi was published, even Terry Branstad, Iowa's Republican governor at the time, shared his support, stating "I think Iowans are very open and accepting to immigrants in situations like this" and noting that Iowa had many jobs to offer refugees, such as those in food processing and meatpacking.[16] Trish recalls how this welcoming energy, coupled with her willingness to say yes to whatever was asked of her, led to the founding of Iowa Bridge:

> I think it actually started out of a book group; [that] was where the conversation actually got started. And then, one of the members went to the session and said, "Hey, we really want to do this."
> And they nodded their heads and said, "Yes."

They called me and asked me if I would chair it. I said, "Sure. That's exactly what I want to do." I called the first meeting, and we had like over 40 people show up.

American support for Syrians during the refugee crisis—a crisis that was far away and, like the family separation crisis on the border, full of innocent children—seemed to be increasing. Perhaps Iowans would see their share of refugees once again. And when they did, Trish would be ready.

≈

On November 13, 2015, shortly after Iowa Bridge was founded, a coordinated attack that included automatic weapons and explosive devices occurred across six sites in Paris, France, killing 130 people and injuring 416.[17] The next day, ISIS claimed responsibility for the attacks, and one perpetrator was found to have entered Greece among Syrian refugees before making his way to Paris.[18]

Reactions were swift among US Republican governors, who raced to halt efforts to accept Syrian refugees. One CNN article summarized the rhetoric of the time, pitting refugees against the safety of Americans: "Shelter the homeless, or protect the host country?," the article asked.[19] The Brookings Institution called the period "a transition in public sentiment from humanitarian sympathy to national security anxiety,"[20] a sentiment reminiscent of the changing mood of the country following 9/11. It seemed the crisis had come too close to home, and Americans fell back into our historical tendency to oppose taking in large numbers of refugees no matter what those refugees were fleeing.[21]

Louisiana Governor Bobby Jindhal ordered his state police to begin tracking refugees who entered his state.[22] Texas Senator Ted Cruz and Florida Governor Jeb Bush advocated for the rejection of Muslim refugees (though they still wanted to allow in Christians[23]). And Trish's own governor, Terry Branstad, reversed his earlier support for refugees and his invitation to fill Iowa's meatpacking plants, stating the following: "We have welcomed refugees from around the world into Iowa.... We must continue to have compassion for others, but we must also maintain the safety of Iowans and the security of our state."[24]

It looked like no Syrian immigrants would be coming to Mount Pleasant after all. Undeterred, Trish pivoted.

While she was ready to accept and support highly visible Syrian refugees and their children, she was equally ready to support the immigrants who were already her neighbors in Mount Pleasant, immigrants who were not in the public discussion, who were not fleeing in rubber boats but still had to survive under the everyday threat of deportation.

As Trish explains to Nicole: "So we broadened our focus to make Mount Pleasant a welcoming place for international students and immigrants and refugees from around the world who live, work, play here." It was this willingness to pivot, combined with her deep roots in the community—and the serendipitous timing of another of Trish's weekly meetings—that proved essential to Trinity Presbyterian's success in supporting families after the raid of Precast Concrete.

Trish shares her memory of the day of the raid:

NICOLE: Can you kind of walk us through your experience that day, starting in the morning?

TRISH: So I got a call probably shortly after 9:00 from one of my members in Iowa Bridge, who had heard that there was a raid at the Mount Pleasant Midwest Precast Plant....

Then I started getting calls from teachers who had students leaving in search of their parents. Or parents coming to the school to take their kids out of school. It was a real day of terror for the immigrants. . . . Basically the immigrant community was in hiding.

As it happened, we already had an Iowa Bridge meeting planned for that night. And I was able to reach out to [someone I knew] from American Friends in Des Moines because we had been talking about the whole Iowa Sanctuary Movement. . . . She reached out to . . . Community Bond people, to the University of Iowa Labor Center, the University of Iowa Law Clinic, to the immigration attorneys, to the counselors.

So that evening, just a few hours after the raid, we had all of these people from around the state in our church. Ready to help these families that were just in tears and so afraid about what had happened to the men in their lives.

Trish's years of dedication to Mount Pleasant's immigrant community brought with it a reputation that multiplied the impact of every phone call she made. Sometimes the person who picked up the phone could provide the service Trish requested. Other times she would contact one of her colleagues, who would agree to join Trish in her church even if they had never met. As the energy to respond to the raid grew, Trish decided to open up the meeting even more. Before long, it wasn't just organizers and advocates who were coming to Trish's church, but the families they wanted to protect as well, as Trish relates: "And because we'd had all these connections with the immigrant leaders in the community, they knew that this would be a safe place that they could bring people. And so they called us and said, 'We want to bring the families together for your meeting tonight.' And we said, 'Yes, that's exactly what needs to happen.'"

As the number inside the church grew, other Iowans also wanted to find a way to help. So Iowans in and around Trinity

THE MULTIPLICATION OF LOAVES AND FISHES

Presbyterian began to donate food to the families who couldn't afford groceries or fled the homes and food pantries they contained. The stockpiles of cans and bags and boxes of food began to grow. Seeing the food beginning to multiply, Trish found something to do with that, too: "You know, we opened the food pantry at our church just because people showed up with food. So we said, 'Okay, we have a Sunday School room we're not using; now it's a food pantry.'"

≈

As church communities throughout the country found ways to welcome immigrant families into their spaces, so, too, did they find ways, often as their faith directed, to keep them fed. While Trinity Presbyterian of Mount Pleasant developed a food pantry, other churches used different strategies to feed the growing number of hungry families seeking safety among their walls.

Sometimes, if a church had the facility, the food was prepared in-house and given directly to those sheltered in the building. Larry, who had spoken with Nicole and compared the psychological impacts of the raid in Bean Station to those of the civil war in Suriname, shared how he and other volunteers used the church kitchen to feed thousands of people in a few days: "So about 11 o'clock Saturday night, [two days after the raid on Thursday], we've served thousands of meals. We probably served 2,000 meals every day nonstop, and all the Latino community, we have a great kitchen back there."

Not every church had a kitchen with the capacity to prepare food for thousands of people. But as word spread that the immigrant community was huddled in churches, these sanctuaries became drop-off locations for fresh food that was prepared elsewhere. In Salem, Ohio, in one of the churches in which families gathered after the raid on Fresh Mark, the first meals were prepared in a school cafeteria and brought over to the church.

After the raid in Bean Station, families originally hid in an elementary school adjacent to the National Guard Armory where detainees were held, and Father Jim entered in search of parishioners. In this case, since families were not hidden in the church, the church brought the food to them, as Sylvia, an educator in nearby Morristown, described: "You're seeing community carrying in water by the cases. One church brought in a bunch of Chick-fil-A. You're seeing pizza—boxes and boxes of pizza to feed these families. Had one baby that the mother was across the road in the armory. No bottle, no formula. Somebody went out and got [formula]."

When school was starting and families could no longer hide in the elementary school, they shifted over to St. Peter's Church, the Catholic church of which Father Jim was the pastor. Sylvia followed them to the church, as did the food. She said: "I mean, we went the next day down [to the church] to work, and that night, and just food. . . . They had a whole room full of infant needs. Formula, diapers, wipes, an entire room just for all of that. Food. Some of the families slept there because they were afraid to go home."

Father Jim described the same scene: "It was triage, you know. People were coming in and they had boxes of food. And other people were coming in. And so you were signing in. And then there were people in the kitchen. You had the Marthas there. You had the Marys there. It was a whirlwind."

≈

When Father Jim referred to the "Marthas and the Marys" bustling around St. Peter's Catholic Church after the raid on Southeastern Provision, Nicole, Julio, and I had to smile and laugh.

THE MULTIPLICATION OF LOAVES AND FISHES

We grew up Catholic, and we had heard the story of Martha and Mary in countless homilies throughout our Catholic school lives. In the story, found in Luke 10:38-42, Jesus and his disciples enter the home of two sisters, Martha and Mary. Martha, as tradition and culture at the time dictated, begins to cook, clean, and prepare her home for her sudden guests. Mary sits at Jesus's feet to listen to him preach, ignoring her hosting responsibilities and leaving them to Martha. Martha feels slighted by Mary and asks Jesus to tell Mary that she needs to take her hosting responsibilities more seriously and not leave them all to her. Jesus replies to Martha, "Martha, Martha, you are worried and upset about many things, but few things are needed—or indeed only one. Mary has chosen what is better, and it will not be taken away from her." Martha is left to continue the preparations on her own.

This story is commonly interpreted in one of two ways, the first much more generous than the second. The first interpretation argues that there are different types of service, active and contemplative, and that God calls some people to one type of service and calls other people to the other type.[25] In this interpretation, Martha and Mary are generally seen to engage in equally important—yet different—types of service. When I heard Father Jim reference the "Marthas and the Marys," I was fairly certain he was referencing the first interpretation of the story: There were many different roles that played out in St. Peter's that day—people writing down names, people talking to the media, people playing with children, people developing legal strategies, people managing money for bonds, people preparing meals—and each of those roles was essential to the raid response in and around Bean Station. Each person who supported the community after the raid simply did so by doing what they did best.

The second interpretation of the Martha and Mary story argues that Christians need to prioritize a deeper relationship with

Jesus and not be distracted by the demands of the world. In this interpretation, Martha allowed herself to become preoccupied with cleaning and cooking, failing to realize that listening to and engaging with Jesus was more important than attempting to make her home a welcoming space for him.[26]

This interpretation—that Mary's contemplative work was superior to Martha's active work—always struck me as particularly harsh. Martha was, after all, cleaning and cooking for Jesus and his disciples, who suddenly showed up at her door, undoubtedly dirty and dusty from their time on the road. And while as a 12-year-old kid in Catholic school I didn't quite have the word "sexist" in my vocabulary, something made me uncomfortable about a male priest lauding the woman who sat at the feet of a man and his male disciples and dismissing the work of the woman who cooked for them. I thought of all the carework I had seen my mother and my aunts do—the cooking, the cleaning, the laundry, the comforting of the crying children—to keep the home running.

In the aftermath of many movements against unjust deportation, it's often the intellectual work of professionals, such as lawyers, judges, advocates, or actors, that circulates in the media. In the public narrative of the Muslim ban, for example, it was the creative and benevolent lawyers who slept on airport floors and developed the legal strategy of flooding the courts with writs of habeas corpus that caused the ban to be overturned. When the family separation crisis unfolded, it was the reporters who broke the story, along with the actors and health professionals who made public statements about the harms of family separation, that ultimately pressured the administration to end the zero-tolerance policy that resulted in separation. To be clear, all these professional roles were essential to the victories that resulted, and I count many friends and colleagues among the reporters, lawyers, and public health professionals who contributed to those victories.

But the work of mothers, like Juana, organizers like Destiny, retirees like Trish, and many, many teachers—most of whom were women—were often hidden from the public narrative. I couldn't help but relate the dismissal of Martha to the invisibility of these women.

≈

A legend surrounding Martha arose in the latter part of the twelfth century, allegedly written by her maidservant, Marcella.[27] The legend states that Martha not only cleaned and cooked for Jesus but later captured a dragon that had been hiding in the river and sinking incoming ships:

> The people of Tarascon implored Martha to get rid of this beast, which no man had been able to defeat.
>
> Upon coming to the dragon eating a man, she threw holy water at it and held up a wooden cross, which froze the dragon in place.
>
> Martha then tied it with her belt and gave it over to the townspeople, who killed it with their spears and stones.

The legend of Martha presents a more dynamic Martha than that of the Bible. Here, Martha is clearly the central character of the story—agentive, strategic, and courageous in her own right—not a foil to a lead male character. In the biblical account, Martha was invited to forgo the culturally ascribed work of women and join the discussion with the men. In the legend, however, the town sought Martha's help specifically because she was able to do what the men could not do, which in this case was to capture a dragon. But importantly, the legend of Martha argues not for a single protagonist but for a collaborative solution. It was not Martha, after all, who killed the dragon. She only captured it, allowing the community to collectively destroy what had been terrorizing it.

I wondered if Father Jim knew about the dragon-capturing Martha, or how aptly the Martha and Mary analogy, including all its interpretations and surrounding legends,[28] described the activity in rural America that summer.

Your Search Has Returned Zero (0) Matching Records

Organizers like Destiny and Trish were lynchpins in their communities' responses to the worksite raids that happened nearby. With phones full of contacts and trusted reputations, they brought together a network of people with experience serving immigrant communities. At the same time, they created the infrastructure for those angered by the raids—or inspired by their faith—to do something practical, like donate money or food or volunteer to take on simple tasks. In each case, churches played a central role in their organizing efforts. First and foremost, undocumented family members felt safe behind church walls, as ICE forbade enforcement efforts in these "sensitive locations" without exigent circumstances (this policy would be rescinded in Trump's second term). Pastors, congregants, and regular church volunteers, many of whom followed their church's centuries-long tradition of serving immigrants, also created a welcoming space for the immigrant families who feared the worst.

Meeting in a church was also a matter of practicality. Churches were spacious, or at least more spacious than the small mobile homes in which many immigrant families lived. This allowed the community to gather in the open rooms, to sleep on pews when they feared going home, and to cook, prepare, and distribute food. And in the rolling plains of the rural US, churches were known landmarks, beacons in a sea of highways connecting a

THE MULTIPLICATION OF LOAVES AND FISHES

few two-lane roads between small towns. You found a church. You got started.

With families and volunteers huddled in churches—and food miraculously showing up to feed them—communities now had to address the complicated task of figuring out who had been taken and where they had been taken to.

Kimberly, a staff member at an immigrant-serving organization in Norwalk, Ohio, recalls the day of the raid at Fresh Mark meatpacking plant in Salem, after which the families of those detained fled to St. John's church.[29]

> So we had husbands and wives and kids coming in who had loved ones detained. And we were just doing intake. It was like triage at that point. There was not really much we could do except get people's information and figure out what the next step's going to be.
>
> And literally we had a notebook, just a regular notebook. And we passed it around, and people just wrote down like everyone they knew who had been detained because nobody even knew at that point. Like, how many was it?

Kimberly calls the Mexican Consulate, but it, like every other organization in the area, has no list of who has been detained. It seems the only way to find out who is missing is to find out who is present and ask them who should be next to them—on the assembly line, in the canning factory, at the family dinner table—but isn't. So Kimberly and other volunteers start the reverse roll call that would come to be a defining feature of community-driven raid responses that summer, tabulating presence for the purpose of discerning absence.

As she scribbles down information, Kimberly runs into a problem. As it turns out, "what was the name of the person who should be next to you" is a more complicated question than it seems, due to the reality of working while undocumented as well as some typical Latino name conventions. Kimberly shares:

> People didn't know full names or maybe they knew the person's nickname, not their given name. Or maybe someone was working under a different name. And that's not their name on their documents.
>
> So, it was very chaotic. But we put this list together, literally handwritten by members of the community, [and] identified most of the people who were detained in one way or another.
>
> But I remember being very skeptical, like, is this even going to be helpful? Because we literally had, like, "Jose," "Maria," like "Paco." It was like, who are these people? How is this going to be helpful?

Nicknames, or *apodos*, are common among Latinos and are sometimes used so often they replace a given name. While sometimes an *apodo* might be related to one's given name—Chuy is widely known as the nickname for Jesus, for example—not all *apodos* map on so clearly. Kimberly wonders how she is going to match these *apodos* with the formal names in government databases, a problem that cannot be solved simply by being bilingual. Kimberly, after all, speaks Spanish just fine. But the help she needs requires problem-solving across cultural differences, Latino and white, formal and informal, work and home, citizen and undocumented. To solve this problem, Kimberly needs other people, people with the cultural knowledge and experience to supplement hers.

The Mexican Consulate, which was unable to provide information on who had been arrested as the raid was unfolding, is quite helpful in telling Kimberly that, for example, Paco is Paco to his friends at work but Francisco to the government, so the Francisco about whom the distraught wife is asking and the

Frank the congregants identified as the man who sometimes shovels their snow are probably the same person. As Kimberly recalls:

> But we gave [the list of names] to the Mexican Consulate, and they were so grateful because they were like, we couldn't get information from ICE. . . . And they were like, "We don't even know how many people, who's there," so that they were so grateful for that list. And then they sent it back to us after they were able to get everybody's full names and identify them. And that's how we started.

Over and over, these moments of cross-cultural translation and collaboration would happen inside church walls across the country, allowing for the solution of problems in creative ways. Unfortunately, however, sometimes these cultural mismatches were too much, the time to address them didn't exist, or they were ignored on purpose, an easy excuse to leave the community without the resources necessary to address their needs.

Figuring out who was missing was just the first step. Once the list of nicknames had evolved into a list of names that could be reasonably expected to exist in a database, it was time to try to locate the missing. But which database would they be in? And what naming conventions would that particular database follow?

≈

According to Freedom for Immigrants, a nonprofit devoted to abolishing immigration detention, there are five possible places someone can end up if they are detained in an immigration raid.[30] Some detainees are quickly deported to their countries of birth. Others are released back into the community, citing humanitarian concerns such as a home full of children with no adult to watch them. If the detainee is not deported or released, he could be held in one of three types of government facilities: a local jail, a federal prison, or an ICE detention facility. If you believe the person is being detained in a jail or prison, you can call the facility or use that facility's offender locator tool. Each jail has a different phone number and locator. Each prison has a different phone number, but each prison in a given state uses the same locator.

If you decide to search jails and prisons, it makes sense to start with those closest to the site of the raid and continue searching in facilities further out. There is no real logical distance from the point of arrest at which one should stop searching, however, as those arrested could be transported hundreds of miles away, especially in rural settings where available beds for detention may be sparse. Many jails and prisons do not have bilingual staff, so calling may be futile if you don't speak English. And some jails and prisons have no idea that they house immigrants and don't know how to navigate that side of the database.

To further complicate matters, none of the five options listed are mutually exclusive, and someone can enter the system in one way and be housed in one location before being moved to another location, being deported, being released, being moved again, being deported and disappearing in their country of birth, or being deported and disappearing in the US after reentry. If the person cannot be found in any database for a significant amount of time, other organizations are available to help find out if the person has died—for example, No More Deaths, or a Red Cross chapter in the town in which the individual may have tried to cross the border.

These five options assume that those in a raided facility are actually detained. Sometimes workers in a raided building manage to avoid being caught by ICE. Some workers hide—in the restroom, under a table, among the cow carcasses[31]—and are able to escape after ICE leaves the property. Others may get injured, perhaps in the raid, perhaps as they flee or drive away, and find themselves in the hospital. Fleeing ICE could also mean you end up in the morgue, perhaps driving away more quickly than you should.[32] And avoiding ICE at one point doesn't mean you can't be detained later, perhaps by a raid that extends to the community, or by a police officer pulling you over as you try to drive away, or by an agent knocking on your door.

If the person in the ICE raid is detained by ICE and placed in an ICE facility, one more major tool can be used to locate them: ICE's Online Detainee Locator System (ODLS). The ODLS is colloquially referred to as the ICE Locator, or just the Locator, without the word "ICE" preceding it. A different word, usually a Spanish expletive, precedes it instead.

Freedom for Immigrants conducted a nationwide study on the functionality of the Locator and found the Locator to be "so erroneous that it routinely fails to identify and locate people in ICE custody." For example, entire facilities do not show up in the database, despite clearly housing detainees. Sometimes the website simply won't load.[33] In a survey of immigration lawyers, many stated that the system functioned so poorly that they avoided it, resorting instead to picking up the phone and calling anyone who may be able to give them information about the person's whereabouts.[34]

Yet the anger over the Locator is not because it simply doesn't work but because it fails to do what it should logically and fundamentally be able to do: locate Latino detainees. A report by the American Immigration Council showed that the majority of those detained by ICE are from either Mexico (43 percent) or the three Northern Triangle countries of Honduras, Guatemala, and El Salvador (46 percent).[35] This means that more than 89 percent of those detained by ICE are considered Latino in the US, with names that generally follow typical Latino naming conventions, including, in addition to the frequent use of *apodos*, having two surnames (an *apellido paterno* and an *apellido materno*), using different names depending on the dominant language of the setting (some are obvious cognates, like Mary and Maria, but others are not, like the English James and the Spanish Jaime or Santiago), or spelling names with tildes or accent marks.[36]

To use the ICE Locator, you have two options. First, you can search using the person's A-number, or Alien Registration Number, a unique identifier given to immigrants when they first encounter the DHS. Most A-numbers are eight digits. Some are seven. Some are nine. If your A-number is fewer than nine digits, you need to remember to enter leading zeros into the ICE Locator. In addition to the A-number, you must enter the individual's country of birth. While most family and friends will generally know the person's country of birth, not every family member knows their A-number. Importantly, an A-number is different from the Bureau of Prisons number, the state number, or the case number, which you may need to identify someone in other databases.

This leaves the second option, searching for the person's "Biographical Information" by filling in three boxes:[37] "Country of Birth," "First Name," and "Last Name." But the ICE Locator is incapable of searching all possible combinations of items in a search box, so you must decide which single name or combination of names go in the "First Name" box and which go in the "Last Name" box. Any combination of names may or may not contain a hyphen. You must also spell the name correctly every time, unless the name has an accent or tilde, in which case you must spell the name incorrectly, omitting the accent or tilde as the Locator cannot recognize them.

Even prison databases are more flexible. For example, the Texas Department of Criminal Justice Inmate Search requires only a last name and the first letter of the first name. The Michigan Department of Corrections (MDOC) Offender Tracking Information System will let you search by first name, last name, MDOC number, age, or "marks, scars, or tattoos." That you can search by tattoos in some state databases but not in the ICE database is perhaps most ironic, as the DHS extensively documents Latinos—and often profiles us as gang members—based on our tattoos.[38]

The ICE Locator brochure warns users about the challenges of naming conventions, though, noting that if you enter "Robert Smith," the system will not return a detention record for "Robert Smyth" or "Bob Smith."[39] While I never saw Kimberly's notebook, I doubted a "Robert Smith" appeared among those detained after the raid of Fresh Mark.

Sometimes entering the name correctly doesn't matter anyway. Prior to 2019, the ICE Locator system would show "Not in Custody" if you searched for someone who had, at one point, been detained but had since been released or deported. Thus, if your search turned up a "Not in Custody" result, you would know you had the name right, that they were in custody at one time, and that you could now move to the next stage of the search.

But shortly after Trump was elected in 2016, a change to this function became a source of yet more deep frustration among friends, families, and advocates using the Locator.[40] Now, if the person for whom you are searching has been deported, is being transferred, was never arrested at all, or if you are just misspelling his name, the system provides the same response: "Your search has returned zero (0) matching records. Please re-check the search terms you entered to ensure they are correct and try your query again. If you conducted a name-based search, please remember that only exact matches to the name you entered will be returned. You may want to try searching any name or spelling variants used by the detainee."

The most generous interpretation of the poor functionality of the ICE Locator is that the systematic ineptitude stems from benign neglect, the product of some ICE official or programmer ignoring the problem, hoping it will go away, or prioritizing some other task they deem more important. The less generous interpretation, however, argues that the poor functionality is a purposeful and strategic attempt to break the will of immigrant families by disappearing their loved ones and ignoring the cultural norms of the exact detainees most likely to be in their facilities.[41] This strategy—what Freedom for Immigrants calls "enforced disappearances"—has a long history of use as a political tool by Central American regimes backed by the US who routinely disappeared "subversives" from the 1960s to 1980s.[42] At a minimum, the poor functionality of the ICE Locator represents yet one more of the complexities of immigrant invisibility and hypervisibility in the rural US. When all you want to do is work unnoticed alongside your Latino immigrant friends, ICE notices you. And when you are stuck in detention alongside those friends, you disappear unnoticed into the system, your Latino name just too confusing for anyone to understand.

CHAPTER 5

Where Do You Stop Being a Teacher?

A Chatty Student

Weekends are sacred for teachers. After five days of early rising, lesson planning, and talkative students giving you headaches, the weekend can be a time to sleep late, spend time with one's own children, and be somewhere different than the inside of your classroom or the teachers' lounge. So it was not lost on us that four educators, including the school's principal, agreed to meet with us on a Saturday morning, in their school building, on the last day of their summer vacation at Mountain View Elementary School.

We arrived at Mountain View, an elementary school in Hamblen County, Tennessee, at about 10 a.m. on a beautiful and warm day in late July 2018. The school is surrounded by trees and set on the peak of a slight hill, allowing you to look outward at yet more trees and an endlessly expansive blue sky peppered by white clouds that were not threatening any rain that day. Hamblen County is a midsized Tennessee county of about 64,000 people.[1] It is a notable 15 percent Latino,[2] more than double the percentage of Latinos in the state of Tennessee as a whole, which stands at only 5 percent.[3] In Hamblen County schools, however, one in three students is Latino.[4]

Many of these students had parents who did the gritty work of dismembering cattle carcasses at Southeastern Provision, 15 miles away, over the bridge and past the boat launch and campground. And many of them, along with all the teachers in front of us, were deeply shaken when the slaughterhouse was raided on April 5, 2018, less than four months before our visit, after a monthslong probe into allegations that the slaughterhouse's owners were paying undocumented immigrants in cash to save $2.5 million in unpaid taxes over three years. On that day, 97 workers were arrested.[5] Many were parents. And many of their children were at school.

The school principal, Sylvia, was among the four teachers meeting with us and invited everyone in attendance into her office. She was joined by three teachers, Leslie, a 55-year-old woman who taught third grade; Cathy, a 41-year-old woman who taught ELL, or English Language Learning for students who needed to improve their English, to grades K through 5; and Ted, Cathy's husband, who had recently taken a job teaching computer programming at a high school in the same district. All were white. Among tiny iron cowboy boots and bookshelves covered with pictures of Sylvia's family, we sat around a small wooden table, one by one getting up to serve ourselves food from the buffet-style side table covered with a platter of pastries and cut fruit Sylvia had carried in a woven picnic basket with blue fabric trim.

Julio, who had arranged the interview with Father Jim, had also arranged these interviews for Nicole and me. Fifteen years ago, Julio had himself attended a middle school in Hamblen County, where Cathy, the ELL teacher with us that day, was his English teacher. The warmth of the unexpected reunion between a teacher and student from a decade and a half ago was evident to everyone in the room, and as Julio and Cathy caught up in front of us all, it was clear that Cathy deeply cared—and still cares—for Julio. Reveling in the small audience now watching them exchange banter back and forth, Cathy and Julio both laughed about how incredibly talkative Julio used to be in school, often distracting his classmates as they were trying to work. I can only imagine how talkative a young Julio must have been, because now he's funny, welcoming, good with people, and, with degrees from Notre Dame and Vanderbilt, likely has a political career in front of him.

But while Julio's chattiness as student was distracting—making it all the more worthwhile when Cathy made it to those liberating weekends—Cathy didn't describe it as a burden. That a Spanish-speaking, Latino immigrant student from Mexico whose mom worked in a lawn mower transmission manufacturing company would be confident enough to be chatty—in English, in a majority-white, English-speaking school—marked at least some sort of comfort in this new rural world in which he found himself. We all knew that Julio's English chattiness was probably a marker of success for Cathy, who, like other ELL teachers, played a key role in the cross-cultural navigation that made kids like Julio, kids they cared about deeply, comfortable in rural Tennessee.

We ate. We got increasingly caffeinated. We chatted. We collectively teased Julio. And when it was clear that we had all been fed and had something to drink, the teachers joined us individually in separate rooms to tell us about April 5, 2018, when ICE engaged in the largest raid it had conducted since the raid in Postville, Iowa, to kick off the Trumpian era of increasingly large and militarized worksite raids. In the days and weeks that followed, Sylvia and her team—like educators in rural school districts throughout the country—would have to figure out how to make sure students weren't going home to empty houses, if they even got picked up at all. Then they would have to convince their students, as well as their students' families, that it was safe to return to school, where the race and language of the teachers matched the race and language of the people who took their parents. And amid the arrest of financial providers, they'd have to consider whether their students would even be able to eat.

Perhaps the politically astute, simple, and even expected role was to continue teaching the best they could and rely on other organizations to address the fallout of the raid. But it was evident to all of us that Cathy, who remembered her chatty student from 15 years ago, was not the type of person to focus only on what was happening in the classroom. None of the educators sitting in front of us seemed to be built that way.[6] They couldn't let their students sob about a deportation, console them, and go back to their lesson plans. And, like those in the churches next to them, they had to make sure their students had something to eat. As Sylvia, the school's principal, later told us, "In the South, you don't let people go hungry."

A Very Good Deterrent

The first problem Sylvia's team encountered was what to tell the students in front of them as the raid unfolded. The likelihood was high that at least some of their students were not going to be picked up by their parents, who were themselves either picked up by ICE or refusing to leave their homes. Sylvia and her team of educators wanted to avoid leaving students in a car-rider line for parents who would never come or having bus drivers drop students off at homes now void of Mom and Dad.

But explaining that a raid was unfolding—in an age-appropriate way—to flustered and terrified students is a nearly impossible task, especially amid rumors, extrapolation, exaggeration, and educated guesses. Raids rely on the element of surprise, with agents intending to catch workers off guard, seal all exits, block all doors, and detain the targets of the raid efficiently. By design, as few people know about worksite raids as possible. When seven poultry-processing plants in Mississippi were raided in 2019, ICE officials did not even inform the White House.[7] Reporters questioned ICE about its lack of a plan to support the children of detained parents afterward, to which an ICE official responded, "We are a law enforcement agency, not a social services agency" and noted that any advance notice to welfare agencies or children's schools could alert their parents to the raid and ruin the operation. A reporter later confronted President Trump as he boarded Marine One en route to fundraisers in the Hamptons two days after the raids.[8]

REPORTER: Why wasn't there a better plan to deal with the migrant children in Mississippi?[9]

PRESIDENT TRUMP: The reason is because you have to go in, you can't let anybody know, otherwise when you get there, nobody will be there. . . . I want people to know that if they get into the United States illegally, they are getting out, they are going to be brought out. And this serves as a very good deterrent.

ICE does not tell anyone about raids, that is. The chaos that results is not only operationally necessary but serves as a useful deterrent. It's up to local police to direct the traffic—perhaps pausing on immigration enforcement that day, perhaps not—and teachers like Sylvia to figure out the rest.

Around lunchtime, Sylvia began to get messages from the district's central office that an immigration raid had occurred that would likely result in the detention of at least some of her Latino students' parents. It wasn't possible for Sylvia to figure out which students were impacted, as at that time it was unclear which or how many businesses were raided, how many people were arrested, or if the raid was even over. Teachers had to wade through layers of conjecture and assumption to arrive at a conversation they didn't know how to have anyway. Then they had to make a plan.

Through social media, emails, and bits and pieces of stories, the staff of Mountain View Elementary eventually determined that the Southeastern Provision factory was raided, or at least was the only one raided so far. Sylvia and the other educators swung into action doing what educators do best: articulating student problems and devising strategies to address them.

Admittedly, however, they had never quite articulated—or addressed—this particularly disastrous set of student problems. Sylvia shared: "We designed a plan. . . . The staff was going to get on the school buses with the children in that afternoon. And the bus drivers were alerted; [we told them], 'You may have children who, when they get home, when you take them to their home, there may not be anyone there.'"

Car-rider lines at elementary schools tend to have tightly regulated guidelines so that children are only picked up by those with permission to do so. It occurred to Sylvia that with caregivers detained and others simply too scared to leave their homes, an influx of caregivers she didn't recognize would likely show up to pick up their students.

> We have a very, very strict system with that [car-rider pickup]. You have to be on the pick up list, you have to have a tag or you have to call. So we had some calls. "This person is going to pick up my children today." A lot of that was due to fear. They were afraid to get out . . . afraid to leave their homes.

≈

Eight hundred miles west of Sylvia's team, Troy Madison, a tall white man with wire-rim glasses and the warm aura of the math teacher who patiently taught you division when you barely understood multiplication, wrestled with many of the same issues as Sylvia. Troy was the superintendent of Orchard Green Independent School District (ISD), located in the town of Orchard Green,[10] population 1,600. Orchard Green is situated about 90 miles northeast of the much larger and more diverse city of Dallas, Texas, and about 20 miles west of Paris, Texas, and Pastor Isaac's church. Like Sylvia, Troy agreed to speak with Nicole and me on the weekend, sacrificing his sacred, nonstudent family time to meet us in front of the school and welcome us into his office.

Orchard Green ISD, like so many school districts in the rural US, is small, with only one elementary school, one middle school, and one high school needed to educate the district's 650 or so students. The district boasts a number of students who have won a livestock scholarship or sold championship steers, hogs, goats, or broilers—a type of chicken bred specifically for meat production. Orchard Green ISD was also the educational home to many of the children of the Latino immigrant parents who worked at Load Trail, which was raided on August 28, 2018.

Whereas Sylvia, the principal of an elementary school, learned about the raid in Bean Station via a call from the district's central office, things worked a little differently for Troy, who also had high schoolers under this authority. Unlike elementary school students, some high schoolers have their own phones, and with those phones comes occasional contact with the outside world during the school day. Troy shared the following:

> We learned about [the raid], basically, from our kids. We had a couple kids that were getting some Facebook messages just saying

that "Hey, have you heard [about] Load Trails?,"[11] [or] "There was a raid at Load Trails today." And so after we got our kids talking, we got the information from them, and then we tried to put together the best plan possible to give all the information to our kids that day.

Like Sylvia and her staff, Troy and his staff frantically tried to figure out an age-appropriate way to tell their students what was happening. This was especially challenging among those with limited English-speaking ability, as well as younger students, who may not be aware of their parents' immigration statuses or the possibility of their arrest or deportation. Troy, as did Sylvia, relied heavily on his ELL teachers. He also decided to rely on the support of older siblings:

> I have two bilingual teachers here in our district that are well engulfed in our Latino Hispanic community, and so they also help drive the information to us as administrators to get it to our kids. [Then] we brought our kids into the library on both campuses, our middle school and high school campus, and we brought our elementary kids into those facilities also. Most of them had siblings, older siblings that helped orientate the conversation, and so we brought them in, explained to them what information we had right now.
>
> We gave them the opportunity to call their parents, call their moms at school to see what information they had. And so we tried to work together and plan as best as possible with them calling their moms, trying to kind of ease the tension that was going on in their minds.

Troy and Sylvia, each with their respective staff, scrambled to explain to their students what might have happened to their parents and to do so across linguistic, cultural, and developmental differences. They leaned on ELL teachers, others with close contact to the Latino community, and sometimes even older siblings, the very siblings who might later have to drop out of school to work. With dedication, creativity, and a complete sacrifice of any learning going on that day ("We started putting a plan in place. I used my planning time," Cathy told us), the staff came up with detailed strategies to avoid the most destabilizing moments for the students who might have just lost their parents: arriving at empty homes, being picked up by strangers, or not being picked up at all. Like the lawyers before them, the educators came together in a moment of catastrophe, fueled by adrenaline, compassion, and commitment to their roles. But had they successfully avoided the worst part of the "very good deterrent" that the Trump administration espoused? Or were they—and the American public—misinterpreting who the administration was actually trying to deter? Perhaps worksite raids were not only aiming to stop migrants from coming into the US but to stop those already in the US from having compassion for them, lest they be mired in chaos and heartbreak as well.

Sylvia and Troy's first job was to get their students safely home. Getting them back to school in the days that followed would be a different challenge altogether.

Absent Parents, Absent Students

For a worksite raid to function, employees must be at work when the raid happens. And during the workday, children and youth between the ages of 5 and 18 will, for most of the year, be at school. This means that nearly every time a worksite raid happens, it's teachers like Sylvia and Troy who must decide what to tell their students and how to get them home from school. Once they are home, it's the parents, like Juana and Elisio, who must decide when or if their children are going to return. While some students will return eventually—whether because the remaining parent adapts to life with one driver or the detained parent is released—some students will never return to the school in which they were enrolled. Instead, they will leave the district altogether, moving to a school farther from the reach of ICE that does not remind them of the day their fathers disappeared into a system that does not acknowledge their names.

Media reports following the worksite raids of 2018 and 2019 described classrooms empty of Latino students in the days after the raids. When Jonathan Blitzer wrote about the raid in Bean Station in *The New Yorker*, he noted that schools in Hamblen County—such as the one in which Sylvia taught—reported 530 absences the day after the raid,[12] a number that made its way both into *Rolling Stone* and CNN.[13] A typical day in Hamblen County sees about 75 total daily absences for students of all races.[14] When the seven poultry plants were raided across Mississippi in 2019, the 680 arrests took place on the first day of school. CNN reported that a quarter of one Mississippi school district's Hispanic students were absent.[15]

Quantitative studies strengthen and support journalists' observations. J. Jacob Kirskey and Carolyn Sattin-Bajaj, researchers at Texas Tech and the University of California, Santa Barbara, respectively, compared absenteeism, academic performance, and school mobility prior to and after the raid of Load Trail in Sumner, Texas. Kirskey and Sattin-Bajaj, who have studied deportation and education for years, succinctly described their reason for considering worksite raids and their relationship to education: "The scale and violence of workplace raids distinguish them from other interior enforcement actions, and they warrant careful scrutiny given their power to produce serious immediate and long-term consequences for entire communities with a single act."[16]

Comparing data from the 2011–2012 school year to data from the 2021–2022 school year, the researchers found that absenteeism increased markedly after the raid among Latinx and English-learner students, while reading and math test scores declined. The study also showed a sharp increase in the number of students who left the school district altogether.

Researchers studying the raid in Bean Station, Tennessee, similarly found a significant spike in school absences in the month of the raid.[17] In addition to educational measures, the researchers considered students' Medicaid data and found an increase in diagnoses of substance use disorder, depression, self-harm, and suicide attempts or ideation in the year after the raid.

Sofia Avila, a sociology and social policy doctoral student at Princeton University, analyzed the test scores of Hispanic students 40 days after the Allen, Texas, raid in which ICE raided a technology repair company and detained 284 workers.[18] Avila found that the raid resulted in lower test scores and passing rates among Hispanic students. Using geographical analysis, Avila also showed that proximity to the raid predicted larger drops in test score performance. Why might those who went to school near the raid site experience the biggest decrease in test scores? Avila hypothesizes, "Those closest to the raid were more likely to physically witness the operation, seeing or hearing the hundreds of ICE agents that came to the location, some by helicopter," a trauma that shook them more deeply than those who heard about the raid only on the news.

Taken together, this emerging research shows that immigration worksite raids keep Latino students out of classrooms, lower their grades, and have tremendously detrimental effects on their mental health.[19] Some students never return to the schools in which they were enrolled when the raid happened, moving to another district, or, possibly, returning with their families to the country to which a parent was deported. These quantitative studies provide powerful evidence of the far-reaching consequences of worksite raids, specifically for Latino students.

These studies imply that it was only a matter of time before students returned to their classrooms. Yet as Sylvia, Troy, and their teams of educators would tell me, returning to school did not happen automatically. Instead, it required incredible effort and personal sacrifice from the teachers whose classrooms stood half empty through no fault of their own. It also required teachers to confront some of the uglier racial tensions emerging in the US at the time.

Knocking on Doors While White

The day after ICE raided Southeastern Provision, Sylvia and her staff called or visited the home of every single one of their absent students. Every single one. The educators hoped to use these visits and phone calls to remind families that school was a safe place for their children to return, with classrooms designated as "sensitive locations" at which ICE could not enforce immigration law (this policy was rescinded shortly after Trump began his second term). But getting their children back in school was low on the list of priorities for families who were still hungry.

At Mountain View Elementary, Leslie and Ted, who taught at Sylvia's school, decided to deliver food to the families of the absent students. Their efforts continued after students had returned to school and continued still after the school year had ended. Leslie shared, "We would load up our cars once a week, and we would take it over to the families, to their homes. And then through the summer, we did it every two weeks, but it was still the same amount of food. We just doubled it up and delivered it every two weeks."

WHERE DO YOU STOP BEING A TEACHER?

In Texas, Troy said that he and his staff did similarly, personally visiting the homes of each student who did not return to the classroom: "The number one thing that's worked well is house visits. After it was over, I visited every family that was associated with this, either myself or part of my administrative team has visited them. . . . We just go to see what they were doing, what they needed."

Many teachers, including Sylvia and Troy, weren't always greeted with open doors when they stood on the stoops of their students' homes. Sometimes, a parent or a child would glance outside, recognize a familiar face, and let them in. As Troy told me:

> BILL: Did you have resistance when you first knocked on the door?
>
> TROY: Oh, without a doubt, without a doubt. I had to identify myself as Mr. Madison, and then my kids would look through the window or blinds and know who it was. . . . It wasn't the bad man at the door, it was just me there lending support. And all my families, as soon as they recognized who I was, let me in with open arms.

But just as often, families would simply refuse to open the door, perhaps not recognizing the person on the other side, perhaps being frightened regardless. We asked Sylvia about the resistance she and her staff encountered from their students and their families:

> Some of the teachers reported [that] someone would peep through the blinds or peep from around behind the curtain. Some opened the door after that because they trust the school, they trust the teachers, they trust me.
>
> But even then, some wouldn't open up. I don't blame them. . . . If I were in that position, I don't know if I would have [opened the

door either], even [for] my teacher. . . . I mean, that's risky. I can't imagine the fear that they felt.

Cathy, the ELL teacher who had taught a chatty Julio so many years ago, also described a looming fear that kept families from opening their doors. Unlike Sylvia and Troy, Cathy hadn't been teaching at the school for long and was not a familiar face to many of her students' families. She described how few families opened their doors to her:

> I don't have all of these students, so some of them didn't know me. Even when I'm knocking on the door and saying "Hey, it's me," they didn't answer. I had a woman talking to me through the crack in the door, and she was just bawling, and she said, "I'm just too scared to send her to school. I just couldn't send her to school today. I just couldn't." . . .
>
> I guess [in] twenty-five home visits, I probably saw five people. Five people opened the door . . . and the others just said they were too scared.

Notably, while both Sylvia and Cathy acknowledged that the closed doors they encountered stemmed from parents' fear, they didn't explicitly describe what caused that fear. Troy, who was much more candid than the other teachers, was more than happy to tell us why the doors remained closed to him and other teachers, even though all they wanted to do was help the families in need. "I drove most of my [students'] dads [to the church] the next day. . . . That was pretty funny, because my [students'] parents had to explain to the [Latino] church who I was because they didn't want to let me in the door, and so here it is, white guy, you know, 'What's he doing here?'"

Troy was clear that it wasn't the knocks on the doors of homes and churches that pushed families further into hiding; it was *who* was doing the knocking. In his case no one wanted to let in the unrecognizable "white guy" standing outside the door of the home of the Latinos gathered in a circle inside, as a few days before, dozens to hundreds of mostly unrecognizable white guys had forced their way past the door of the workplace to arrest the Latinos gathered in a circle inside.

Sarah, who taught at Mountain View Elementary with Sylvia, expanded on Troy's description of knocking on the doors of Latino students while white. Sometimes, she told us, being recognized as a teacher actually worked against you, as you became a representative of the government. And at the end of the day, you were white, and it was mostly white representatives of the government who were responsible for this chaos in the first place.

> SARAH: [Students' parents] still see me as an authority figure and a professional and probably in some ways a representative of the government, so . . . it doesn't matter who I am; they're still not gonna trust me completely.
>
> BILL: What do you think affects when someone trusts you?
>
> SARAH: First of all, they're smart to not trust automatically because as amazing as the response has been, there's still a lot of racism [against Latinos] in this community and there's still a lot of misinformation. . . . I think it's just like protection; you shouldn't just trust everyone you see. . . . The government is not always out there to care about you so you should be wary of governmental organizations. I don't know. I mean, I'm white, why would they trust me?

Deciding to open the door became an exercise in extremes for immigrant parents. If I open this door, will it be, as Troy described, "the bad man," the ICE agent, taking me away from my kids, or the good man, the teacher, hand delivering a sandwich to my hungry daughter?

≈

The raid of Southeastern Provision that sent Sylvia and her team scrambling occurred amid a growing wave of anti-immigrant sentiment across the US. At this point, it had been over two years since President Trump gave his first campaign speech, descending down the escalator with the Make America Great Again sign behind him. After taking digs at China and Japan, he brought up immigration from Mexico, sharing his now famous lines, "When Mexico sends its people, they're not sending their best. . . . They're sending people that have lots of problems, and they're bringing those problems with us. They're bringing drugs. They're bringing crime. They're rapists."[20]

With a political figure in the highest office actively stoking racial tensions and xenophobia, the public became increasingly comfortable expressing their own xenophobia, and rates of anti-immigrant and anti-Latino hate crimes climbed.[21] The anti-immigrant fervor was even higher in rural areas, like those in which Sylvia and Troy taught. A 2018 poll found that 57 percent of rural residents, compared to 35 percent of urban residents, agreed that "the growing number of newcomers from other countries threatens traditional American customs and values."[22] Rural Republicans also tended to have a higher percentage of "very warm" views on President Trump (56 percent) compared to suburban (48 percent) or urban (46 percent) Republicans.

Yet educators like Sylvia and Troy—in white, Republican, rural school districts throughout the country—visibly supported the families of those detained in the immigration raids that were specifically designed by the Trump White House, the very White House about which their neighbors felt warmly and for which many of those same neighbors undoubtedly voted. Sheltering immigrants after a raid became a political gesture for churches. Would feeding the children of immigrants become political for teachers in the same way?

To justify or defend their efforts, educators distanced themselves from the politics of the support they provided, often describing the work of feeding students as a fundamental part of their roles as educators that had nothing to do with race or political party.

Sylvia described the support she gave after the raid simply as an extension of the care she provided to every student, every day, no matter who they were and no matter what they needed:

> Morally, ethically, I take care of my kids. If a kid comes in, we start school, our tardy bell rings at 7:55, I've got a kid that comes in at 8:05 and they've not had breakfast, they're offered breakfast.
>
> We take care of our kids.
>
> They don't have shoes? We find shoes. We have a whole closet full of clothes. So it doesn't matter [if they are] red, yellow, black, or white. That's what we do. That was our stance, and still is our stance, and will be our stance.

At the close of the interview, Sylvia again described her motivation: "We're not serving politics. We're not supporting political agendas. We're here for the kids." Leslie, who taught at Sylvia's school, similarly justified her efforts to support her students as part of her role as a teacher, asking rhetorically, "Where do you stop being a teacher?"

Other educators similarly noted that their support for the students and their families was based on a higher ethical standard that was apolitical and race neutral. Troy told us: "You know, we have a lot of undocumented people. . . . I have a relationship with my kids. I love them to death. I've never blamed the kids for the position they're in. . . . People get into education for kids, and it doesn't matter if they're black, brown, purple, white kids. We get in it for kids."

Sylvia, Troy, and other educators attempted to distance themselves from a political interpretation of the help they were providing. Anger over children in cages, grief at the sight of a drowned two-year-old refugee child, or giving food to hungry students, it seemed, were permissible no matter your political persuasion. As these teachers told us, supporting families in moments of crisis was not about race and politics; it was about humanity.

But not everyone was able to distance themselves from the racial politics of providing support to Latino immigrants. For many who would support immigrant families long term, or deal with challenges related to their own immigration statuses, it was undeniable that the trauma immigrant families experienced was not accidental but a feature of a system designed specifically to make their lives so miserable that they would choose to leave on their own. Absenteeism wasn't increasing among white students; it was increasing among Latino students. White families weren't leaving the district. Latino families were. Immigration raids happened because the parents of those students were called rapists and murderers, job stealers, and social service leeches, gang members and narcotraffickers, labels that stuck because those parents were Latino. For some, an admission of the purposeful cruelty of the system was too much to bear.

CHAPTER 6

A New Overground Railroad

Meeting Human Needs

Kimberly is kind and welcoming as she invites us into the waiting area of Bienvenidos, a nonprofit organization in Ohio that works to increase opportunities for Latino families in the area. Started in the 1990s, Bienvenidos formed in response to the growing influx of immigrants from Mexico who worked in Ohio's horticultural nurseries. While immigrant agricultural labor mostly takes place in fields, a notable portion of it occurs in enormous greenhouses that grow plants for grafting, planting, and sale. These greenhouses employ hundreds of people, who spend their days watering, pruning, and moving dozens to hundreds of plants and the heavy soil needed to sustain them.

Kimberly is the volunteer coordinator for Bienvenidos, and as she invites Nicole, five students, and me to sit in a circle around her and talk about the raids in Ohio, her skills as an organizer and people person are on full display. Knowledgeable and well-connected, she is also humble and inclusive, and she encourages the students with us to ask her any questions they have as well.

Kimberly has also invited other Bienvenidos volunteers to join us, allowing us to tap into a network of people who have seen the fallout of immigration worksite raids firsthand.

As we sit in the wood-paneled waiting room, evidence of the tone of the organization's raid response strategy surrounds us. Folding tables covered with paper towels, diapers, and children's blankets line the walls. A basket holds a knitted hat, liquid baby soap, a small pair of knitted booties, a bar of soap, and a few toothbrushes. On one wall a sign reads *"No importa de dónde eres, estamos contentos que seas nuestro vecino* / It doesn't matter where you are from, we are happy that you are our neighbor"— in Spanish, English, and Arabic.

Bienvenidos is located on the second floor of an old and drafty building in the downtown area of a medium-sized Ohio town, neither all that close nor all that far from many of the Ohio cities and towns—like Cleveland, Akron, Columbus, or Sandusky— with which non-Ohioans are familiar. The town's location midway between here and there was either quite serendipitous or extremely unfortunate, depending on whom you asked and when. About half an hour southeast of Sandusky and two hours northwest of Salem, staff and volunteers at Bienvenidos responded to a once-in-a-lifetime raid twice in a few months, first when two Corso's Flower and Garden Center locations in Sandusky were raided on June 5, 2018, then, exactly two weeks later, when Fresh Mark in Salem was raided on June 19. In total, 260 workers were detained.

Surrounded by pictures of Latino families that Bienvenidos had served over multiple decades, Kimberly tells us about herself, her work with Bienvenidos, and her role in the organization's response to the two Ohio worksite raids. Kimberly began as a volunteer for Bienvenidos before the organization hired her as the volunteer coordinator. She was originally drawn to Bienvenidos by the grassroots, authentic connection she observed between the organization and the community. She shares,

> We would have our community meetings where we just get to know the community, hear from them exactly what their concerns are, what's going on in their life and the course of those meetings we would find out about [everything]. Often the stories we would hear are: This person has a chronic medical condition that, you know, maybe it's diabetes or something that's treatable, but they have not gotten treatment because they've been so afraid or haven't known where to go. And so often we would find out about it when it's gotten so serious that it was an emergency.
>
> So, we would do a lot of coordinating access to medical care. But then as we're in communities longer, people know where to come and then they come to us earlier. So, it's not necessarily an emergency at that point, hopefully.

Though she doesn't use the phrase, Kimberly is articulating well the core beliefs of community-minded public health: When you spend time in a community, you learn about its problems; when you address those problems early, you can prevent them from becoming emergent; and if, despite your efforts, those problems become emergencies, the community will trust you to address the emergencies as well.

Kimberly and the team at Bienvenidos realized early that the needs of the community following the raids in Sandusky and Salem would shift as time went on, so she and others at Bienvenidos did what they could to address those evolving needs before they resulted in emergencies. When people needed to be fed, keep their children fed, and keep their infants healthy, Bienvenidos organized a food pantry and handed out food and diapers. When people needed to bail their loved ones out of detention, Bienvenidos set up a bail fund—which quickly received an anonymous $25,000 donation—to get detained workers back with their families as they awaited the results of their court cases. And when those detained workers were back home, Bienvenidos created a rideshare system to address an entirely new set of problems before those, too, became emergent.

When undocumented immigrants are released from detention, they are faced with a catch-22. Though they are usually unable to drive legally, the federal government asks them to show up to any number of different locations to fulfill a range of requirements. In the rural US, these locations can be over an hour away, across counties, across state lines, and across the highways with which they have no familiarity. While there are a few exceptions, most everyone released from detention to await his immigration trial at home must check in periodically with ICE and return to court for the result of his trial. Between each of these requirements are also an unpredictable number of formal and informal duties, such as additional paperwork, signatures, thumbprints, more check-ins, and doctors' approval forms.

In the days immediately following a worksite raid, those who wanted to support immigrant families would converge on the church in which those families sought safety from ICE. But as the days turned into weeks and weeks turned into months, families who had not left the town altogether returned to their homes, slowly reintegrated their children into school, and awaited the final outcomes of their deportation cases, all while the list of places they needed to go grew. Responding to a raid was no longer about getting things to people. It was about getting people to a new range of ever-changing places.[1] Immigrant families no longer needed the stone walls of the church to protect them from ICE. They needed the driver's licenses, cars, and free time of others in their community to take them to the places they couldn't take themselves.

A NEW OVERGROUND RAILROAD

≈

Scott and Lisa join us in the Bienvenidos waiting area shortly after we wrap up our interview with Kimberly. Like Kimberly, Scott and Lisa are happy to share their experiences with a room full of professors and students. Their willingness to speak in front of a crowd isn't surprising. Though both are retired now, Scott was once a professor himself at a nearby college in Ohio, and it was easy to imagine him lecturing a group of students in an auditorium. The pair had been ingrained in immigration advocacy for decades and are well-known as leaders in their community, even winning an award from the college at which Scott taught for their contributions to global change. In fact, the pair had played a significant role in the Sanctuary Movement in Ohio.

The centuries-old tradition of church sanctuary was brought to the US in the 1980s, when Central American migrants fled the US-backed civil wars that resulted in hundreds of thousands of deaths. The US government did not grant asylum to those fleeing the death squads of US-supported government regimes, however, and rejected 97.4 percent of asylum claims from Salvadorans and 98.2 percent from Guatemalans.[2] To prevent the deportations—which likely would have resulted in their deaths— of Central American refugees, about 500 faith communities formed the Sanctuary Movement, inviting these refugees to shelter behind the stone walls of their churches, safe from Immigration and Naturalization Services (or the INS, the precursor to ICE).[3] A subset of these churches organized what they called the Overground Railroad,[4] which moved immigrants from one church to the next as they sought asylum in Canada.[5]

Scott served in the role of citizen coordinator for the Overground Railroad at his church and, with the help of Lisa and other congregants, provided refuge to 20 individuals and 4 families fleeing Central American violence. Hosting refugees sought by the INS was both dangerous and expensive, with volunteers risking fines and arrest while transporting refugees and providing them with food, medicine, clothing, and living expenses.

Lisa details Scott's role in the early days of the Overground Railroad, drawing from his network to holistically care for those living in his church. "Scott and a number of people from the community came together and located volunteers who would take on language instruction, grocery shopping, [and] cooking," she tells us. An article written about Scott's church claims that the church further provided refugees with tutoring, transportation, and work opportunities, often paying for the expenses by bringing in playwrights focused on Central American politics or selling prints of artwork made by refugees themselves.

Thanks in part to the public pressure of the Sanctuary Movement,[6] in 1990 the George H. W. Bush administration announced it would no longer automatically deport Salvadoran and Guatemalan asylum seekers.[7] With the need for sanctuary declining, the movement slowed until it ceased in the mid-1990s. It wasn't until President Trump was elected in 2016 that a large-scale need for sanctuary—or at least some version of it—emerged once again.

After the raids in Salem and Sandusky, Scott and Lisa hoped to build on their experience with the Sanctuary Movement and the Overground Railroad of the1980s and 1990s. But as families returned to their homes to await the outcomes of their deportation cases, it was clear that the couple's experience supporting families hidden in churches was not enough. The situation had changed. Lisa was aware of this shift: "[That was] a different context because we knew that the people in sanctuary could not leave their quarters." Now, the challenge was that everyone needed to "leave their quarters" by order of the US government.

I point this change out to Lisa: "So, it sounds like what you did for Bienvenidos was almost the opposite of what you had planned for sanctuary, from bringing everything in, [to] transporting and moving things around."

In my head, this is a major change in what it means to support immigrants and refugees, an evolution that is likely to be documented in the history books, just as church sanctuary had before it. But Lisa clearly isn't concerned with the difference: "Well, I was just thinking about [your] question. It's an interesting way to think about those problems being different. Because, the truth is what you're doing is meeting human needs, and there's really not a whole lot of difference."

For Scott and Lisa, the decision to become a driver in the newly developed rideshare program was very simple. When their pastor said he needed help "transporting people to ICE appointments and medical appointments and immigration court" and asked if they were interested, they jumped right in. They didn't quantify it or weigh the cost. They just drove. Transportation had become a human need, one they were uniquely positioned to address.

Soon, other churches came to Scott and Lisa and asked how their congregations could also support the families impacted by the raids in Salem and Sandusky. So Scott and Lisa recruited congregants from those churches to volunteer at Bienvenidos, growing a network of people to address immigrant needs, just as they had in the 1980s and 1990s.

Lisa shares an example of one of the rides she provided:

LISA: Now, I will say that we took one woman and her six-year-old son to Detroit to a hearing, and it happened to be during the government shutdown. And we drove them to Detroit—

SCOTT: —from here.

LISA: —picked them up early in the morning from here, and got to Detroit, went to the hearing. There was no hearing. They said "government shut down, go home." So, we went home and all the way up the road, I think all the way to Detroit, I don't think the woman said more than three or four words.

But, on the way back, relieved from [her court hearing being delayed], both she and her son engaged us in conversation. We stopped at McDonald's and we had, you know, we just had a really open good time.

Lisa's emphasis is not on the logistical demands of the ride she provided nor on the fact that the entire trip was ultimately for naught and had to be made again. The trip from Bienvenidos to Detroit is two hours with tolls, meaning the trip was four hours plus whatever time it took Lisa to pick up and later drop off the mother and her daughter, plus the time it took to park the car and walk to the courthouse only to be turned away. I imagine that the ride took no less than six hours. But Lisa doesn't focus on any of this. Instead, Lisa tells us this particular story to illustrate that the human connection across race, culture, and immigration status could happen not only in the original Overground Railroad of the 1980s and 1990s, but the new one of the 2020s.

≈

After our full team interviewed Scott and Lisa, we each went off alone or in pairs to interview more of the volunteers who Kimberly had invited to share their stories with us. Katie Collins, a public health and social work student at the time, joined me in an adjacent room to interview Sal, who also volunteered to give rides with Bienvenidos. Sal graduated from Ohio State University (despite being rival University of Michigan graduates, we spoke to him anyway), received a master's degree in natural resources, and worked for the Department of Natural Resources in Ohio until he retired six years before we met him. Like Scott and Lisa, he and his wife were at church on the fateful day in which their pastor announced that Bienvenidos was in search of drivers. "So, I just called them up and said I was available. Basically it," Sal told us.

Sal was like Lisa and Scott in many ways. Among the most obvious, he was religious, white, retired, and had a driver's license. But he differed drastically in his experience working with immigrants. While Lisa and Scott had helped to provide sanctuary to some of the first Central American refugees to pass through Ohio, served as human rights monitors during a civil war in Guatemala, and had taken students to Guatemala during winter breaks at the college, Sal had never worked with immigrants before. With more freedom in his recently retired hands, he found himself "floundering," unsure of how to spend his free time and feeling like he no longer found the fulfillment in life he had once enjoyed. So, he asked himself, why not do something with purpose? He found that purpose and fulfillment in the long drives across Ohio, "the first time I've really volunteered to do anything," he said.

Throughout these drives, Sal learned that very little about the trips was straightforward and predictable. One ride he described to Katie and me was very much like the ride Lisa detailed: unpredictability coupled by bureaucratic frustrations:

> Well, for the last time we went to Detroit. I picked up a young lady here in [town]. She was supposed to meet with her lawyer at 7:30 [in the morning] at the courthouse, and it was in the spring. It was pretty cold and rainy. And so, we got up there around a little before 7:30 so we could meet with the lawyer. We walked across the

parking lot to the building, and it turns out that the federal building doesn't open till 8:00. They don't let anybody in until 8:00. So there was a whole group of us, maybe 50 people out there standing in the cold, rain freezing.

Then they open the doors and we all kind of funneled in and went through the line, snaked around, sort of like waiting for a ride at that Cedar Point [amusement park] or whatever. They finally got everybody through, and the young lady and I went upstairs to the particular courtroom waiting room. When we got up there, she gave her name, and [the clerk] told the lady who she was supposed to see. The [clerk] looked at her list and said, oh, that judge is sick today. So we'll reschedule you for six months later. So, we came back.

Sal didn't live in the town, though, so he had to first drive there to pick up the person he would then drive to the courthouse in Detroit, where he would park, to wait in the Cedar Point–style line, then turn around and retrace his steps, knowing he would need to do it all again in six months. If I had to estimate, I would say that Sal's trip took no less than eight hours. Yet nothing in his words, body language, or tone made me feel like the extensive, unsuccessful trip bothered him.

When the stated purpose of a ride changed or burgeoned into more, Sal was quick to adapt: "And one young guy I had, I drove to the Mexican embassy because in order to get medical help, I took him to the doctor, but they couldn't see him because he didn't have any ID. So we took him to the Mexican Consulate in Detroit, and they were able to issue him a temporary passport."

Sal seemed to measure the success of a trip not by predictable, efficient progress toward a goal but by the entire set of interactions that took place. When I asked Sal, Scott, and Lisa how long their trips took, they all seemed to react as if they had never considered that question. It was the accompaniment itself[8]—the driving, the sitting, the waiting, the quick pivot to address a need you didn't predict for someone who couldn't address the need herself—that mattered most to them.

≈

The most effective responses to worksite raids across the country match specific needs of the community with the volunteers who have the personalities, skills, and life circumstances to address them. Perhaps nowhere was this more evident than in the rideshare system Kimberly and Bienvenidos organized that thrived on the freedom of retired Ohioans armed with driver's licenses, tanks of gas, and a desire to make the lives of their immigrant neighbors a little easier. Whether they had witnessed human rights violations in Guatemala or never spoken to an immigrant in their lives was not the issue. They had a pickup location, a destination, and a willingness to pivot, adapt, and smile amid a sea of frustrations.

Systems like the rideshare organized by Bienvenidos would also lead to new relationships across communities that had not crossed paths as deeply before, like Sal and the many immigrant passengers who told him about their lives from the passenger seat of his car. But the life-giving trips to McDonald's with the immigrant mother and daughter would come at a cost, as volunteers who came to see the immigrant families who lived among them as their neighbors had to reckon with the possibility of their deportation.

La Gente Nos Conoce Ahora

Lesley, the daughter of migrant workers, came to the US when she was 7 years old. Except for a short stint in another state after she graduated from high school, Lesley had lived in Ohio all her life, helping her parents at the grocery store they owned that was frequented by the Latinos in the area. About 11 years before we met Lesley, she became a US citizen. Lesley was working as a line manager at Corso's in Sandusky, Ohio, when she began to feel that she and her coworkers were being exploited. She would regularly see those who worked next to her pulling 80-hour weeks for a company she felt didn't value their labor. "I felt like my life was just fading away," she told Nour and Katie, the two student interviewers who spoke with Lesley in the Bienvenidos office at Kimberly's request.

Lesley's daughter, who had not entered kindergarten yet, barely saw her hardworking mother. Lesley shared,

> It got to the point where I would go to work at seven o'clock in the morning. I would come home at two o'clock in the morning. And then we had to be back at seven in the morning again. So it was more of, like, I would see her asleep and that's it. She would [see me] only on Sundays. And then Sundays, all I wanted to do was just sleep, instead of like taking her out someplace.

Lesley made a conscious decision to spend more of her waking hours with her daughter and take time off work from Corso's when she could.

One Sunday in June, Lesley took her daughter to an ice cream parlor in Port Clinton, about 25 minutes from where Leslie lived. Brown Dog Gelato—which Lesley humorously referred to as The Wet Dog—was a favorite of her daughter, who was lactose intolerant and appreciated the savory, lactose-free ice cream served by Brown Dog staff.

If you drive just 2.3 miles north from Brown Dog, you'll run right into Lake Erie, a lake so big that if you were to look out from the coast, all you would see is water. Canada sits on the other side of the lake, thus making Port Clinton an international border city with its own headquarters for Customs and Border Protection. As Lesley and her daughter licked their lactose-free ice cream, Lesley began to see buses and trucks piling into the parking lot of the Border Patrol headquarters across the street. The feeling was sinister, but Lesley allowed herself to enjoy the rest of the day with her daughter, looking forward to spending even more time with her during the week.

On Tuesday, which Lesley had taken off from work, she was sitting at home when she picked up her phone,

> and I saw my phone, and . . . I went on Facebook, and I saw this message that said, "God, pray for Corso's." You know, and I keep seeing over and over and over, like all of these "Pray for Corso's," "Pray for the people at Corso's."
>
> So, I was actually like, what is going on? So, I called one of my friends and she said, "Immigration is here and they're picking up everybody."

The buses that Lesley had watched from her seat at Brown Dog Gelato were now filled with the coworkers from Corso's who had not serendipitously taken the day off, many of whom were, like Lesley, mothers. But unlike Lesley, many were not citizens and might never again share ice cream with their daughters in the US. Lesley explained that unlike most other facilities that were raided in 2018, Corso's employed more women than men. The women worked in a separate location than Lesley, tagging plants and making them look presentable to the public, who would walk through one of the greenhouses on the front of the property, a greenhouse we visited earlier that week.

On the day of the raid, it was the plant-tagging crew—the mothers, like Lesley—who were taken. Lesley continued, "I think there was at least four buses just for women. And most of these moms are single moms being taken all the way to Michigan." Women detained in Sandusky were taken to Calhoun County Jail,[9] two and a half hours away.

In some ways, the arrests, detentions, and deportations of mothers resemble those of fathers.[10] Losing a parent, no matter which, is a traumatic experience for children, often with lifelong impacts. When mothers are also financial providers, income is significantly diminished, with all the same repercussions as the loss of the breadwinning father. But sometimes, the aftermath of immigration enforcement is unique to detained mothers, who are more likely to be the heads of single-parent households,[11] provide direct care for children, and cope with immigration stressors while breastfeeding.

Some of the mothers detained in Ohio were the sole parents in the home, leaving children without parental supervision, as Gordon, an immigration attorney in Ohio, described: "In the Corso's raid . . . until we got the women out, there were people without a parent for quite a while." Among mothers' greatest fears was that Child Protective Services (CPS) would become aware of their absence and take their children into custody. If this happened, mothers would face overwhelming challenges to regaining custody of their children. For example, when a parent is detained or deported, she cannot attend child custody hearings. ICE has no obligation to inform CPS that a parent has been detained or deported,[12] leaving the judge to assume that the parent is uninterested in regaining custody. Further, when parents cannot comply with court orders—including regularly visiting their children or finding employment—their rights may be terminated.[13]

For many mothers, it was the "stretching and strengthening" of their social networks that allowed them to avoid having their children placed in CPS custody. Lesley shared: "So, [having children removed from homes] was our concern. But most of the kids either had an older sibling, or they had somebody like a neighbor that would go over and watch for them, or cook for them. But that's mainly how the kids were taken care of, until Mom got back."

After women are released from detention, they must further balance motherhood with a new range of bureaucratic demands.[14] Martina, who had worked with the Latino community for over 30 years and responded to both the Sandusky and Salem raids, described what it was like to accompany mothers to their mandatory ICE check-ins after they had been released from detention. Whether because no other parent was in the home, they couldn't afford a babysitter, or their infant was still nursing, many mothers brought their children with them to the waiting room. As Martina told Nicole:

> We have ... these big vans that we have to, you know, fill it with the women, with the children. It was like going to a trip early in the morning, seven o'clock in the morning or 7:30, and then get there at 8:30 for the check-in, then go through security and then go with all the kids and then moms with their bags with food and diapers and moms with babies and milk. That's, you know, Mom breastfeeding. I mean, we were sitting waiting for hours.

With supplies in tow, mothers fed, nursed, and diapered their children while they attended their biweekly or monthly ICE check-ins, hoping to be granted permission to continue to live and raise their families in the US. Reasonably, with children as young as those described, the deportation of the mother would likely mean the relocation of her children as well.

Breastfeeding mothers may also be unable to continue breastfeeding their children, whether for the short period of detention or permanently after deportation if their child does not return with them. Anneka, a student intern at a law firm who responded to the raids in O'Neill, Nebraska, shared the following story, one that would eventually cause her to feel physically ill: "The moms would be saying, 'I have a baby, a newborn baby and she's getting breastfed and I'm not able to breastfeed her.' And then, there was some moms that the babies were breastfeeding when they got detained, so then they had no food for that night for the baby, [and] the mom was in pain."

While Anneka did not specify whether the "pain" from being unable to breastfeed was emotional or physical, both were most certainly possible. When Maria Domingo-Garcia was detained after ICE raided the poultry plant at which she worked in Mississippi, she was separated from her four-month-old daughter. Speaking of Domingo-Garcia's case, Heather Marcoux wrote in the well-known parenting website, Motherly:[15]

> Earlier this week, when Domingo-Garcia had been separated from her daughter for 12 days, her lawyers told media that she was in a lot of pain as she had not been able to breastfeed or pump for nearly two weeks.
>
> Not being able to drain one's breasts can lead to engorgement, which can lead to mastitis. Both engorgement and mastitis are painful, and mastitis can even be deadly if mothers cannot get medical help.

No empirical research clearly establishes the link between a particular type of immigration enforcement action and one's inability to continue breastfeeding. But, when I spoke with Fernanda after her apartment was raided in 2013, she explained it succinctly and factually: "Se me fue la leche" or, "the milk just left my body," she told me. "I couldn't produce good milk for my son because of the fright. But that's what happens when ICE comes into the house, right?"

And rare was the mother who could find the time to care for her own health amid the myriad new stresses placed upon her children. Sonia and Liz, two nurses who worked in Ohio, shared,

> SONIA: And a lot of the women, I think, kind of avoid taking care of themselves because they're focused on the kids, which is good, but you also have to take care of yourself. So, you know, there were a lot of them that hadn't had routine women's health checks—
>
> LIZ: —[like] mammograms and things—
>
> SONIA: —for a long time.

≈

Lesley found herself driving back to Port Clinton, but this time she didn't go for ice cream. She went instead to the Border Patrol office across the street, where she had seen the buses piling up, with the hope of finding out more about who was detained. Unfortunately, she wasn't Father Jim in his liturgical collar or National Guard fatigues. Border Patrol agents wouldn't tell her anything, and she left empty-handed. "They wouldn't give us any information," she said.

Lesley's good friend Sara was among the single moms who was taken when Corso's was raided. Sara's son had no other immediate caretaker and had to move around from house to house after his mom was detained. Lesley welcomed Sara's son into her home when she could but knew it wasn't a long-term solution.

Lesley contacted Bienvenidos to see if the organization could help Sara get out of detention. But Sara had a previous illegal entry into the US on her record that meant, despite Bienvenidos's best efforts, she was unable to do anything to prevent or even slow her removal, and she was deported seven days after being removed from Corso's, packed into a bus, and taken to Calhoun County Jail.

Sara's son's birthday came shortly after his mother was removed. Lesley tried to help him celebrate the day, despite his mother's absence:

> And it was so sad, because his birthday came around, pretty much a couple of days after Mom was deported. So, I actually have pictures where we took him out to eat and we got him a little gift.
>
> And I know that it still wasn't the same, because Mom was not there. But we tried to make him feel good, at least on his birthday, and he had fun. So, my daughter and him played out in the rain that day. So, they enjoyed it. Yeah, they had fun.

Lesley observed how dedicated Bienvenidos was to helping Sara and everyone else—including the many women—detained in the raid, so she started volunteering with Bienvenidos whenever she could. She shared, "I started volunteering more and more with them, going to the clinics, translating, doing transportation, helping with their bond fund, and that's pretty much how that evolved."

Eventually, the executive director of Bienvenidos offered Lesley a job, one that built upon her long list of contacts, bicultural and bilingual skill set, and friendship with Latinos throughout the area, including those who were taken in the Corso's raid. So on the Fourth of July, less than a month after her coworkers were detained, Lesley left her job at Corso's to take a job with the organization supporting the families who were separated at Corso's. In her new role, Lesley helped to arrange a mobile clinic that served a small community heavily impacted by the Sandusky raid. We visited the mobile clinic in November of 2019.

≈

Calling it a "mobile clinic" is a bit of a misnomer. I described the clinic in my field notes very technically as "the mobilest of mobile clinics." In fact, the "clinic" wasn't so much a facility but people with black suitcases full of medical supplies who would come every three months into the meeting space in a few trailers at the front of the mobile home community. I have a photo of three students, Katie, Nour, and Lupe, taking notes on a folding table covered with empty bottles of water, paper plates, red and green Lofthouse cookies, and a centrifuge waiting to spin the vials of blood sitting next to it.

From my perch on a plastic chair in the waiting area, it's clear that the space is also used for school-aged children to meet, learn, or hang out. Homework is taped to a long piece of yarn that is stuck at the ends with tape to the wall. The inverted arch of homework dangling from the yarn looks like a goofy-toothed smile, especially with two windows that look like eyes right above it. I have to imagine that the seventh graders learning English in the space chuckle a little, like me, when they see it.

As I make small talk in Spanish with another woman in the waiting room, she tells me that the father of her children was taken in the Corso's raid a year ago. There is almost no chance that he has been detained this long, so he has probably been deported. She worked at Corso's too. But as tends to happen after a raid, her employers suddenly decided to care about immigration law and asked her to produce the papers they didn't ask her to produce when they hired her. When she couldn't produce those papers, she was also let go. One parent deported. The other without a job. Two incomes gone. I don't want to pry, so I don't ask if she has come to the mobile clinic to see a counselor because of stress, a nurse because of high blood pressure, or a social worker because she needs more resources. All are plausible.

A collaboration with Ohio Friends in Health, an independent nonprofit that serves Ohioans in low-income areas who lack access to medical care, this mobile clinic—or really, this highly mobile group of people making a multiuse space into a clinic—was meant to bring health care staff to those who were too scared to leave their neighborhoods after the raids. Notably, Alicia, a Latina behavioral health counselor whose first language is Spanish, numbers among the health care professionals in the clinic. Someone like Alicia, in a small, rural town like this one, outside a major city, is quite a rarity. I have no doubt that most people in that mobile home community have never met a bilingual Latina therapist like Alicia in their lives and, if not for the organizing efforts of people like Lesley, probably never would.

Residents of the mobile home community realized that they suddenly had health care professionals just a few feet away from where they lived, including a Latina mental health counselor who spoke Spanish, and that all the counseling, medications, and treatment were covered on a sliding scale. For an immigrant community, most of whom were uninsured or underinsured by their employers, ineligible for the Affordable Care Act Marketplace or Medicaid, and spoke Spanish, this clinic was a gift from heaven.[16]

Many residents were unsure of what to make of all the symptoms that flooded their bodies after the raid, a problem that Alicia helped them address: "People that have never experienced what was anxiety, what was depression, they didn't even know what was happening to their body, what was happening to their mind. So that's when we came in and just describe what was happening after the raid, what was happening to their system . . . They didn't recognize it."

Notably, on-site, accessible, culturally sensitive health care also meant that other residents could address pre-existing chronic conditions that were around well before the Corso's raid. As Lesley described, the clinic helped patients determine "a lot of health issues that women didn't even know they had. Yeah, a lot of them [have] diabetes or [high] blood pressure, and never before had they been checked by any doctor." The mobile clinic, first designed to support families after the raid, had become a staple in the community, drawing Latino families with a range of health needs unrelated to the raid itself.

Plus, with a sliding fee scale, residents of the mobile home community could now afford to treat the ailments they were discovering. A full 22 percent of Latino adults in the US have diabetes, compared to just 12 percent of our white counterparts. And while many attribute our high rates of diabetes to our diets and lack of exercise, these high rates are also attributable to factors outside our direct control, like socioeconomic status, educational disadvantage, and neighborhood discrimination,[17] all factors that intertwine with immigration status. Diabetes medication is also simply expensive, especially for folks without insurance. Latinos are significantly more likely to be uninsured than their white peers, with rates at 18 percent compared to just 7 percent.[18] Lesley shared,

> So, the most things that we see is diabetics. That is like our main thing. I feel just because diabetic medication is so expensive, and a lot of these people are working under the table right now.
>
> So, going to a doctor and paying $130, I'm not sure like, you know what it costs to go. But, for them coming to this clinic and being on a sliding scale and be able to get medications every three months for 25 bucks, it's amazing.

The positive ripple effects of these community-organizing efforts were not limited to health resources. Just as immigrants with health concerns unrelated to the raid began to use the mobile clinic and those who did not have deportation cases pending signed up for Bienvenidos's rideshare, the sudden influx of lawyers from big cities also meant other immigrants could finally begin to work through long-standing immigration issues they could never address because of the absence of lawyers in their towns.

In Morristown, Tennessee, Father Jim described how the presence of immigration lawyers allowed others in the community to prepare for an immigration disaster they now saw as imminently possible.

> After we had all those people pretty much taken care of, everybody else in the community that felt that they might be the next ones, they got down there [to the church] and they started doing all of the paperwork. That's why, after the initial wave, it just never ended, it seemed like it.
>
> That's when I realized people are now being proactive. There were legal people down there, and so they're being proactive. So they went down there and that's why we ran out of toner and Xerox and paper and everything else. Because I don't know how many people that they processed paperwork for, but it had to have been, I don't know, maybe a 1,000 or something.

Jay, the executive director of North Texas Immigration Alliance, noticed something similar after he drove from the lawyer-heavy Dallas-Fort Worth area to isolated Paris, Texas, to screen people after the raid on Load Trail. While the legal response was designed to help those whose loved ones had been detained, others in the community saw an opportunity to address their own immigration issues, the lawyers they so desperately needed driving the high-risk highways to come to them. As Jay described:

> When I went to that other church and screened people, some of them weren't the people from the raid, they were just people in Paris that heard there were lawyers giving screenings and showed

up and said, "Hey I'm a welder and I really, I just wanna get a job. How can you help me? What's the mechanism for me to get some kind of visa to work here?"

These new systems of support, right in the middle of where they were needed most, allowed many to make sense of and address their health needs, to prepare for the worst—should another raid happen—and to prepare for the best, setting themselves up legally to move forward in the future.[19]

≈

Such community mobilization and organizing efforts also played a role in shifting the story of immigration enforcement, as well as that of immigrants themselves. As more and more media began to cover worksite raids, reporters began to extend their stories beyond tragedy (albeit tragedy was the focus of most) and feature exposés on the rural communities in which these raids occurred. Pieces such as "ICE Came for a Tennessee Town's Immigrants. The Town Fought Back" in *The New York Times*, for example, began with descriptions of the town, Southeastern Provision, and the raid but also covered the support provided by St. Patrick's Catholic Church and the strategy and sacrifice of local teachers before closing with a description of a procession through downtown organized by white and Latino Tennesseans.[20] *The Des Moines Register* detailed the pressure the Mount Pleasant, Iowa, community exerted on the police to be transparent about their role in immigration enforcement.[21] *The Mississippi Clarion Ledger* published a report focused on church response after the worksite raids in 2019, highlighting local opposition to ICE operations: "Churches on ICE Raids: 'Mississippi didn't ask for this. It doesn't come from the people.'" Even *Bloomberg* shined light on the invisible corners of immigrant and white relations, describing the "unlikely bond" that formed between the people of Mount Pleasant and the rural Guatemalans who came to the town to work.[22]

Taken together, these stories often illustrated a side of the rural immigrant community with which many across the country were unfamiliar. While the national narrative Trump continued to spin was of violent immigrant criminals covered in tattoos, wielding machetes, and selling drugs, suddenly stories began to appear of immigrants as resilient, creative, hardworking, and, perhaps even more importantly, just like everyone else, enjoying activities like eating meals with their families and going to church.

These community-organizing efforts also created opportunities for white and Latino residents to be physically together in the same spaces. While some volunteers, like Scott and Lisa, had extensive connections with Latino immigrants, others, like Sal, had little or no previous contact with Latino immigrants at all. Sitting in the car together, or in the church together, or in the school together, or joining in on a march together, changed this.

After the raid on Midwest Precast Concrete, Trinity Presbyterian Church of Mount Pleasant, like other churches throughout the US, opened a food pantry staffed by volunteers to support the families of those with a family member detained in the raid. Due in part to the demographics of the church and town, most of the volunteers were white. But it wasn't long before Juana volunteered, handing out food alongside the white Iowans next to her. As Juana shared:

> [The food pantry] is when Americans and Latinos connect. In fact, after the raid, we were like a small little circle under a set of spotlights / Un circulito en frente de unos grandes reflectores. . . . We are a very small community of Latinos in this town, but now,

most people know us. And they know we are good people / Pero la mayoría de la gente nos conoce ahora. Pero también se da cuenta que somos gente de bien. It's not like we are trying to do bad things; we just had the bad luck of being in a raid.

Now, according to Juana, even though the town's residents will remain politically divided, they at least see their Latino neighbors as members of their community, as "good people" who happened to have a bad thing happen to them: "If you ask someone, 'Hey do you know this [Latino] person?,' I don't think they are going to say anything negative about the person. I know the people may be divided, but, thank God, most people have realized who we, as Latinos, really are."

≈

Social scientists have shown that humans tend to engage in what they call *infrahumanization*, or the belief that the group one belongs to experiences a range of emotions that other groups do not. According to the theory, we assume that people who are similar to us feel secondary emotions—emotions like the vulnerability, regret, anxiety, confusion, frustration, guilt, and hope that come after initial reactions to situations—while people unlike us do not feel these emotions. When a group of people are denied their full human range of emotions, it's a short step to perceiving them as some sort of lesser human or, when spurred on by people in power with strategically selected stories, as animals.[23]

This process of dehumanization—or the denial of various aspects of a person's humanity, such as personality traits, emotions, warmth, or mental capacity[24]—is a well-documented tactic that makes it easier to hurt or kill those positioned as members of the dehumanized group—for example, the Japanese or Jews in

World War II or Muslims during the war on terror.[25] In a chapter in the book *The Criminology of War*,[26] Kelman describes dehumanization as a fundamental component of what he calls "sanctioned massacres": "The special features of sanctioned massacres are that they occur in the context of a genocidal policy, and that they are directed at groups that have not themselves threatened or engaged in hostile actions against the perpetrators of the violence."

That is, dehumanization not only allows for violence against one's opponent in war but also, with the right policy conditions, for violence against those who have shown no aggression at all.

How do we stop infrahumanization? What can we do to better empathize with and understand those who are different from us and therefore insulate ourselves from their dehumanization? Research suggests one possible answer. Promoting intergroup contact can prevent infrahumanization.[27] Put another way, being familiar with those different from you, learning about their lives, and drawing similarities between your group and theirs can prevent you from seeing them as less than fully human. And if you can't deny their humanity, it's harder to perpetrate—or consent—to violence against them.

In the lead up to the worksite raids of 2018 and 2019, the Trump administration did everything in its power to dehumanize undocumented immigrants, comparing them to animals and constantly highlighting acts of violence.[28] For those who had never met immigrants and took Trump's stories at face value, worksite raids and all their related trauma were easier to accept, as those harmed by these raids were either dangerous and deserving of what they got or, at a minimum, lacked the emotional capacity to experience what was happening to them.

But when you allow yourself to feel empathy, the violence that depends on dehumanization is no longer possible. For those who saw Latino immigrants as their peers—whether historically or for the very first time, whether in person or through stories on the news—their removal from the life they had built began to seem inhumane and cruel.

Throwing Up in the Bathroom

We wrap up our conversation with Kimberly, excited to split our seven-person team among the multiple interviewees who have joined us at her invitation. Before we close the interview, Nicole invites Kimberly to take a step back from her description of the rich organizational response of Bienvenidos to the Salem and Sandusky raids and comment on the personal impact of the work, asking Kimberly: "We're going to wind up. . . . I just wanted to ask one more time, just about [your] experience, personally, through all of this. . . . How has it affected you?"

Kimberly pauses and takes a breath before answering Nicole's question. She stutters a bit as she starts to respond. It's the first time in the interview that she's seemed a little unsure of herself, as if what she's about to say is entirely unpredictable, even to her:

> Um . . . it's . . . it's really, it's awful to see. These first few meetings, I mean, these are young boys who literally came to us crying and sobbing and adults coming and crying and sobbing. And you feel like there's very little that we can offer.
>
> It's infuriating. It's devastating. We were working around the clock until midnight every day for months. And it was completely exhausting. Like to me, it felt like just the, like, vicarious trauma . . .
>
> It's hard to sleep at night when you hear those crying teenagers or kids come to you and you have to tell them "I'm sorry, but your mom's going to be deported."
>
> It's—it's hard.

It was clear in speaking to Kimberly—and directly benefiting from her skill at organizing—that she was good at what she did. She also seemed to be fulfilled by her work and expressed joy and satisfaction when she could support families in crisis and build the infrastructure to do so at a larger scale. But it was also clear that Kimberly's work came at a major cost to her own emotional and psychological health. An English major who had taken master's level courses in social work, Kimberly's choice of words—"vicarious trauma"—was apt and unsurprising and, in all likelihood, a correct assessment of what she and so many others experienced as they bore witness to the impact of worksite raids throughout the summer of 2018.

Much research has considered vicarious trauma, or the "post-traumatic stress reactions experienced by those who are indirectly exposed to traumatic events."[29] This trauma, McNeillie and Rose write, is "a cumulative and pervasive process in which the helper's inner experiences are negatively and permanently transformed through listening to traumatic material frequently and repeatedly over time."[30] Among those who commonly experience secondary trauma are family; friends; coworkers, like Lesley; volunteers, like Destiny, Trish, and Sal; and professionals, like Kimberly, Melanie, or Fathers Isaac or Jim, who care for those who experienced the trauma firsthand.

While most work considers the numerous harms of trauma exposure, a growing body of research highlights that the harms of vicarious trauma can approach those of the experience of the trauma itself. For example, a review of vicarious trauma in therapists found that therapists who experienced vicarious trauma presented with emotional, physiological, and cognitive symptoms.[31] Emotional symptoms included anxiety, sadness, guilt, shame, and fear. Physical symptoms included exhaustion, pain, nausea, dizziness, headaches, and shortness of breath. Cognitive symptoms included cynicism, hopelessness, and a shift in worldview that allowed them to better recognize humanity's capacity for cruelty. It's notable, however, that this study excluded what the authors called "shared experiences of trauma," which they defined as war, natural disaster, and terrorism, all examples interviewees used when they explained to us what a worksite raid was like.

An integrative review of the vicarious trauma from working with refugees found that many professionals who continually hear narratives of human rights violations and brutality eventually want to do something beyond face-to-face counseling to address the atrocities their clients describe. Yet with no change in legislation in the foreseeable future due to political "impasses," they are left feeling "shattered, drained and impotent."[32] While this research seems to accurately characterize the efforts of people like Kimberly, Destiny, Scott, Lisa, and Trish—who hear the narratives of trauma from the immigrants they serve and hope for systemic change—it would be hard to describe the efforts of the Trump administration as "impasses" when there was never an attempt to create more humane immigration policy. As Kimberly stated, perhaps her exhaustion was part of the plan: "We're such a small organization, and we're all having to respond to this great need. To me, it feels like maybe intentional to try and wear down all of us who are trying to assist in this."

If political impasses could be psychologically harmful to those who want a better world, what about deliberate efforts to work them past the breaking point?

≈

The last state we visited was Ohio, so by the time we made it there we had seen the vicarious trauma that Kimberly described echoed in many ways in interviews with organizers, volunteers, and advocates throughout the country. Whether interviewees were working with immigrants for the first time or had done so before; were bilingual or only spoke English; were Latino or white; were lawyers, priests, or drivers; the massive amount of need coupled with the feelings of uselessness and the specter that all of it was part of the plan left an indelible mark on those who attempted to do something about it.

Sometimes, interviewees described being caught off guard by their own responses to the trauma around them, working so hard and so intensely for so long that they had no capacity to reflect on the personal impacts of what they observed until later. Stacy was the director of an immigrant rights organization based in Nashville, Tennessee, who responded to the raid of Southeastern Provision in Bean Station, over three and a half hours away. Like other advocates, Stacy spent most of her interview detailing the organizational systems created in the immediate aftermath of the raid. When she brought up what it was like to work in Father Jim's church, however, she started to speak about how it impacted her personally. It was clear to her that volunteers needed to take care of not only immigrant families but also each other: "It was completely the most overwhelming experience. . . . I've never been in that concentrated amount of human suffering in my life. You walked through the church and there were literally hundreds of people. I couldn't go to the bathroom without 10 people asking me a question; kids were crying everywhere. So it was really intense at every turn."

Later in the interview, I asked Stacy more about how the "concentrated human suffering" had affected her:

BILL: It sounds like you were there [in the church for] . . . multiple weeks and . . . all day long.

STACY: Yeah.

BILL: I was wondering what kind of toll that took on you.

STACY: It was just so busy that we were running on adrenaline, but we were definitely sleeping three hours a night. It was awful. Luckily, a lot of the staff in the church were making sure everybody was staying fed. We tried to incorporate more self-care. There was a nap room; we started to try to manage that. It was just that we were almost too busy to take care of ourselves.

Notably, Stacy's attempts at self-care involved yet more advocacy for her community, as she directed her energy into disseminating the stories of those with her and soliciting more donations. She continued:

I remember me and my colleague, we started doing almost nightly Facebook Lives just to give updates on what was happening, what was needed, and what we were learning; thanking people for their donations, or asking for more donations, or whatever it might be. I remember it was the only time that we sort of stopped, or talked in a coherent way about what was happening. There was one [Facebook Live broadcast] where we ended the broadcast because we just started crying.

Stacy was also aware that, as emotionally overwhelming as it was for her, the vicarious trauma was probably worse for those of her staff who could directly relate to what they were seeing. Either way, she notes, the feelings of helplessness wear you down: "Then for a lot of our staff who come from immigrant families and were sort of reliving trauma that they had had previously with immigration enforcement or things like that. So I think it really does take a toll, and just hearing the stories and feeling a bit helpless."

Anneka, the law student who responded to the O'Neill raids, related personally to the affected families she was helping. When Anneka, whose father was a Guatemalan immigrant, heard about the raids, she immediately rushed over from Lexington—a two-hour-and-forty-five-minute drive—because she "was angry," as the raid "hits really close to home."

Anneka shared very specific examples of the situations that she carried with her that pushed her over the edge until she, too, finally broke down, including the story of the nursing mothers who were detained:

> Like one person was saying that they sent dogs after them at one of the farm locations, and that one person was trying to escape from the dogs, so he was crawling through like a pigpen or something. So he was covered in pig feces and stuff; he didn't escape. The dogs got him and they ripped up his clothes and stuff. So he spent hours, he spent overnight in detention with these clothes.
>
> And then, there was some moms that the babies were breastfeeding when they got detained, so then they had no food for that night for the baby.

When Anneka first heard about the raid, she said, "I just knew I had to be there. I wanted to do anything that I possibly could." But like so many others, she felt that even if she did everything in her power, it simply wasn't enough, as everything that was happening was by political design. She described these situations of injustice as a "power imbalance . . . like a huge looming power that I couldn't do anything about."

Like Stacy, it wasn't until Anneka had a moment of downtime that she realized the toll her work was taking:

> At one point I didn't even realize how stressful it was. We hardly took any breaks, like we hardly sat down to eat or anything, and

I took a bathroom break at one point, and I didn't realize how intensely emotional it was until I had to throw up in the bathroom because I was so anxious and stressed from hearing all the things that the people were telling me.

To exacerbate the situation, advocates often had to explain to families that their needs were not as urgent as the needs of another family. This meant that advocates had to articulate the reasons behind their decision to "triage" care that would be inadequate anyway. Diane, a white woman who served as the managing attorney of a nonprofit law firm that responded to the raids in O'Neill, Nebraska, recounted through tears the challenge of explaining to families that their needs were not yet critical enough to garner help:

> It felt like a nurse in the emergency room having to triage who's the most important to help even though everyone deserves help. That was really hard because we'd have to explain to individuals who had been released in O'Neill, you know, it was almost like saying, "I'm sorry, your case is not as important as someone else's right now." That was really difficult to say, you know, [for example], "You're out of jail, someone else isn't, we have to get to them more quickly than you."

When Diane characterized her work as "triage," she echoed the word choice of advocates throughout the country but specifically described the type of triage as that of a nurse in an emergency room. While we didn't meet any ER nurses who responded to the raid, we did meet Ruth, who had worked as a hospice nurse before joining Scott, Lisa, and Sal as another retired driver for Bienvenidos's rideshare.

I interviewed Ruth after wrapping the interview with Kimberly and asked Ruth what it was like to observe so many traumatic stories unfolding as she drove people across the state.

BILL: What has it been like for you to be a volunteer, to be driving, to be witnessing?

RUTH: I've been a hospice nurse, so I've been with many people as they've left this world. And I will tell you, there's nothing that has wrecked me like this. And I've been a nurse a long time.

I journal it. I write poetry about it. I do whatever I can to release it myself because nothing has wrecked me, probably, like this has. There's been no basis in my life for what I've seen, and it's deeply disturbing to me.

As Ruth implied, secondary trauma also had to be managed. If not, it only stood to make an already emotional situation even worse. Reginaldo, who coached youth soccer in a small town in Iowa, shared with Nicole how he learned to "cry in silence" to avoid escalating the situation for the children whose parents had been detained.

Born in Mexico, Reginaldo had lived in Iowa for 19 years when Nicole interviewed him in a coffee shop downtown. He started his time in Iowa like so many other Mexican immigrants by working as a cook, but he didn't like the work and said he just wasn't good at it. "Creéme, lo traté, pero, eh, no pude! / Believe me, I tried it, but I just couldn't!" he told Nicole through laughter. After a short stint cleaning parks around Iowa, he found his dream job: "Dios me dió la oportunidad de ayudar con los equipos de fútbol / God gave me the opportunity to help out with the soccer teams."

As a coach, Reginaldo could support Iowa's Latino youth on the soccer field and also serve as one of the few Latino male role models they had outside of their own families. Being a role model was important to him, and he tried to always model motivation, discipline, and professionalism to his players.

A NEW OVERGROUND RAILROAD

When the raid on Midwest Precast Concrete hit his hometown, removing the parents of players on his soccer teams, Reginaldo brought the families together to see what could be done. It was then that he saw one of his teens break down:

> I called everyone, called all the families so that we could get together at my house. And [one of my soccer players], he threw himself on the floor and cried and cried and screamed, asking why God had forgotten about him.
>
> You know, it was something so impactful, and now that I am thinking about it, I remember clearly that I started to cry. But later, I started thinking that if I don't stop crying, that's not going to help him, you know? I have to be stronger. So that's what I did.

Reginaldo composed himself the best he could—"me puse más fuerte"—and, when he was ready, engaged the young soccer player again.

> And he told me, "Coach, just tell me why this happened to me? Why has God forgotten me? Why did this happen to my dad? He didn't deserve this."
>
> It's something so impactful, impactful and so sad. Óyeme, te parte el corazón . . . / Listen, it just breaks your heart. . . . Hay veces que tienes que llorar en silencio. / There are times you just have to cry in silence.

≈

"And this serves as a very good deterrent," Trump said about the immigration raids that resulted in the arrest of 680 workers on the first day of Mississippi public school. A deterrent for whom? Are worksite raids—and all the chaos and cruelty that define them—meant to deter immigrants from crossing the border?

Or to deter others in their community from seeing them as human and supporting them? The answer, unfortunately, is both: If you cross the border, you'll be separated from your family and deported. If you help someone who crossed the border, you might find yourself throwing up in the bathroom.

CHAPTER 7

It Was the Bed Bugs That Broke Her

The Perfect Immigrant

Edith, or Edie to her friends and neighbors, is 83 years old when she welcomes us into her modest home in a small town in the southeast corner of Iowa. It is an unseasonably warm Saturday, with a low of just 24 degrees, significantly warmer than the low of 2 degrees the day before and the −19 degrees the day before that. It seems the historic polar vortex is coming to an end. A Midwesterner through and through, Edie does what she can to make us feel comfortable in her house, offering us quilts made with her own hands and coffee with "a little something"—not whiskey but French vanilla powdered creamer—to keep us warm. Edie was a theater major in her youth and still acts the part, commanding the room with her presence and embellishing her one-person routine as she gets more comfortable with her audience. She's boisterous, funny, and a little unpredictable. She answers questions but also just lets her mind wander, talking about something that is related, or tangential, or, if she wants, unrelated. Everyone in the town seems to know who Edie is and has an opinion about her. Whether they formed that opinion before or after she invited an undocumented Guatemalan teenager into her home after his father was detained in the raid on Midwest Precast Concrete—a gesture that would also capture the attention of a range of reporters[1]—I can't be sure.

I've interviewed people like Edie before, and I know they can get carried away, even making some social faux pas. An interview is not the same as a conversation between friends, and it's easy to interpret the silence of a good interviewer as an invitation to continue expanding upon a topic without reservation. This can result in interviewees saying things they would never say in public. I'm pretty good at reacting—or, more often, biting my tongue and not reacting—when interviewees tread down these paths, as their unfiltered commentary often provides another level of insight into what I'm studying. But I have never interviewed someone like Edie with students present, let alone Latino students from immigrant families, like Juan and Bella, who sit beside me.[2]

Edie cares deeply for others in her community and seems to have a keen intuition about who is in need and what it is they need. She is known for daringly attempting to address those needs in ways that others find inspiring, petrifying, ill-informed, or all three at the same time. So it wasn't completely out of character that, even though she did not speak Spanish or cook any Guatemalan dishes, she offered her home to Edgar after his father was detained so that Edgar would not be placed in foster care or, like his father, deported.

Edgar and his father were two of the 724,000 undocumented Guatemalans living in the US in 2019.[3] Edgar's father had been working in Mount Pleasant for three years, sending money back to Guatemala to provide for Edgar, his sisters, and his mother, when the family decided that Edgar should join his father in Iowa. This way, the family hoped, gangs could not pressure Edgar to traffic drugs.

IT WAS THE BED BUGS THAT BROKE HER

As a young teenager, Edgar trekked through Guatemala and crossed all of Mexico to arrive at the Texas–Mexico border, where he crossed the Rio Grande in a raft. Because he was legally a child, Edgar was taken in by the Office of Refugee Resettlement, or ORR, and released into the care of his father in Iowa.

For about a year, things went smoothly enough for Edgar and his father. Edgar enrolled in a local high school and began to learn English while his father worked at Midwest Precast Concrete, where his work provided vital resources to the Iowan economy and building materials to a construction-hungry Midwest. Edgar's father made more money than he ever would in Guatemala and continued to send funds to his family. Many Guatemalan immigrants did the same, with their collective remittances accounting for 14 percent of Guatemala's gross domestic product in 2018.[4] Edgar and his father lived together, ate together, and slowly adapted to life in Iowa, even surviving a blisteringly cold polar vortex.

Everything changed on May 9, 2018, when Midwest Precast Concrete was raided and Edgar's father, along with 31 other workers, were detained by ICE. Three months later, his father was sent back to Guatemala. Without family in Iowa to care for him, Edgar would likely be deported as well. While Edie didn't want to do the guardianship paperwork, she was more than willing to "just be the grandma with a bed." So Trish, at Iowa Bridge, did the paperwork for her. Soon after, Edgar had a bed, a home, an adult caretaker, and was safe—for the moment—from deportation.

This means that in less than two years, Edgar had left his mother and sisters to avoid being recruited by gangs as a drug trafficker, crossed Guatemala and all of Mexico, been transferred by the ORR from the Texas–Mexico border to Iowa, begun living with his father, survived his first Iowan winter, started school in English, and lost his father to deportation. He was now living in his third radically different home—headed by a radically different caretaker—in two years.

While some of the costs—like groceries—were what Edie expected, others were not. Edie recalls when Edgar felt a tension in his chest that surprised him:

> I think it was just anxiety. I don't know. He thought he had a little heart palpitation, and he had not seen a doctor or anything. Then I called my doctor and she said, "Come on in."
>
> Well, of course there's no insurance, and then they gave him an EKG. And so, his bill ended up being about $400–500 or so. And, I went and paid for that.

Edgar is not the first immigrant Edie has supported. In about 2005 she began sponsoring a man from a country in West Africa. She tells us:

> I—about 12, 13 years ago—started sponsoring a young man from [West Africa] just through the magic of the Internet, which I was probably stupid to do. But, I was very lucky, and he has had such an adventure.
>
> And, he has gotten to the United States legally, and he is married. He was married in one of my friend's backyards here in [town]. And they have two children now. They both have their citizenship, and he has his nursing degree, and she's working on hers. And they are the perfect immigrant. He's like my son, and they live in [a city about two hours away].

In truth, Edie did something enormously generous and risky for both Edgar and the West African man she now considers family, acts that were likely foundational in the positive life changes that would follow. Yet I notice Edie's use of the phrase "the perfect immigrant." I know that Edie is using it as a compliment, an acknowledgment of his successful climb up the career ladder, his two children, his marriage, his nursing degree, and, as she'll later describe, his creative entrepreneurship that included traveling on a bike with a battery to allow people to charge their cell phones for a small fee. I also notice that she uses the singular form for three people—the man, his wife, and their child are, collectively, the perfect immigrant.

I can't help but wonder if Edgar is "perfect," or if it is even possible for him to be so. Given that he is a teenager, jobless, barely knows English, is obsessed with video games and shoes—and is Guatemalan—my guess is that he is not.

Edie's exuberance only grows as she shares more and more emotional stories with us. We listen, sipping away at our French vanilla–flavored coffee while wrapped in quilts that, we would find out shortly, had been infested with bed bugs earlier that year. She is clearly getting more comfortable in front of us, which in turn puts me on edge. I am not sure if Juan and Bella are on edge as well. I look over at them often, more often than I should. So far, they've been fine.

The raid that took Edgar's father was the same one that took Juana's husband, and Edie, a member of the church in which Juana volunteered, detours into a memory about the food pantry in which Juana worked. She describes how the food pantry operated:

> Each family, their problems were that most of these guys [who were detained] were the breadwinners of the family. And so, they hear there were a lot of moms that didn't have anything coming in. They had rent to pay and all these kinds of things. And so, every Monday, we have two people that sit out at the church and dole out money. But what we've done, and I think this was, as somebody said, "Well that doesn't seem very fair," but I think it's very smart. Each family gets

the same amount of money. It doesn't make any difference if you're a single guy, or if you got 10 kids, you all get the same amount of money. And, the reason for that is that it was going to be too difficult to try and figure out, this person, should they get more, then somebody will say . . . there's some haggling going on within the people. They're not perfect.

My skin bristles a little bit. There's that word again, "perfect," and this time the imperfection comes from the inclination of the families visiting the food pantry to "haggle." Haggling is common in many non-Western countries—countries like those in which most immigrants in Iowa were born—where individual sellers have authority over pricing and can raise and lower the price without needing oversight from anyone else. This is not to say that haggling is uncommon in the US. While we may not haggle to buy individual servings of laundry detergent in the *pulpería*, I don't know of a flea market or garage sale in which haggling is not expected. When I was growing up, my grandmother dressed my brother and me in clothes she bought from garage sales. Sometimes, family lore has it, she would buy the item and then resell it at her own garage sale, pocketing some spending money herself (which, God bless her, she probably then used to dress my brother and me).

Edie seems to be bothered by something I understand to be very common, Latino, immigrant, and, yes, I admit, familial behavior. Edie returns to Edgar, recapping a conversation she had with him and some of his friends:

> Now, he's only 16, and one day he was going with somebody to somewhere, this friend. I said, "How old are you?" And he said, "18," or so. I said, "Let me see your driver's license." Man, he didn't have one. I said, "Edgar, you're not going." Although, if he'd been caught, he would have been taken probably into the police station. I don't

think he would've been charged particularly with anything. But I said, "You are not to drive with anybody who does not have a driver's license."

And I said, "And keep your nose clean." I said, "If you do anything, you're going to be out of here. You're going to be out of my house, and you're also probably going to be out of here [the country]." Because he has no family. Now, that's been another thing is that we've gone through a lot of . . . that's been an experience.

It's highly unlikely that Edgar's friends have licenses. If they are undocumented and in Iowa, like Edgar, it's not even legally possible to have a license. I know Edie is trying to protect Edgar by keeping him out of a car in which he could get racially profiled, taken to jail, and deported. I was worried when Pastor Isaac shared with me how much time he spent in the car driving the highways between his two churches. Yet even though she was asking about his license to protect him, all I can think about is how hard it was for Edgar to have yet another white adult asking him and his friends for their papers.

≈

Edie's use and embrace of the ideals of the perfect immigrant are not uncommon and are likely not meant to be malicious. To be described as a "perfect immigrant" is to be seen as successful, entrepreneurial, and a hard worker who contributes to the US economy. It generally implies a level of assimilation into US culture that means white, non-immigrants feel comfortable around you; that they can talk about TV shows, music, and food and you will be able to relate. It often has a family component, as we see in Edie's example, that suggests you are married, usually to a person of the opposite gender, and have what is considered a reasonable amount of children.

The archetype of the perfect immigrant shifts over time with the political and social moment. In the contemporary US, the qualities of the perfect immigrant are probably best represented by the idea of the immigrant "Dreamer," a term that originated from the Development, Relief, and Education for Alien Minors Act, or DREAM Act,[5] first proposed in 2001 by Senators Dick Urban and Orrin Hatch. The DREAM Act aimed to grant a path to citizenship to undocumented immigrant Dreamers who arrived in the US when young and met certain criteria. While differences exist over the 20-plus versions of the DREAM Act introduced in Congress, the act generally provided a reprieve from deportation and a work permit to those who came to the US as children, graduated from high school, and went on to a college or university or joined the military.[6]

The DREAM Act was introduced in Congress many times but never passed. In 2012, President Obama used his authority to institute Deferred Action for Child Arrivals, or DACA,[7] largely based on the ideals of the act. As an executive order, Obama didn't need the support of the House and Senate but couldn't propose as drastic a step as offering a path to citizenship to undocumented immigrants. Instead, DACA provided two years of relief from deportation and a work permit to undocumented youth who arrived in the US before their 16th birthdays and met certain criteria similar to that of the DREAM Act. And while "DACAmented" would be used in some circles for undocumented youth who received DACA, the term "Dreamer" had stuck around, crystallizing the image of a young immigrant, brought to the US through no fault of her own by her undocumented parents. Dreamers were smart. They were assimilated. They spoke English. They went to college or joined the military. US citizens rooted for them to reach the American dream they so fervently chased. And while the government still used it extensively throughout the country, deportation was too cruel for them, a fate meant for other immigrants, not these.

When President Obama gave his talk in the Rose Garden after the institution of DACA,[8] he began,

> Good afternoon, everybody. This morning, Secretary Napolitano announced new actions my administration will take to mend our nation's immigration policy, to make it more fair, more efficient, and more just—specifically for certain young people sometimes called "Dreamers."
>
> These are young people who study in our schools, they play in our neighborhoods, they're friends with our kids, they pledge allegiance to our flag. They are Americans in their heart, in their minds, in every single way but one: on paper. They were brought to this country by their parents—sometimes even as infants—and often have no idea that they're undocumented until they apply for a job or a driver's license, or a college scholarship.
>
> Put yourself in their shoes. Imagine you've done everything right your entire life—studied hard, worked hard, maybe even graduated at the top of your class—only to suddenly face the threat of deportation to a country that you know nothing about, with a language that you may not even speak.

Even President Trump supported Dreamers. When asked about DACA recipients in his Person of the Year interview with *Time* magazine in November 2016[9]—even though he actively tried to dismantle DACA throughout his presidency[10]—Trump shared: "They got brought here at a very young age, they've worked here, they've gone to school here. Some were good students. Some have wonderful jobs. And they're in never-never land because they don't know what's going to happen."

Everyone loves a Dreamer.

To be clear, DACA was incredibly helpful for hundreds of thousands of undocumented immigrants, who, researchers show,[11] had greater access to employment, health care, and educational opportunities. While undocumented immigrants are not legally barred from having credit cards or bank accounts, without Social Security numbers the application process is often too cumbersome or aroused too much suspicion for many to undertake. But with the Social Security numbers granted by DACA, undocumented youth were able to access credit cards and open bank accounts alongside their citizen peers. Many could also, for the first time in their lives, get behind the wheel of a car and legally step on the gas.

But the main problem with the category of the perfect immigrant is not in the category itself but in what it creates by extension; that is, one is either a perfect immigrant—meeting all the criteria the category requires—or does not deserve to be in the US. While US citizens are allowed a range of activities, religious beliefs, health statuses, family arrangements, and even feelings about their country, there is no category for an "imperfect but still acceptable immigrant," an immigrant who works hard but stops at 40 hours if he's not going to get paid overtime and demands his boss give him the required safety equipment. An immigrant who uses supplemental food assistance because her citizen child is entitled to it. An immigrant who made it through high school, but just barely, and doesn't want to join the military. There's the perfect immigrant and then there's the villainous, dangerous one who must be removed at all costs.

As we learned in the summer of 2018, other immigrants may also merit humanitarian treatment, like the provision of food and water or the right to be in a cell with their parents. But these immigrants all tended to be young children—children the public viewed as raceless and innocent—and public support did not extend beyond meeting their basic needs. As children, they were not old enough to be either perfect and protected nor imperfect and deported. The true judgment would come when they became adults.

As a teenager, Edgar is on the brink of adulthood. Still an undocumented immigrant child in the state's eyes, I know he is inching perilously closer to becoming an undocumented Latino man in the eyes of the public, to being brought to the town square where he will be weighed and measured against the elusive criteria of the Dreamer.

As I sit across from Edie, I steal a glance at Juan and Bella, trying to get a sense of what's going on in their heads. I can see the writing on the wall. Edgar can't be "perfect." I know this. When an undocumented immigrant slips up in any way—from a broken law to a mistimed joke to a failed class—they are precluded from perfection. From there it's a quick step to dehumanization and a quicker one to justification of their removal. When Edie gets to this point in the story, how will she talk about the imperfect Edgar?

It Was the Bed Bugs That Broke Her

On July 6, 2015, as Trump was setting the stage for his defeat of Hillary Clinton, he released a three page, 881-word statement updating his views on the "rapists" who immigrated from Mexico:[12] "The largest suppliers of heroin, cocaine and other illicit drugs are Mexican cartels that arrange to have Mexican immigrants trying to cross the borders and smuggle in the drugs. The Border Patrol knows this. Likewise, tremendous infectious disease is pouring across the border."

While Trump's focus remained on the role of the immigrant as the drug smuggler, he made another notable evolution in his anti-immigrant language, describing the immigrant not only as the trafficker of drugs but also of infectious disease.

He would use this language often at future campaign stops, including a stop in Grand Rapids, Michigan, on April 2, 2024,[13] as he prepared for a rematch with Biden, the presidential nominee for the Democratic Party at the time. In a speech described by *The New Republic* as "off the rails," Trump detailed immigrants crossing the US–Mexico border: "People were sick, we don't want them coming into our country with contagious diseases, and they have it. All of a sudden you see these contagious diseases spreading, and everyone is saying, 'I wonder where they came from.' I can tell you where they came from."

Trump's association of infectious disease with immigrants is not new. In fact, associating immigrants with infectious disease is a tried-and-true method for policymakers to restrict the entry of immigrants into the country without having to disclose other, less publicly palatable reasons to prevent their entry.[14] The rate of infectious disease among an immigrant population does not determine when this association is made. It's the story of the infectious disease that's important.

As researchers explain,

> At many points over the past century, some people have wanted to exclude persons perceived as foreign, inassimilable, and dangerous to the country's social, political, or economic fabric. Metaphors of germs and contagion have never lurked far beneath the surface of such rationales. . . .
>
> More often than not these arguments have been motivated by, and closely intertwined with, ideologies of racialism, nativism, and national security rather than substantiated epidemiological or medical observations.

That is, it's much easier to convince the public to prevent the entry of immigrants carrying a disease that is a threat to the country's health than immigrants whose skin color is a threat to the country's whiteness.

The closing of the US–Mexico border during the COVID-19 pandemic serves as an example. As rates of COVID-19 climbed, the Trump administration searched for ways to limit migrant entry at the US–Mexico border, despite being encouraged by disease experts to focus on internal pandemic mitigation strategies, such as masking mandates, social distancing policies, and contact tracing.[15] In March of 2020, Pence ordered the director of the Centers for Disease Control and Prevention to use emergency powers to seal the US borders, leveraging an obscure federal law from 1944 called Title 42 to do so. Title 42 allowed for rapid asylum dismissals based on the potential spread of disease.[16] This meant that those on the border, despite having the legal right to make an asylum claim, could not, resulting in 1.7 million unheard asylum cases in just two years.[17] Doctors for America and Physicians for Human Rights circulated a letter drawing out the social ramifications of the policy, saying "The decision to halt asylum processes 'to protect the public health' is not based on evidence or science. In fact, this order directly endangers tens of thousands of lives and threatens to amplify dangerous anti-immigrant sentiment and xenophobia."[18]

And while immigrants were being turned back at the border, they were also dying at rates that far outpaced their US-born counterparts inside the US. The media documented the spike in immigrant deaths in meatpacking plants due to their close quarters, inability to take breaks to wash hands, and lack of personal protective equipment, deaths in exactly the type of places that ICE had raided the summer before. The deaths in meatpacking plants eventually rose so high that many plants, including Tyson, halted production.[19] (Trump ordered Tyson back to production a few days later.[20]) And as COVID-19 continued to spread in the cramped, poorly ventilated quarters of detention centers, public health professionals, including Nicole and me, wrote a brief in support of a lawsuit against Chad Wolf, the acting secretary of the Department of Homeland Security at the time, to force detention centers to release detainees at heightened risk of COVID-19.[21]

Perhaps it's because I have been reading about the infectious diseases allegedly carried by immigrants since I was a doctoral student over a decade ago. Perhaps it's because of the disproportionate deaths of so many immigrants in meatpacking plants and detention centers from COVID-19. Perhaps it's because I saw public health—via Title 42—used against a community I love. Or perhaps it's because the story of diseased immigrants harkens back to words I heard in my youth—"dirty Mexican," which wasn't *exactly* about infectious disease but kinda was— but I *hate* when people talk about immigrants carrying disease.

So when Edie says that what ultimately pushed her over the edge with Edgar was the bed bugs he brought into her home, I get angry. She recalls:

> I was up at Cedar Rapids [for Edgar's dad's] first hearing, and it got very mixed up, very badly handled. And . . . it's the first time I'd ever seen Edgar just break down and cry and cry and cry. And you see all these families are there trying to wonder what's going to happen. Edgar's hearing, his next hearing is in [quite a while now].
>
> All of this got to be a little much for me.
>
> We went through a very interesting situation. We found that we had bed bugs, and I know that Edgar had brought them in. When he moved in, he brought bags and bags and bags of stuff that had been his dad's, and all this kinds of stuff. And, all of a sudden,

IT WAS THE BED BUGS THAT BROKE HER

Edgar was being bad and so forth. And, of course, we had the guys come in, and so we had to take all of our clothing and wash all of our clothing, and take everything, all bed clothing, everything.

We had to take all my quilts and wash all my quilts, everything. And I really thought I was going to go nuts. It was really too much for me.

I feel a metallic taste in my mouth from the adrenaline. I am thankful that Edie took Edgar to his dad's court case over an hour away, as Edgar probably would not have gone otherwise. She didn't have to do that. But my heart aches as I think about what Edgar went through when his dad was taken away. I imagine Edgar taking everything he owns and stuffing it into a garbage bag, then taking everything his dad wasn't wearing when he was detained and stuffing that into a garbage bag too. I imagine Edgar leaving the house that had, for not even two full years, become his home in Iowa away from his home in Guatemala, a home that kept them warm through more snow than they knew possible, a home that, perhaps, brought a notion of comfort while Edgar made his way through a new school in a new language without his mother and siblings.

But what broke Edie was the bed bugs, not the thought of Edgar washing his dad's scent off the clothes he left behind, not the sight of his dad's poorly handled case, not seeing Edgar himself break down and sob.

It was the bugs.

The infection.

The dirtiness, grime, and disease.

What had been a tenuous feeling in the room for most of the interview starts to shift cataclysmically. I no longer wonder where the interview is going. I know.

Edie continues.

And, at that point my kids said, "Mom, I think you've done your part." But, Edgar is still here. That was very traumatic, and it was something that couldn't be helped. They'd lived in a hovel with a bunch of other people, and that just happened. But I don't want to do that again. I'd sooner burn the house down than to do that. So, I don't know where I was from there. Go ahead and ask me something else.

From Edie's perspective, her life was turned upside down by a sacrifice she willingly made for Edgar. Who knows where he would be without her? But at that moment, my well of empathy just isn't deep enough to care.

The bugs are not Edgar's fault. His dad's deportation is not Edgar's fault. The risk of driving while Latino is not Edgar's fault. It's the circumstances. Immigration policy. Worker exploitation. Like being in a meatpacking plant during a raid. The illness is social, the infection political.

I am very worried about Juan and Bella, and as I try to figure out how to redirect the conversation—a hovel, yes, he came from a hovel, what else can you afford when you work at a factory?—my tunnel vision makes it hard to be the agile interviewer I usually am. How were they handling this? Did they wonder if Edith was glancing at their skin to see if anything was crawling on it?

As I move us toward the end of the interview, Edith brings up DACA. Then, looking at Juan and Bella, she asks, "Do you have DACA?"

≈

Stephen Miller, the great-grandchild of Jewish immigrants, was born in 1985 and a youthful 33 years old when he became the senior adviser for policy to President Trump. Miller began working as communications director for Jeff Sessions—the public face of the family separation policy—in 2009 while Sessions was the US senator for Alabama. When Sessions rose to the position of the US attorney general under President Trump in 2016, Miller was right there with him. Sessions had brought Miller along, but Miller moved over to communications director for President Trump.

Miller was known for his racist and xenophobic beliefs, but he had always been careful about presenting them publicly. Then in 2019 a trove of leaked emails offered a glimpse into the depth of Miller's anti-immigrant beliefs. Among the emails were discussions showing Miller's belief in replacement theory, or the idea that the white population of the US will eventually be replaced by racial minorities.[22] Many of the ideas that Miller cited and circulated were rooted in the idea that whites were genetically superior to people of color. This idea, called biological or genetic determinism, argues that behavior is determined by genes more than culture or circumstance. Accordingly, some people—whites—are born with superior genes, and others—Central Americans, Mexicans, Africans—are inherently inferior. Allowing the latter into the country will pollute the bloodline of the former, the diluted skin color only a representation of the diluted intellect and virtue.

But while Miller did everything he could to keep his perspective out of the public, Trump didn't—or couldn't—keep his beliefs about biodeterminism out of the public discussion. As far back as 1988, he told Oprah Winfrey that you need "to have the right genes" to succeed.[23] In a campaign speech in Minnesota in 2020, Trump told the Minnesotan audience, "You have good genes, you know that, right? You have good genes. A lot of it is about the genes, isn't it, don't you believe? The racehorse theory, you think we're so different? You have good genes in Minnesota."[24] The racehorse theory to which Trump referred is the belief that selective breeding improves performance.[25]

In a campaign rally in New Hampshire in December of 2023, Trump said that immigrants coming to the US were "poisoning the blood of our country," which many decried as a reference to Adolf Hitler's *Mein Kampf*. Trump then posted on his social media website, Truth Social, that "illegal immigration is poisoning the blood of our nation. They're coming from prisons, from mental institutions—from all over the world."[26]

By the end of the Trump administration, it had become clear that Miller and Trump had made it publicly acceptable to support biological determinism. Indeed, it was foundational in many of their policy proposals. Policies like the Muslim ban, the elimination of asylum, or the use of immigration raids were much easier to accept when those they impacted were genetically inferior subhumans with a stunted range of emotion. Preventing their integration into the US would make America white again.

It was clear to me that many who supported Trump's policies supported this idea of biological determinism. But what about others who had never met an immigrant? Others who helped immigrant children because they felt sorry for them? Who saw the aid given after raids as apolitical? Was it possible to support immigrants even if you found them to be biologically inferior?

≈

I wrap up the interview and turn off the recorder, trying to move toward the end of our time with Edie so I can check on Juan and Bella. Like I usually do after I formally end an interview, I engage in a bit of small talk to allow the interviewee to slow down and extricate herself from emotional topics before returning to her daily life. Interviewees often open up more when the recorder is turned off, and since there is no record of what they say, I jot down field notes to summarize the conversation as soon as I can.

Edie continues to speak freely, continuing down the trajectory she was already on. She tells us that Edgar is having a hard time in school. He's getting into trouble. He's hanging around with a group he shouldn't. And he, or someone he was hanging around with, stole something from someone. "But what can you expect?" she asks us rhetorically. "It's in their blood."

The Porch Test

About a year after she invited us into her home, we find out that Edie has passed away, having lived a full life of 85 years. Her obituary described her as a dedicated Democrat, bridge player, and quilter, who stayed up-to-date on world events. She was a teacher and sang in the choir. The virtual guestbook on her obituary page is lined with words of praise from an array of people who loved her.

In October 2022, about four years after Midwest Precast Concrete was raided, I flew from Ann Arbor, Michigan, to Des Moines, Iowa, to meet with Juan and Nicole. Nicole flew in from Los Angeles, where she had since relocated with her husband and two young children. Juan, who was born in Iowa and relocated to Washington state, had returned to visit his family and joined us for breakfast and a long, important conversation. Juan had been a master's student in public health when he sat across from Edie that day. Since then, he had graduated with a master of public health in epidemiology and had begun his doctoral studies in public health. He had also started working for Nicole on a project she codirected, examining histories of forced sterilization in the US, often of women of color, often with disabilities, including nearly 2,000 Iowans. The records of these sterilizations sat in the archives of Iowa's State Historical Building, which we planned to visit later during the trip.

We had decided we needed to meet in person to figure out how—or if—to tell Edie's story, a complicated tale of generosity, material support, cultural mismatches, racial stereotyping, and the cost of inclusion in rural communities. It was a very specific story, but we had sensed it may also be a larger one, an immigration story that repeated itself hundreds if not thousands of times across the rural US every year. And while the purpose of the visit was legitimately to figure out how to handle her interview, especially after her death, I selfishly needed to see if I had failed Juan that day, letting him sit in a space in which he was told he was biologically inferior and had thievery in his blood. If I had let him down, I wanted to tell him how sorry I was.

We enjoy our coffees and eggs and catch up on each other's lives at a popular breakfast restaurant in downtown Des Moines, then walk around the city a bit, getting something to drink at Gong Fu Tea, whose hundreds of glass canisters filled with tea leaves of every kind line the light-green walls. Up-to-date on each other's work and families, we drive over to the State Historical Building, where Juan and Nicole are working on their sterilization project. We take a seat outside the building on two stone benches arranged in a semicircle. I'm thankful we are sitting in a semicircle instead of around a table. While we are partially facing each other, we can also look away if we need to without it being too obvious.

I place my small audio recorder between the three of us and start to record. The State Historical Building seems to also serve as a transit center of sorts, and our conversation is occasionally broken up by the sound of buses pulling in. We can see Iowa's capitol building in the distance. The Holocaust memorial sits across the street, out of view.

We talk for a few minutes about our team dynamic before I clunkily try to bring us to the question at hand.

IT WAS THE BED BUGS THAT BROKE HER

BILL: So I think it's a good time to talk about it now since we're here, but let's talk more about what you remember with, I've asked you about it before, but with the woman with the quilt in Iowa. Are you okay digging into that a little more?

JUAN [AFFIRMATIVE]: Let's talk about that situation.

BILL: Yeah . . . so she was talking to us and answering most of our questions. And then she went to this point where she said, you know, I remember pretty distinctly, and I wish I had the quote, but it wasn't recorded, but something about that "stealing is in their blood"—

Juan mercifully cuts off my meandering, poorly formulated, nonquestion. I realize I'm nervous. I can't articulate why.

JUAN: Yeah. "It's in their *DNA*."

I remembered Edie's quote incorrectly. Edie said stealing was in the *DNA* of Edgar and his friends, not in their blood. But I am not sure there is a difference. "Yes, in their DNA. What do you remember she said, and what do you remember thinking at the time?" I ask Juan.

At that moment, a little early in our recap of what Edie said about Edgar and his friends, Juan and I are both saying "they." We haven't brought ourselves to say "we" yet, as in "*We* have thievery in our blood, thievery in our DNA," but we will. Maybe we are just making sure to quote Edie correctly, to not repeat the mistake I had made. Or maybe we are subconsciously distancing ourselves from the bad immigrant archetype. Edie hadn't, after all, said, "*You* have thievery in your DNA." She had left Juan, Bella, and me out of it.

Juan continues: "Honestly, I think that the way that she said it felt like she was just talking [normally]. . . . I hear that, and then literally I feel like everything after she said [that] I just couldn't listen. At first it was like, 'What did she just say?! I can't believe she just said that in this room.'"

He means, I assume, in a room full of Latinos.

I was right that Juan was shaken by Edie's words. I was also right that Juan was expecting me to do something about it: "And then we were looking at you as the person with more authority and experience.... You kind of weaved around it, but I felt like you, we could tell like you felt that too."

I have a pretty good poker face during interviews. I've talked to law enforcement officers about police killings, talked to former immigration agents about separating families, talked to wives about their husbands disappearing, and talked to mothers about raids that shook them so deeply their bodies stopped producing breast milk, and I generally know when and how to express what I'm feeling or when and how to hold it back. So I wonder what it was that gave it away to Juan that Edie's words had made my blood boil.

Juan goes on:

> After that, I was so disengaged. I felt I was judged immediately when she said that.
>
> I was like, "Dang, I can't believe she would say that" and then selfishly I was like, "How am I here? Is that what she thinks when she talks to everyone like this?"
>
> I'd grown up in Iowa and experienced some similar situations.... Sometimes people think like this, and it's when you're in their own home, and they might consider you in that group or not. But I identify in that group so . . .

Clearly, Juan had wrestled with some of the same questions I had in the year since we had our French vanilla coffees with Edie. Why did she feel so comfortable saying that thievery was in Latino DNA, so comfortable asking Juan if he had DACA, so comfortable saying aloud that it was the bed bugs that put her over the edge? Is it because we were foreigners in her home? Or was it, as Juan had reflected, because she thought we were different from Edgar in some notable way? When Edie asked Juan if he had DACA, was she suggesting to him that he was different, giving him the chance to affirm that he is a Dreamer? I ask Juan about it:

> BILL: That's something I struggle with. Did she read us as "not Latino," or did she read us as "not *that kind* of Latino"?
>
> JUAN: She read us as "not that kind of Latino."

He takes advantage of the semicircle in which we are sitting to stare out into the distance.

It feels so invalidating to be lopped off as a different kind of Latino, as if somehow something about me—my lighter skin? My lack of accent? The degrees after my name?—changed my family heritage, changed the struggles of my ancestors, changed the very blood in my body, and could so easily allow me to abandon others like me.

Juan continues. "I have this problem in Seattle . . . not Latino enough, 'white passing.'"

Juan compares his time in Iowa to his time in Seattle and how the interpretation of his Latino-ness is so context dependent. "I think I'm fairly white passing, but growing up in Iowa, everybody said, 'You're Latino! You're Mexican!' That was my identity. And that *is* my identity, but then coming to Seattle, I've encountered situations where people are like, 'Oh you're white.'"

This dichotomy—purposefully fomented by anti-immigrant politicians—between the perfect, white-passing Latino and the biologically criminal one often results in infighting in our own communities. Some of us choose to paint ourselves as different from "those Latinos." "We did it the right way," the story goes, even when a "right way" doesn't exist or clearly exists only for certain groups at certain times. That division is painful; painful to watch; painful to have to negotiate. Yet Edgar's experience illustrates why we do it. "Those" Latinos have thievery in their DNA. Deportation is just fine. Kick in their door and take them. "We" Latinos get welcomed into the house—the country—with coffee and quilts. It was Trump's Angel Moms all over again.

I finally bring myself to ask Juan whether I should have done something, should perhaps have gotten him out of the situation, or even outright confronted Edie for her incorrect belief that thievery was in Edgar's—in our—DNA. But Juan says he would have done the same thing I did.

> I think I would have done something similar, because at that point we're in that community . . . [and] if the goal is to build trust and to work toward that, it's such a meticulous thing.
>
> And it's kinda shitty, but, [laughs] if you start going off, then what if she has all this power; all of a sudden she starts telling people and like *bada bing* you're out of the town—nobody wants to talk to you. So it's very sensitive; like I really want to [say something], but what's the larger goal?

Despite both being angry, humiliated, and shocked by the comments made in front of us, we agree that confronting Edie at that moment was not in the interest of our larger goal. It was her town. She welcomed us into it. We wanted to talk to people in it so we could tell a fuller, richer story about immigrant life in the rural US, a richer story about America itself. Feeling judged and inferior in her house was a trade Juan and I were willing to make for the material benefits she offered.

It's clear we all agree that there is a story here, but do we tell it? How? I ask Juan and Nicole what they think. Is our responsibility to speak well of those who have passed and to honor the good they've done while sanitizing the bad or to tell a messy, complicated, authentic story?

Juan shares first: "She's a person but she also represents the ideology, and I think that is what we're critiquing, really. Like, how is it that we admire the saviorism and then acquiesce to everything else? I think it's the ideology really that we're talking about, not the individual. Because this is public health, you know?"

I'm struck by the wisdom of Juan's point. As a study team, yes, we are talking to individuals to bring to light what communities experience. That's also what is happening here. What we—as Latinos—are told by one of the most welcoming women in rural Iowa is very likely to play itself out thousands of other times across the country. It's not Edith we are talking about. It's the ideology she held at that moment in time. It's the biological determinism. It's the story that allows so much violence to unfold on people we love. It's an ideology that, I'm forced to admit, can be held even by the people who provide for the immigrants around them. And yes, we are public health professionals. It's our job to bring to light the stories and beliefs that make people sick. Nicole agrees.

So how do we decide if we share Edie's story? Juan suggests we use the same decision-making process he used when he was choosing schools for his PhD: the porch test. In the porch test, you imagine yourself on a porch at 75 years of age, and you reflect on the life you have lived up to that point. How satisfied are you, sitting in your rocking chair looking at the sunset, having chosen Path A? What about if you had chosen Path B?

"In this case, Path A is, you omit the story," Juan says, prompting us to reflect on what we would all feel like, at 75 years old and sitting on a porch—in Iowa, in Texas, in Michigan—having chosen to leave out Edie's story. We could also choose another path, Juan reminds us: "Path B is, you tell it. . . . And I feel like the story is not complete without it. . . . Iowa is not a living, breathing entity. It is a place that we love and cherish because of the memories we hold. And sometimes places that we love are also places that we criticize."

We aren't sitting on a porch. We sit instead on a pair of stone benches in front of a museum that holds the records of Iowans who were sterilized for their purported biological inferiority, right across from the Holocaust memorial. We know which path we are choosing.

≈

When Edie died, the same pastor who welcomed Juana into the church when Elisio was detained presided over Edie's memorial. Her obituary requested that gifts of love and friendship be given to Iowa Bridge.

EPILOGUE

A Beautiful Morning in the Heartland of the US

NICOLE AND I SIT in the far back row of St. Peter's Catholic Church and watch as parishioners and their families fill the pews.[1] By the time mass begins, the church is about two-thirds full, a strong showing for a Catholic service at 9:00 a.m., even if it's less crowded than it was after the raid in nearby Bean Station. The stained-glass windows that line the left side of the church shine brilliant blues and greens, a bright sky over multicolored grass on which stand three crosses. The priest begins to greet the congregation and asks visitors to raise their hands and share where they are from. Nicole and I both raise our hands—"Iowa," "Texas," we say in turn—and are joined by visitors from Seattle, Pittsburgh, and Kansas City. The priest also asks for those who are not visitors to share their hometowns or home countries. Congregants born in the Philippines, Canada, Mexico, El Salvador, Honduras, Guatemala, and elsewhere compose the Tennesseans in the crowd.

In the pew in front of us sits a short woman with black hair and brown skin. Bustling around her are three children who look just like her. The woman—who I assume to be their mother—lets them play in the pew, reacting only when their antics grow loud enough to distract the congregation from the priest's story about how Jesus fed the crowd gathered around him by multiplying the loaves and fishes. The woman is visibly pregnant.

I can't help but think about the timing of this woman's pregnancy. Since ICE raided Southeastern Provision just four months ago, she will likely give birth to her baby before the ICE agents celebrate the first anniversary of what was, at the time, the biggest raid since Postville.

What kind of world will she bring this child into? As studies suggest, will her child begin his life at a disadvantage? Will he be born at a lower birth weight than the white infants born next to him? Will he be chronically absent while his white classmates continue to go to school?

Before he is 10 years old, he will see a president call for a return to the immigration enforcement operation of Dwight D. Eisenhower, Operation Wetback, when the country brought in Mexicans for short-term labor while US citizens were away in World War II, only to round up those laborers using raids and roadblocks and deport them by the hundreds of thousands when the US soldiers returned.

He will grow up in a world in which the White House will circulate a video of shackles being lifted from a plastic basket. Agents in "POLICE ERO" jackets and black winter utility gloves will bind the ankles, waists, and bare hands of waiting immigrants. No words will be spoken during the video. Instead, the faceless immigrants will walk up the stairs to board a plane for deportation as the viewer listens to the clinking of their chains. The video will be called *ASMR: Illegal Alien Deportation Flight.*

He will grow up in a world in which Guantanamo Bay is used once again to disappear Latino immigrants, in which Texas officials will offer thousands of acres to be used to process a projected record-breaking number of detainees, in which birthright citizenship is up for debate.

He will grow up in a world in which the Venezuelans we invited to take refuge in our country are deported to a Salvadoran prison.

But that is only a tiny fraction of the world in which he will grow up.

He will also grow up in a world in which the very people detained in Southeastern Provision will sue for racial profiling and excessive use of force and, with the help of the National Immigration Law Center and the Southern Poverty Law Center, win $1.175 million for their fellow meatpacking plant workers. The suit will be historic, the largest and only known class settlement related to an immigration raid, and will become a new tool for tireless lawyers to combat large-scale worksite enforcement.

He will grow up in a world in which his teachers will deliver meals to his home when his mother is too afraid to bring him to school; in which his pastor will welcome him into the church so his mother can eat, change his diaper, and strategize; in which his father's lawyer will sleep in hotels and work on the floor to complete his paperwork; in which those who have cars and licenses will sign up to drive those who don't.

He will grow up in a world in which his mother and father will do anything for him, even if it means crossing a border. Again.

But mostly, he will grow up in a world that understands that mass deportation requires mass public consent. And I like to believe the public will refuse to consent.

The service ends and we leave the church and see a group of teens sitting on picnic tables under a wooden pavilion. They all look Latino. A young boy twirls a girl about his age, their hands linked delicately over her head. While I don't know for sure, I imagine they are meeting in this wooden pavilion, right outside the church in which their families huddled when their fathers disappeared, to get ready for her quinceañera.

It's a beautiful morning in the heartland of the US.

Acknowledgments

Grief and rage inspired this book, but love and community brought it to fruition.

I'll begin by thanking every person across the US who spoke with us, inviting us into moments of heartbreak, humor, and hope. Research ethics and a desire for safety in a political moment that seeks the removal of many of you prevent me from listing your names, but they don't prevent me from sharing your stories everywhere I can. I intend to spend my life doing so. Thank you.

This book would not have happened without Nicole Novak, my public health colleague, immigration advocacy co-conspirator, and friend. Nicole was incredibly kind and graceful during the writing of this book and all the twists and turns we encountered during the process. She is a brilliant epidemiologist, immigrant advocate, and mother.

Alongside Nicole, I frequently wrote and advocated with sheroes and hero Alana LeBrón, Maria-Elena De Trinidad Young, and Nolan Kline. Their dedication to keeping immigrant communities healthy, happy, and whole is inspiring and ceaseless. They are the academics, advocates, and people I aspire to be.

The meals, church services, coffee, and *baleadas* would not have happened without the support of many people who, just months after a raid, invited us into their lives. You know some of them from the stories here, but there are so many others, Julio, Dalila, Kyle Southern, Kelsey, and Gladys Godinez among them. The research literature calls you "interlocutors." What an awkward word for cool, funny people who put you in touch with other cool, funny people. Thanks.

ACKNOWLEDGMENTS

I love teaching, and nothing surpasses the joy I find when I see the next generation of public health students and know that their work will be more visionary, diligent, and kind than anything our generation ever produced. Nour Eidy, Ronnie Alvarez, Aissa Cabrales, Madeline Simone, Lupe Cervantes, Naomi Marroquín, and Bella Reyes, you are that next generation. Katie Collins, you were a wonderful collaborator on this project; thank you also for the field-note margarita. Juan Gudino, you are going to change the field of public health. But more importantly, you crack me up, hermano. I was sad to see Twitter go because I needed my skim-milk updates.

Thank you to Robin W. Coleman and the team at Johns Hopkins University Press for their support, organization, and steadfast belief in the value of this project.

A portion of this work was developed into graphic art by two incredible artists, Carolina Jones and Dalia Harris, and presented to local schools by Irving Suarez, Hannah Rice, and Darin Stockdill. Thank you for your dedication to the cause and your willingness to brave the unpredictability of high school student questions.

A number of authors supported me in the writing of this book or in the transition from the first to the second. These include Jason De León, Heide Castañeda, Joanna Dreby, Gary Rivlin, Heather Ann Thompson, and Myriam Gurba. Thanks also to Adam Goodman; your book, *The Deportation Machine,* was particularly influential.

Speaking of the period between the first and second book, special thanks to Jean Guerrero and Jacob Soboroff. When I had dinner with you in downtown Los Angeles, it was a mind[trip] to be physically together for the first time despite all that had transpired among us in that period sandwiched between the two Trump administrations. You are dedicated, creative, gracious people, and I'm thankful to have each of you in my life. You make me wish I knew how to surf.

ACKNOWLEDGMENTS

Shout out to our weekly, then daily, Writing Accountability Groups! What started as just a few people writing together once a week grew into a network of dozens of folks meeting up every day to move our projects along in solidarity. It was great to see your grants, applications, books—and families!—grow (I'm in a Zoom room with you right now, Lauren and Craig!). Thanks Michael, Alexis, Lisa, Hillary, Rachel, Lydia, and so many others for staring at your cameras as I stared at mine, and we wrote quietly together.

An army of friends provided me with all types of support while writing, including Liz Mosley, Riana Elyse Anderson, Sara Ableson, Jeff Grim, Richard Nunn, Nick Espitia, Lee Roosevelt, and Aleck Stephens. In addition to emotional support, Raúl Gámez and Carlos Robles-Shanahan were always available to help with translations; thanks.

Thanks to my barber, Uzy K. Nothing beats looking clean for a presentation.

Paul Fleming and Melissa Creary were constant sounding boards for my writing as well as anything else I had going on in life. They each have books of their own in the works, and I look forward to packaging our books and selling them with a photo of that time we *almost* won an Emmy for talking about racism but were beaten out by the sportscasters who were much more fun than we were to have around in bars.

Reporters were critical to the work I did as well as to the change in perceptions of immigrants in 2018, 2019, and beyond. Thank you to Jonathan Blitzer for covering the raid in Bean Station so well, and thank you for your book, which is way too heavy—physically and emotionally—for a beach read. Thanks to Caitlin Dickerson at *The Atlantic* and Monte Reel at *Bloomberg* for your incredible coverage of immigration events. Thanks also to Julia Preston and Dara Lind, whose work I have followed for years.

Thanks yet again to Lin Manuel-Miranda, whose work got me through moments in which I didn't think the book I envisioned

ACKNOWLEDGMENTS

was possible. At times I felt it was unreasonable to weave together the stories of people and communities all over the country. But then I heard "We Don't Talk About Bruno" and thought that if you could weave stories together in two languages with music, dancing, and syncopation, I could surely do it in writing. Thank you for pushing so many boundaries. Adelante.

The data collection for this book and related projects was funded in part by the Prevention Research Center for Rural Health at the University of Iowa College of Public Health, Cooperative Agreement Number 1 U48 DP005021-01, the Institute for Research on Women and Gender at the University of Michigan, and the Documenting Criminalization and Confinement Project at the University of Michigan Humanities Collaboratory.

Thank you to my department, Health Behavior and Health Equity, at the University of Michigan School of Public Health. The place and the people have been a great home for over a decade and have made for a wonderful place to learn and write about health.

Thanks to Glenda and Armando for giving my daughter the best damn quinceañera we could have imagined. This is *my* acknowledgment section, and yes, I want to thank you for something unrelated to the book in it. If you, dear reader, had seen the quince decorations, you would understand.

Let's be honest—behind every writer is a good therapist(s). Thanks to Amy M. and Dr. Kiley for keeping my family and me healthy.

This paragraph is for Oso, our family doggo. No one has spent as many waking (or sleeping) hours next to me while I write than he has. And if we hadn't gone for midday walks, I might have gone a full nine hours without getting up from my chair. You are the bestest boy.

Traveling the country to talk to folks as soon as you can in the aftermath of unpredictable events resulted in sporadic absences from my family. But any challenges this brought were addressed with love and logistical flare. Mom and Dad, Bill and Linda, your

ACKNOWLEDGMENTS

support as parents and parents-in-law is the village that makes the writing possible. Thanks also to my brother Ben, his wife, Celena, and my sister-in-law, Ellen, for being such good aunts and uncles to the kiddos when we needed yet a bigger village.

I want to specifically thank my mom for translating all kinds of things at any hour with no context and no punctuation and my dad for responding to my constant texts of "What kind of car/tank/helicopter is this?" Your love of cars and military history worked out great for me.

Most importantly, I want to thank my wife, Katie, and my children, Mia and Miguel. You are my reason for doing what I do, my reason for believing that, above all else, families deserve to be together.

Notes

Introduction. Documenting Cruelty in the US Heartland

1. Officially, the Midwestern US, often referred to as the "Midwest," is a census region that refers to 12 states in the northern central US: Illinois, Indiana, Iowa, Kansas, Michigan, Minnesota, Missouri, Nebraska, North Dakota, Ohio, South Dakota, and Wisconsin. I also refer to the "heartland" of the US, which does not correspond to an official Census region. No formal consensus on what it includes has been reached, but it can comprise all the states in the Midwest plus those that do not border the Atlantic and Pacific oceans. See also "How Is the Heartland Region Defined?," Heartland Forward, 2021, https://heartlandforward.org/faqs/how-is-the-heartland-region-defined/.
2. US Census Bureau, "RACE," Decennial Census, DEC Redistricting Data, PL 94-171, table P1, 2020, accessed March 5, 2025, https://data.census.gov/table/DECENNIALPL2020.P1?q=salem+ohio.
3. Michael Fix and Wendy Zimmermann, "All Under One Roof: Mixed-Status Families in an Era of Reform, 1," *International Migration Review* 35, no. 2 (2001): 397–419.
4. Suzanne Gamboa, "Americans Way Off on Number of Latinos They Think Are Undocumented, Poll Finds," NBC News, September 30, 2021; Victoria E. Rodriguez, Laura E. Enriquez, Annie Ro, and Cecilia Ayón, "Immigration-Related Discrimination and Mental Health Among Latino Undocumented Students and US Citizen Students with Undocumented Parents: A Mixed-Methods Investigation," *Journal of Health and Social Behavior* 64, no. 4 (2023): 593–609.
5. Lexi Lonas, "Americans Overestimate Number of Undocumented Latinos: Poll," *The Hill*, September 30, 2021, https://thehill.com/latino/574783-americans-overestimate-number-of-undocumented-latinospoll/.

6. Marta Maria Maldonado, "Latino Incorporation and Racialized Border Politics in the Heartland: Interior Enforcement and Policeability in an English-Only State," *American Behavioral Scientist* 58, no. 14 (2014): 1934, 1927–1945.
7. ICE, or Immigration and Customs Enforcement, is the branch of the US Department of Homeland Security responsible for enforcing immigration law in the interior of the US. For a breakdown of the Department of Homeland Security and the department's relationship to immigration law enforcement, see Rachel H. Adler, "'But They Claimed to Be Police, Not La Migra!' The Interaction of Residency Status, Class, and Ethnicity in a (Post–PATRIOT Act) New Jersey Neighborhood," *American Behavioral Scientist* 50, no. 1 (2006): 48–69.
8. See also Sujey Vega, *Latino Heartland: Of Borders and Belonging in the Midwest* (New York University Press, 2015).
9. Parija Kavilanz, "ICE Arrests More than 100 Workers in Raid on Ohio Meat Supplier," CNN, June 19, 2018, https://www.cnn.com/2018/06/19/us/ice-raid-meat-supplier-fresh-mark/index.html.
10. Fresh Mark (website), n.d, www.freshmark.com.
11. Debbie Berkowitz and Patrick Dixon, "An Average of 27 Workers a Day Suffer Amputation or Hospitalization, According to New OSHA Data from 29 States: Meat and Poultry Companies Remain Among the Most Dangerous," Economic Policy Institute, March 30, 2023, https://www.epi.org/blog/an-average-of-27-workers-a-day-suffer-amputation-or-hospitalization-according-to-new-osha-data-from-29-states-meat-and-poultry-companies-remain-among-the-most-dangerous/.
12. William Kandel and Emilio A. Parrado, "Restructuring of the US Meat Processing Industry and New Hispanic Migrant Destinations," *Population and Development Review* 31, no. 3 (2005): 447–471.
13. Maria Sacchetti, "ICE Raids Meatpacking Plant in Rural Tennessee; 97 Immigrants Arrested," *Washington Post*, April 6, 2018, https://www.washingtonpost.com/local/immigration/ice-raids-meatpacking-plant-in-rural-tennessee-more-than-95-immigrants-arrested/2018/04/06/4955a79a-39a6-11e8-8fd2-49fe3c675a89_story.html.
14. Jonathan Blitzer, "An ICE Raid Has Turned the Lives of Hundreds of Tennessee Kids Upside Down," *New Yorker*, April 24, 2018, https://www.newyorker.com/news/dispatch/an-icesmall-raid-has-turned-the-lives-of-hundreds-of-tennessee-kids-upside-down.

15. Trip Gabriel, "An ICE Raid Leaves an Iowa Town Divided Along Faith Lines," *New York Times*, July 3, 2018, https://www.nytimes.com/2018/07/03/us/ice-raid-iowa-churches.html.
16. John Bowden, "Undercover ICE Officers Reportedly Gave out Donuts Before Raid," *The Hill*, June 6, 2018, https://thehill.com/latino/391057-undercover-ice-officers-gave-out-donuts-before-rounding-up-workers-in-raid/.
17. Meagan Flynn, "ICE Raid Targeting Employers and More than 100 Workers Rocks a Small Nebraska Town," *Washington Post*, August 9, 2018, https://www.washingtonpost.com/news/morning-mix/wp/2018/08/09/ice-raid-targeting-employers-and-more-than-100-workers-rocks-a-small-nebraska-town/; "ICE vs. Nebraska Nice: An Account of the Immigration Enforcement Raid in O'Neill," ACLU Nebraska, August 15, 2018, https://www.aclunebraska.org/en/news/ice-vs-nebraska-nice-account-immigration-enforcement-raid-oneill-1.
18. Kathryn Lundstrom, "ICE Arrests More than 100 Workers at North Texas Plant," *Texas Tribune*, August 28, 2018, https://www.texastribune.org/2018/08/28/ice-arrests-more-100-workers-north-texas-plant/.
19. "Worksite Immigration Raids Terrorize Workers and Communities Now, and Their Devastating Consequences Are Long-Term," National Immigration Law Center, April 11, 2019, https://www.nilc.org/articles/worksite-immigration-raids-terrorize-workers-and-communities-now-and-their-devastating-consequences-are-long-term/.
20. "ICE Arrests 284 Workers in Allen in Largest Workplace Immigration Raid in a Decade," KERA News, April 3, 2019, https://www.keranews.org/news/2019-04-03/ice-arrests-284-workers-in-allen-in-largest-workplace-immigration-raid-in-a-decade.
21. Dianne Gallagher, Catherine E. Shoichet, and Madeline Holcombe, "680 Undocumented Workers Were Arrested in Record-Setting Immigration Sweep on the First day of School," CNN, August 8, 2019, https://www.cnn.com/2019/08/08/us/mississippi-immigration-raids-children/index.html.
22. "ICE Executes Federal Criminal Search Warrants at Fresh Mark, 146 Arrested on Immigration Violations," ICE.gov, October 16, 2018, https://www.ice.gov/news/releases/ice-executes-federal-criminal-search-warrants-fresh-mark-146-arrested-immigration.

23. "Care of Children a Priority After Fresh Mark Immigration Raid in Salem," *Intelligencer*, June 23, 2018, https://www.theintelligencer.net/news/top-headlines/2018/06/care-of-children-a-priority-after-fresh-mark-immigration-raid-in-salem/.
24. For more on the relationship between police and immigrant communities, see Noland Kline, *Pathogenic Policing: Immigration Enforcement and Health in the US South* (Rutgers University Press, 2019).
25. Erin Blakemore, "The Largest Mass Deportation in American History," *History*, September 1, 2018, https://www.history.com/news/operation-wetback-eisenhower-1954-deportation.
26. Heide Castañeda, Seth M. Holmes, Daniel S. Madrigal, Maria-Elena D. Young, Naomi Beyeler, and James Quesada, "Immigration as a Social Determinant of Health," *Annual Review of Public Health*, 36, no. 1 (2015): 375–392.
27. Andrés Reséndez, "National Identity on a Shifting Border: Texas and New Mexico in the Age of Transition, 1821–1848," *Journal of American History* 86, no. 2 (1999): 668–688.
28. Becky Little, "Why Mexican Americans Say 'The Border Crossed Us,'" *History*, October 17, 2018, https://www.history.com/news/texas-mexico-border-history-laws.
29. Adam Goodman, *The Deportation Machine: America's Long History of Expelling Immigrants* (Princeton University Press, 2020).
30. David Cortez, "Latinxs in La Migra: Why They Join and Why it Matters," *Political Research Quarterly* 74, no. 3 (2021): 688–702.
31. Jessica Haynes, "Ann Arbor Restaurant Says ICE Agents Ate Breakfast, Then Detained 3 Workers," Mlive, May 24, 2017, https://www.mlive.com/business/ann-arbor/2017/05/ann_arbor_business_owner_says.html.
32. William D. Lopez, Kerry Martin, Laura Sonday, Alexander M. Stephens, Anna C. Lemler, Maria Ibarra-Frayre et al, "Team-Based Urgent Response: A Model for Community Advocacy in an Era of Increased Immigration Law Enforcement." *Journal of Community Practice* 28, no. 1 (2020): 56–65.
33. William D. Lopez, *Separated: Family and Community in the Aftermath of an Immigration Raid* (Johns Hopkins University Press, 2019).
34. Laura Sanders, Ramiro Martinez, Margaret Harner, Melanie Harner, Pilar Horner, and Jorge Delva, "Grassroots Responsiveness to Human

Rights Abuse: History of the Washtenaw Interfaith Coalition for Immigrant Rights," *Social Work* 58, no. 2 (2013): 117–125.

35. Alana M. W. Lebrón, Ivy R. Torres, Nolan Kline, William D. Lopez, Maria-Elena de Trinidad Young, and Nicole Novak, "Immigration and Immigrant Policies, Health, and Health Equity in the United States." *The Milbank Quarterly* 101, supplement 1 (2023): 119–152.

36. US Census Bureau, "RACE," Decennial Census, DEC Redistricting Data, PL 94-171, table P1, 2020, accessed March 5, 2025, https://data.census.gov/table/DECENNIALPL2020.P1?g=010XX00US.

37. Nicole L. Novak, Arline T. Geronimus, and Aresha M. Martinez-Cardoso, "Change in Birth Outcomes Among Infants Born to Latina Mothers After a Major Immigration Raid," *International Journal of Epidemiology* 46, no. 3 (2017): 839–849.

38. For more insight on the methods we used, see also William D. Lopez, Juan Gudino, Tamara Shull, Gladys Godinez, and Nicole L. Novak, "Large-Scale Immigration Worksite Raids: Community Disaster, Community Response," *Journal of Community Practice* 32, no. 1 (2024): 86–106; William D. Lopez, Nicole L. Novak, Nourel-Hoda Eidy, Tamera L. Shull, and Angela Stuesse, "Challenges to Addressing Mental Health Repercussions of Large-Scale Immigration Worksite Raids in the Rural United States," *Journal of Rural Mental Health* 47, no. 1 (2023): 59.

39. Kristin Elizabeth Yarris and Whitney L. Duncan, eds., *Accompaniment with Im/migrant Communities: Engaged Ethnography* (University of Arizona Press, 2024).

40. The Institutional Review Boards of the Universities of Michigan and Iowa (HUM00146458) and Iowa (201811206) approved this study. Interviewees were aged 18 years and older and provided material, emotional, or professional support following the six large-scale worksite raids that occurred in 2018 as identified in the study. We did not limit participation based on race/ethnicity, gender, immigration status, or personal involvement in each raid. Thus, while some interviewees provided support on the day of the raid, others may have been involved at a later time. Similarly, some individuals were detained themselves, while others, for example, supported the children of detained parents or may not have had a personal connection to a noncitizen in the community. For more about our sampling, data collection, and coding

strategies, see William D. Lopez, Katherine M. Collins, Guadalupe R. Cervantes, Dalila Reynosa, Julio C. Salazar, and Nicole L. Novak, "Large-Scale Immigration Worksite Raids and Mixed-Status Families: Separation, Financial Crisis, and Family Role Rearrangement," *Family & Community Health* 45, no. 2 (2022): 59–66.

41. Jeffrey S. Passel and Jens Manuel Krogstad, "What We Know About Unauthorized Immigrants Living in the U.S.," Pew Research Center, July 22, 2024, https://www.pewresearch.org/short-reads/2024/07/22/what-we-know-about-unauthorized-immigrants-living-in-the-us/.

42. Alexis R. Miranda, Amaya Perez-Brumer, and Brittany M. Charlton, "Latino? Latinx? Latine? A Call for Inclusive Categories in Epidemiologic Research," *American Journal of Epidemiology* 192, no. 12 (2023): 1929–1932.

1. Raid a Factory, Tell a Story

1. Tanya Maria Golash-Boza, *Immigration Nation: Raids, Detentions, and Deportations in Post-9/11 America* (Routledge, 2015).

2. Adam Goodman, *The Deportation Machine: America's Long History of Expelling Immigrants* (Princeton University Press, 2020); Wendy Cervantes, Rebecca Ullrich, and Vanessa Meraz, "The Day That ICE Came: How Worksite Raids Are Once Again Harming Children and Families," Center for Law and Social Policy, July 2020, https://www.clasp.org/publications/report/brief/day-ice-camehow-worksite-raids-are-once-again-harming-children-and (2020).

3. Julia Preston, "U.S. Raids 6 Meat Plants in ID Case," *New York Times*, December 13, 2006, https://www.nytimes.com/2006/12/13/us/13raid.html; Mike McPhee, "Largest Workplace Raid Ever," *Denver Post*, December 13, 2006, https://www.denverpost.com/2006/12/13/largest-workplace-raid-ever/.

4. Susan Saulny, "Hundreds Are Arrested in U.S. Sweep of Meat Plant," *New York Times*, May 13, 2008, https://www.nytimes.com/2008/05/13/us/13immig.html.

5. Zolan Kanno-Youngs, Maggie Haberman, Michael D. Shear, and Eric Schmitt, "Kirstjen Nielsen Resigns as Trump's Homeland Security Secretary," *New York Times*, April 7, 2019, sec. US, https://www.nytimes.com/2019/04/07/us/politics/kirstjen-nielsen-dhs-resigns.html.

6. Sarah Pierce, "The Obama Record on Deportations: Deporter in Chief or Not?," Migration Policy Institute, March 22, 2017, https://www.migrationpolicy.org/article/obama-record-deportations-deporter-chief-or-not.
7. Priscilla Alvarez, "Biden Administration Ends Mass Worksite Immigration Raids," CNN, October 12, 2021, https://www.cnn.com/2021/10/12/politics/ice-workplace-raids/index.html.
8. Marc Cooper, "Lockdown in Greeley," *Nation*, February 15, 2007, https://www.thenation.com/article/archive/lockdown-greeley/.
9. Matthew D. LaPlante, "Swift Justice," *Salt Lake City Weekly*, December 7, 2011, https://www.cityweekly.net/utah/swift-justice/Content?oid=2159187.
10. Rebecca Boyle, "ICE Raids Swift Plant," *Greeley Tribune*, December 12, 2006, https://www.greeleytribune.com/2006/12/12/ice-raids-swift-plant/.
11. Christina Fernández-Morrow, "Postville Raid Brought Devastation; 15 Years Later, It's a Sign of Resilience," *Iowa Capital Dispatch*, May 12, 2023, https://iowacapitaldispatch.com/2023/05/12/postville-raid-brought-devastation-15-years-later-its-a-sign-of-resilience/.
12. Spencer S. Hsu, "Immigration Raid Jars a Small Town," *Washington Post*, May 18, 2008, https://www.washingtonpost.com/wp-dyn/content/article/2008/05/17/AR2008051702474_2.html.
13. See Mark Grey, Michele Devlin, and Aaron Goldsmith, *Postville U.S.A: Surviving Diversity in Small-Town America* (GemmaMedia, 2009), for an in-depth description of the raid.
14. Julia Preston, "270 Illegal Immigrants Sent to Prison in Federal Push," *New York Times*, May 24, 2008, https://www.nytimes.com/2008/05/24/us/24immig.html.
15. "Immigration Raids: Postville and Beyond," American Civil Liberties Union, July 31, 2008, https://www.aclu.org/documents/immigration-raids-postville-and-beyond.
16. Erik Camayd-Freixas, "Interpreting After the Largest Ice Raid in US History: A Personal Account," *Latino Studies* 7, no. 1 (2009): 123–139, https://doi.org/10.1057/lst.2008.54.
17. "Identity Theft Penalty Enhancement Act," Public Law 108–275, 18 U.S.C. §1028A.
18. "President Bush Signs Identity Theft Penalty Enhancement Act," George W. Bush White House Archives, July 2004, https://

georgewbush-whitehouse.archives.gov/news/releases/2004/07/20040715-3.html.
19. George W. Bush, "Remarks by the President at Signing of Identity Theft Penalty Enhancement Act," White House Press Release, July 15, 2004, https://georgewbush-whitehouse.archives.gov/news/releases/2004/07/text/20040715-2.html.
20. Nils de Jesús Hernandez, "Ten Years After Postville Immigration Raid, a Priest Calls for Solidarity," *Des Moines Register*, May 10, 2018, https://www.desmoinesregister.com/story/opinion/columnists/iowa-view/2018/05/10/priest-remember-postville-ice-raid-Immigrants-Solidarity-Deportation/596622002/.
21. *Immigration Raids: Postville and Beyond*, Subcommittee on Immigration, Citizenship, Refugees, Border Security, and International Law, 110th Congress, July 24, 2008, https://www.govinfo.gov/content/pkg/CHRG-110hhrg43682/html/CHRG-110hhrg43682.htm.
22. Adam Gabbatt, "Golden Escalator Ride: The Surreal Day Trump Kicked Off His Bid for President," *Guardian*, June 14, 2019, https://www.theguardian.com/us-news/2019/jun/13/donald-trump-presidential-campaign-speech-eyewitness-memories.
23. *Time* staff, "Here's Donald Trump's Presidential Announcement Speech," *Time* magazine, June 16, 2015, https://time.com/3923128/donald-trump-announcement-speech/.
24. A. Gabbatt, "Golden Escalator Ride."
25. Nate Cohn, "Why Trump Won: Working-Class Whites," *New York Times*, November 9, 2016, https://www.nytimes.com/2016/11/10/upshot/why-trump-won-working-class-whites.html.
26. Jim Tankersley, "How Trump Won: The Revenge of Working-Class Whites," *Washington Post*, November 9, 2016, https://www.washingtonpost.com/news/wonk/wp/2016/11/09/how-trump-won-the-revenge-of-working-class-whites/.
27. Diana C. Mutz, "Status Threat, Not Economic Hardship, Explains the 2016 Presidential Vote," *Proceedings of the National Academy of Sciences* 115, no. 19 (2018): E4330–E4339.
28. Adam Serwer, *The Cruelty Is the Point: The Past, Present, and Future of Trump's America*, 1st ed. (One World, 2021).
29. Adam Serwer, "The Cruelty Is the Point," *Atlantic*, October 3, 2018, https://www.theatlantic.com/ideas/archive/2018/10/the-cruelty-is-the-point/572104/.

30. Maya Goodfellow, *Hostile Environment: How Immigrants Became Scapegoats* (Verso Books, 2020).
31. Donald Trump, "Transcript of Donald Trump's Immigration Speech, *New York Times*, September 1, 2016, https://www.nytimes.com/2016/09/02/us/politics/transcript-trump-immigration-speech.html.
32. "Transcript: Donald Trump's Full Immigration Speech, Annotated," *Los Angeles Times*, September 2016, www.latimes.com/politics/la-na-pol-donald-trump-immigration-speech-transcript-20160831-snap-htmlstory.html.
33. "Presidential Candidate Donald Trump Remarks on Immigration Policy," C-SPAN, September 2016, accessed March 1, 2025, www.c-span.org/program/campaign-2016/presidential-candidate-donald-trump-remarks-on-immigration-policy/453078; Tara Golshan, "Donald Trump Introduced Us to 'Angel Moms.' Here's Why They Matter," *Vox*, September 2016, https://www.vox.com/2016/9/1/12751434/donald-trump-angel-moms-explained.

2. Choreographed Chaos

1. I lived in Houston and was working at a homeless services center while obtaining my master of public health when Hurricane Katrina hit. It was an experience that was formative to my public health worldview, and I have taught about our public health response to Katrina to hundreds of students. Sarah's analogy was one I found quite personally impactful, as it helped me to understand both the scale of the disaster of a raid and the racial tensions that are formative—yet often invisible to the general public—involved in a response.
2. Zoe Carpenter, "What Happens When ICE Shows Up?," *Rolling Stone*, December 17, 2018, https://www.rollingstone.com/politics/politics-features/ice-raid-tennessee-769293/.
3. "IRS, I.C.E. Officials Raid Grainger County Meat Packing Plant," *Citizen Tribune*, April 6, 2018, https://www.citizentribune.com/newsnow/irs-i-c-e-officials-raid-grainger-county-meat-packing-plant/article_1ec55d96-39be-11e8-9d40-db8d656f86da.html.
4. John North, "Records: Grainger Plant Septic Failure Caused Contamination Scare in March," WBIR, April 6, 2018, https://www.wbir.com/article/news/local/records-grainger-plant-septic-failure-caused-contamination-scare-in-march/51-536016536.

5. Travis Dorman and Jamie Satterfield, "ICE Raids Grainger County Meatpacking Plant amid Charges Owners Avoided $2.5M in Payroll Taxes," *Knoxville News Sentinel*, April 5, 2018, https://web.archive.org/web/20180408010250/https://www.knoxnews.com/story/news/crime/2018/04/05/ice-raids-meatpacking-plant-grainger-county/490673002/.
6. Liz Kellar, "Case Involving Workers Arrested at Tennessee Slaughterhouse ICE Raid Ends with Payout," *Knoxville News Sentinel*, February 28, 2023, https://www.knoxnews.com/story/news/local/2023/02/28/workers-arrested-at-tennessee-slaughterhouse-ice-raid-receive-settlement/69949336007/.
7. While ICE never releases an official count of how many children have a parent detained, Larry's estimate—about one to two kids per person detained—was probably right, if not a little low, based on the fact that Hispanic mothers have an average of 2.6 children by the time they are 44. See "Family Size Among Mothers: Pew Research Center's Social and Demographic Trends Project," Pew Research Center, May 7, 2015, https://www.pewresearch.org/social-trends/2015/05/07/family-size-among-mothers/.
8. Black shirts or vests and khaki pants are a typical uniform for ICE agents in the field.
9. "Southeastern Provision Owner James Brantley Pleads Guilty to Federal Information," Justice.gov, September 12, 2018, https://www.justice.gov/usao-edtn/pr/southeastern-provision-owner-james-brantley-pleads-guilty-federal-information.
10. Robert Moore, "Southeastern Provision Owner Sentenced to 18 Months," *Citizen Tribune*, August 2019, https://www.citizentribune.com/news/local/southeastern-provision-owner-sentenced-to-months/article_b35cf000-b3c4-11e9-8be5-f72523389472.html.
11. Olivia Exstrum, "New Lawsuit Details Allegations of Violence, Illegal Searches During ICE Raid," *Mother Jones*, February 21, 2019, https://www.motherjones.com/politics/2019/02/lawsuit-immigration-workplace-raid-tennessee/.
12. Kristen Gallant, "Court Approves Settlement of Civil Rights Lawsuit Challenging 2018 ICE Raid," WATE 6 on Your Side, February 28, 2023, https://www.wate.com/news/tennessee/settlement-reached-in-2018-bean-station-ice-raid-lawsuit/.

13. "AbUSed: The Postville Raid," IMDb, February 4, 2011, https://www.imdb.com/title/tt1737082/.
14. "History of AirCare," University of Iowa Health Care, 2025, https://uihc.org/history-aircare.
15. Julia Preston, "U.S. Raids 6 Meat Plants in ID Case," *New York Times*, December 13, 2006, https://www.nytimes.com/2006/12/13/us/13raid.html.
16. The National Council of La Raza (NCLR), the largest national Hispanic civil rights and advocacy organization in the US, works to improve opportunities for Hispanic Americans. See NCLR, *Paying the Price: The Impact of Immigration Raids on America's Children*, 2007, https://www.urban.org/sites/default/files/publication/46811/411566-Paying-the-Price-The-Impact-of-Immigration-Raids-on-America-s-Children.PDF.
17. Liz Steward and Gladys Godinez, "Recalling the O'Neill Raid, One Year Later," Center for Rural Affairs, August 20, 2019, https://www.cfra.org/blog/recalling-oneill-raid-one-year-later.
18. Most states and localities possess a mix of inclusive and exclusive policies. See Maria-Elena de Trinidad Young and Steven P. Wallace, "Included, but Deportable: a New Public Health Approach to Policies That Criminalize and Integrate Immigrants," *American Journal of Public Health* 109, no. 9 (2019):1171–1176.
19. US Census Bureau, "ACS Demographic and Housing Estimates," American Community Survey, ACS 5-Year Estimates Data Profiles, table DP05, 2019, accessed March 5, 2025, https://data.census.gov/table/ACSDP5Y2019.DP05?q=paris+texas.
20. The issue also shows how faulty our notion of race is. Neither "Latino" nor "Muslim" are categorized as "race," but experience tells us—and the data show, when they exist—that Latinos and Muslims are pulled over at rates higher than their white peers.
21. N'dea Yancey-Bragg, "Tyre Nichols' Death Is the Latest Example of a Minor Traffic Stop Turning Deadly, Experts Say," *USA Today*, February 7, 2023, https://www.usatoday.com/story/news/nation/2023/02/05/tyre-nichols-experts-say-routine-traffic-stops-can-turn-deadly/11154961002/; Bethany Brunelle-Raja, "One Year Later: A Look at the Antonio Valenzuela Homicide and What's Happened Since," *Las Cruces Sun-News*, March 1, 2021, https://www.lcsun

-news.com/story/news/2021/03/01/timeline-antonio-valenzuela-homicide-christopher-smelser-las-cruces-police/4561813001/.
22. Emma Pierson, Camelia Simoiu, Jan Overgoor, Sam Corbett-Davies, Daniel Jenson, Amy Shoemaker, et al., "A Large-Scale Analysis of Racial Disparities in Police Stops Across the United States," *Nature Human Behaviour* 4, no. 7 (2020): 736–745.
23. David A. Harris, "Racial Profiling: Past, Present, and Future?," American Bar Association, 2020, https://www.americanbar.org/groups/criminal_justice/resources/magazine/archive/racial-profiling-past-present-future/.
24. Jesse Barber, "Black, Latinx People Were 90 percent of Those Arrested in NYPD Traffic Stops," New York Civil Liberties Union, March 23, 2023, https://www.nyclu.org/commentary/black-latinx-people-were-90-percent-those-arrested-nypd-traffic-stops.
25. H. Cherone, "New Illinois Guidelines Aim to Boost College and Career Readiness," WTTW News, 2017, https://doi.org/1002587/c2n_sitewide_300x250_3.
26. "Equality Before the Stop: Analyzing Racial Bias in Traffic Stops and Identifying Solutions to End Racial Profiling," American Civil Liberties Union Nebraska, August 2019, https://www.aclunebraska.org/sites/default/files/field_documents/aclu_of_ne_equality_before_the_stop.pdf.
27. Luis Noe-Bustamante, Ana Gonzalez-Barrera, Khadijah Edwards, Lauren Mora, and Mark Hugo, "Half of U.S Latinos Experienced Some Form of Discrimination During the First Year of the Pandemic," Pew Research Center, November 4, 2021, https://www.pewresearch.org/race-and-ethnicity/2021/11/04/half-of-u-s-latinos-experienced-some-form-of-discrimination-during-the-first-year-of-the-pandemic/.
28. "'If Everybody's White, There Can't Be Any Racial Bias': The Disappearance of Hispanic Drivers from Traffic Records," *ProPublica*, November 23, 2021, https://www.propublica.org/article/if-everybodys-white-there-cant-be-any-racial-bias-the-disappearance-of-hispanic-drivers-from-traffic-records.
29. Emma Pierson, Camelia Simoiu, Jan Overgoor, Sam Corbett-Davies, Daniel Jenson, Amy Shoemaker, et al., "A Large-Scale Analysis of Racial Disparities in Police Stops Across the United States," *Nature Human Behaviour* 4, no. 7 (2020): 736–745.

30. Pierson et al., "Large-Scale Analysis of Racial Disparities in Police Stops."
31. Robert Courtney Smith, Andrés Besserer Rayas, Daisy Flores, Angelo Cabrera, Guillermo Yrizar Barbosa, Karina Weinstein, et al., "Disrupting the Traffic Stop–to-Deportation Pipeline: The New York State Greenlight Law's Intent and Implementation," *Journal on Migration and Human Security* 9, no. 2 (2021): 94–110, https://doi.org/10.1177/23315024211013752.
32. "ICE Executes Federal Criminal Search Warrants in North Texas," Ice.gov, February 25, 2025, https://www.ice.gov/news/releases/ice-executes-federal-criminal-search-warrants-north-texas.
33. "ICE Arrests More than 100 Workers at North Texas Plant," KERA News, August 28, 2018, https://www.keranews.org/news/2018-08-28/ice-arrests-more-than-100-workers-at-north-texas-plant.
34. Rachel H. Adler, "'But They Claimed to Be Police, Not La Migra!': The Interaction of Residency Status, Class, and Ethnicity in a (Post–PATRIOT Act) New Jersey Neighborhood," *American Behavioral Scientist* 50, no. 1 (2006): 48–69.
35. Bess Chiu, Lynly Egyes, Peter L. Markowitz, and Jaya Vasandani, "Constitution on ICE: A Report on Immigration Home Raid Operations," Cardozo Immigration Justice Clinic, 2009.
36. "ICE Administrative Removal Warrants (MP3)," Federal Law Enforcement Training Centers, 2024, https://www.fletc.gov/ice-administrative-removal-warrants-mp3.
37. "ICE Ruses—Immigrant Defense Project," n.d., https://www.immigrantdefenseproject.org/ice-ruses/; see also Min K. Kam, "ICE Ruses," *Columbia Law Review* 122, no. 1 (2022): 125–172.
38. Kam, "ICE Ruses," 125–172.
39. Pastor Isaac states that the "boss of the sheriff" was there. Some of this is lost in translation, but it also reflects Pastor Isaac's general lack of clarity about which law enforcement departments are which, what each does, and who leads each, a lack of clarity shared with most of the public. When he says the "boss of the sheriff," I'm confident he means "the boss of the sheriff's department," which is the sheriff.
40. "Rumors, Lies and Threats: The Aftermath of an ICE Raid," MyParisTexas, August 31, 2018, https://myparistexas.com/rumors-lies-and-threats-the-aftermath-of-an-ice-raid/.

3. Para Uno Que Tiene Familia, Es Más Difícil

1. "Home—Midwest Precast Concrete," Midwest Precast Concrete, January 18, 2023. https://mpcent.com/.
2. I used the word *pistola*, which is sometimes used to mean a firearm generally. *Pistola* is also the word for the English cognate "pistol," or a small firearm that you can use with one hand. While I used *pistola* to mean any firearm, Elisio interpreted it to mean "handgun," which is why he confirmed my question that ICE did have *pistolas* but carried rifles as well.
3. Lisseth Rojas-Flores, Mari L. Clements, J. Hwang Koo, and Judy London, "Trauma and Psychological Distress in Latino Citizen Children Following Parental Detention and Deportation," *Psychological Trauma: Theory, Research, Practice, and Policy* 9, no. 3 (2017): 352.
4. Brian Allen, Erica M. Cisneros, and Alexandra Tellez, "The Children Left Behind: The Impact of Parental Deportation on Mental Health," *Journal of Child and Family Studies* 24 (2015): 386–392.
5. Children of incarcerated US citizens fare similarly. See Rosalyn D. Lee, Xiangming Fang, and Feijun Luo, "The Impact of Parental Incarceration on the Physical and Mental Health of Young Adults," *Pediatrics* 131, no. 4 (2013): e1188–e1195.
6. J. Tellez Lieberman, L. Bakely, C. Correa, C. Valdez, A. Asadi Gonzalez, J. E. Gonzalez-Fagoaga, et al., "They Just Took Him: Impacts of Immigration Enforcement on US Citizen Latino Adolescents' Well-Being," *European Journal of Public Health* 30, no. S5 (2020): ckaa166–759; Katrina Brabeck and Qingwen Xu, "The Impact of Detention and Deportation on Latino Immigrant Children and Families: A Quantitative Exploration," *Hispanic Journal of Behavioral Sciences* 32, no. 3 (2010): 341–361; Lauren E. Gulbas, L. H. Zayas, Hyunwoo Yoon, Hannah Szlyk, Sergio Aguilar-Gaxiola, and G. Natera, "Deportation Experiences and Depression Among US Citizen-Children with Undocumented Mexican Parents," *Child: Care, Health and Development* 42, no. 2 (2016): 220–230.
7. Joanna Dreby, Florencia Silveira, and Eunju Lee, "The Anatomy of Immigration Enforcement: Long-Standing Socio-Emotional Impacts on Children as They Age into Adulthood," *Journal of Marriage and Family* 84, no. 3 (2022): 713–733.
8. As a researcher, I know how critical any research that can help us diagnose and identify levels of trauma can be. As a parent of children

aged 11 and 15 (that is, one child in the most vulnerable stage and one just past it) at the time of this writing, it feels like differentiating shades of death. A parent can only be as happy as their most despondent child.
9. The direct translation is "It was desolation." But the English word "desolation" implies a scene of destruction, which I did not take to be Juana's intention. The English phrase "The place was desolate" is closer to what I believe Juana was relaying to me: emptiness, loneliness, bleakness, or an absence of anyone or anything at all.
10. Juana's description here again emphasizes the relational aspect of what she sees. It's not simply the absence of activity; it's the loneliness, the emptiness, the fracturing of people and relationships. In this case, *soledad* best translates into loneliness, solitude, or isolation.
11. In the exchange I used the word "gringos" to describe the white workers. "Gringo" is a common Spanish or Spanglish term used for people who are white. While it may be considered derogatory in some settings, among Latinos it's generally used jokingly to emphasize a racial difference or a behavior seen as particularly white or non-Latino. In this case, I probably should have stuck with the more formal *personas blancas* but was carried away by the intensity of the exchange such that I didn't monitor which type of Spanish I was using.
12. Over a quarter of families in which one parent is undocumented have a second undocumented parent as well. See "Profile of the Unauthorized Population: United States," Migration Policy Institute, 2019, https://www.migrationpolicy.org/data/unauthorized-immigrant-population/state/US.
13. Joanna Dreby, *Everyday Illegal: When Policies Undermine Immigrant Families* (University of California Press, 2015.
14. The raid of Midwest Precast Concrete occurred on May 9, 2018. I spoke with Juana on February 3, 2019, 260 days later. Juana stated that the fathers had been detained for 8 months, or about 240 days. I imagine Juana was simply not counting the month of February in her total. Either way, her point was the same, even if the number of days we believed the men to be detained differed by about a month: These fathers were gone for a long, long time, and the women they left behind were overwhelmed because of their absence.
15. Immigrants' Rights Clinic at the Stanford Law School and Immigration Law Clinic at the UC Davis School of Law, "Following the Money: New Information About the Federal Government's Billion Dollar

Immigration Detention and Bond Operations," Stanford Law School, May 9, 2019, https://law.stanford.edu/publications/following-the-money-new-information-about-the-federal-governments-billion-dollar-immigration-detention-and-bond-operations/.

16. ICE manages to make a small fortune off bonds that are paid but never returned to the families who paid them. A *Washington Post* article found that more than 18,000 bond payments were unclaimed in a four-year period, leaving ICE with $204 million of unreturned money. See Meagan Flynn, "ICE Holds Millions in Bond Money Owed to Immigrants," *Washington Post*, April 29, 2019, https://www.proquest.com/newspapers/ice-holds-millions-bond-money-owed-immigrants/docview/2216006178/se-2.

17. Jessica Merritt, "The Average Savings Account Balance," *US News & World Report*, February 15, 2024, https://www.usnews.com/banking/articles/the-average-savings-account-balance.

18. Of course, there are details and exceptions to the path I lay out here, but the point remains. Family decisions around deportation involve impossible choices with extreme repercussions, the weight of which often rests upon the shoulders of immigrant mothers.

19. For more on guilt and immigration status, see Leisy J. Abrego, "Relational Legal Consciousness of U.S. Citizenship: Privilege, Responsibility, Guilt, and Love in Latino Mixed-Status Families," *Law & Society Review* 53, no. 3 (2019): 641–670, https://doi.org/10.1111/lasr.12414; Tara Fiorito, "Learning to Be Legal: Transition Narratives of Joy and Survivor Guilt of Previously Undocumented 1.5-Generation Latinx Immigrants in the United States," *Citizenship Studies* 25, no. 8 (2021): 1096–1111.

20. Tanya Golash-Boza, "Punishment Beyond the Deportee: The Collateral Consequences of Deportation," *American Behavioral Scientist* 63, no. 9 (2019): 1343, 1331–1349.

21. "Attorney General Jeff Sessions: 'If You Are Smuggling a Child, We Will Prosecute You,'" NBC News, YouTube video, May 7, 2018, https://www.youtube.com/watch?v=MCSeeAB7g3A; "Attorney General Sessions Delivers Remarks Discussing the Immigration Enforcement Actions of the Trump Administration," Justice.gov, May 7, 2018, https://www.justice.gov/archives/opa/speech/attorney-general-sessions-delivers-remarks-discussing-immigration-enforcement-actions.

22. "Prosecuting Migrants for Coming to the United States," American Immigration Council, December 28, 2018, https://www.americanimmigrationcouncil.org/research/immigration-prosecutions.
23. Most researchers and advocates would argue that detention is intended to be disciplinary, and the threat of detention and its terrible conditions—alongside time away from family—is a tool of social control.
24. Ginger Thomas, "Listen to Children Who've Just Been Separated from Their Parents at the Border," *ProPublica*, June 18, 2018, https://www.propublica.org/article/children-separated-from-parents-border-patrol-cbp-trump-immigration-policy.
25. Madison Park and Kyle Almond, "This 2-Year-Old Has Become the Face Of 'Zero Tolerance,'" CNN, June 2018, https://www.cnn.com/interactive/2018/06/us/crying-girl-john-moore-immigration-cnnphotos/.
26. Sorboroff would go on to film a documentary version of *Separated*, directed by Errol Morris.
27. Elizabeth Egan, "Jacob Soboroff Saw Kids in Cages. Then He Started Talking—and Writing," *New York Times*, July 23, 2020, https://www.nytimes.com/2020/07/23/books/review/separated-jacob-soboroff.html.
28. Laura Bush, "Laura Bush: Separating Children from Their Parents at the Border 'Breaks My Heart,'" *Washington Post*, June 17, 2018, https://www.washingtonpost.com/opinions/laura-bush-separating-children-from-their-parents-at-the-border-breaks-my-heart/2018/06/17/f2df517a-7287-11e8-9780-b1dd6a09b549_story.html.
29. "Celebs Read Mother's Account of Child Separation," CNN, July 11, 2018, https://www.cnn.com/videos/entertainment/2018/07/11/maggie-gyllenhaal-aclu-celebrities-read-mirian-letter-vstan-vpx.cnn.
30. *Politico* staff, "Biggest U.S. Doctors Group Condemns Family Separation Policy," *Politico*, June 20, 2018, https://www.politico.com/story/2018/06/20/american-medical-association-family-separation-policy-655677.
31. "APHA Opposes Separation of Immigrant and Refugee Children and Families at U.S. Borders," American Public Health Association, January 29, 2019, https://www.apha.org/policies-and-advocacy/public-health-policy-statements/policy-database/2019/01/29/separation-of-immigrant-and-refugee-children-and-families.

32. Caitlin Dickerson, "An American Catastrophe," *Atlantic*, August 7, 2022, https://www.theatlantic.com/magazine/archive/2022/09/trump-administration-family-separation-policy-immigration/670604/.
33. Madeline Halpert, "'Like a Kidnapping': Migrant Family Separated Under Trump Reunited After Four Years," BBC News, May 8, 2023, https://www.bbc.com/news/world-us-canada-64959802.
34. Geoff Bennett, Saher Khan, and Kyle Midura, "Hundreds of Migrant Children Remain Separated from Families Despite Push to Reunite Them," *PBS NewsHour*, February 6, 2023, https://www.pbs.org/newshour/show/hundreds-of-migrant-children-remain-separated-from-families-despite-push-to-reunite-them.

4. The Multiplication of Loaves and Fishes

1. US Census Bureau, "ACS Demographic and Housing Estimates," American Community Survey, ACS 5-Year Estimates Data Profiles, table DP05, 2019, accessed March 5, 2025, https://data.census.gov/table/ACSDP5Y2019.DP05?q=Sumner+CCD,+Lamar+County,+Texas.
2. Trip Gabriel, "An ICE Raid Leaves an Iowa Town Divided Along Faith Lines," *New York Times*, July 3, 2018, https://www.nytimes.com/2018/07/03/us/ice-raid-iowa-churches.html.
3. Sarah Burr, "Why Are Children Representing Themselves in Immigration Court?," *The Hill*, October 24, 2021, https://thehill.com/opinion/judiciary/578076-why-are-children-representing-themselves-in-immigration-court/.
4. Erica Bryant, "Immigrants Facing Deportation Do Not Have the Right to a Publicly . . . ," Vera Institute of Justice, February 9, 2021, www.vera.org/news/immigrants-facing-deportation-do-not-have-the-right-to-a-publicly-funded-attorney-heres-how-to-change-that.
5. Ingrid Eagly and Steven Shafer, "Access to Counsel in Immigration Court," American Immigration Council, September 27, 2016, www.americanimmigrationcouncil.org/research/access-counsel-immigration-court.
6. Vera Eidelman, "We Sued for Records About Trump's Muslim Bans. Here's What We Found Out," American Civil Liberties Union, October 24, 2017, www.aclu.org/news/immigrants-rights/we-sued-records-about-trumps-muslim-bans-heres.
7. Evan Perez, Pamela Brown, and Kevin Liptak, "Inside the Confusion of the Trump Executive Order and Travel Ban," CNN, January 29,

2017, www.cnn.com/2017/01/28/politics/donald-trump-travel-ban/index.html.
8. C. Scudder, Eline de Bruijn, and C. Jaramillo, "Prayers and Protests as Dallas Faithful React to Trump's Immigration Orders," *Dallas Morning News*, January 29, 2017, https://www.dallasnews.com/news/faith/2017/01/29/prayers-and-protests-as-dallas-faithful-react-to-trump-s-immigration-orders/.
9. Nahal Toosi, "Protesters and Lawyers Scramble in Response to Trump Refugee Order," *Politico*, January 28, 2017, www.politico.com/story/2017/01/airport-protests-lawyers-trump-immigration-order-234317.
10. "Darweesh v. Trump," American Civil Liberties Union, www.aclu.org/cases/darweesh-v-trump.
11. Kristin Garrity and Emily Crnkovich, "From Bigotry to Ban: The Ideological Origins and Devastating Harms of the Muslim and African Bans," *Southern California Interdisciplinary Law Journal* 29 (2019): 571.
12. Dahlia Lithwick, "The Lawyers Showed Up. And They Won," *Slate*, January 29, 2017, slate.com/news-and-politics/2017/01/lawyers-take-on-donald-trumps-muslim-ban.html.
13. Robin Shulman, "The Syrians Next Door," *Time* magazine, November 3, 2016, https://time.com/desmoines/.
14. "Iowa Invites Southeast Asian Refugees," Iowa PBS, n.d., https://www.iowapbs.org/iowapathways/mypath/2499/iowa-invites-southeast-asian-refugees.
15. Paul Slovic, Daniel Västfjäll, Arvid Erlandsson, and Robin Gregory, "Iconic Photographs and the Ebb and Flow of Empathic Response to Humanitarian Disasters," *Proceedings of the National Academy of Sciences USA* 114, no. 4: 640–644, https://doi.org/10.1073/pnas.1613977114 (2017).
16. Lee Rood, "Syrian Refugees Could Begin Arriving to Iowa Next Year," *Des Moines Register*, September 30, 2015, https://www.desmoinesregister.com/story/news/2015/09/30/syrian-refugees-could-begin-arriving-iowa-soon/73035480/.
17. Eyder Peralta, "Paris Attacks Live Updates: French Authorities Identify Key Players," NPR, November 16, 2015, https://www.npr.org/sections/thetwo-way/2015/11/16/456181539/paris-attacks-live-updates-french-authorities-identify-mastermind.

18. CNN Editorial Research, "Paris Terror Attacks Fast Facts," CNN, December 8, 2015, https://www.cnn.com/2015/12/08/europe/2015-paris-terror-attacks-fast-facts/index.html.
19. Christiane Amanpour and Thom Patterson, "Passport Linked to Terrorist Complicates Syrian Refugee Crisis," CNN, November 15, 2015, https://www.cnn.com/2015/11/15/europe/paris-attacks-passports/index.html.
20. Elizabeth McElvein, "What Do Americans Really Think About Syrian Refugees?," Brookings Institution, March 4, 2016, https://www.brookings.edu/articles/what-do-americans-really-think-about-syrian-refugees/.
21. Jeffrey M. Jones, "Americans Again Opposed to Taking in Refugees," Gallup.com, November 23, 2015.
22. Matthew Teague, "Louisiana Police Deny Governor Ordered Them to 'Track' Syrian Refugees," *Guardian*, November 18, 2015, https://www.theguardian.com/us-news/2015/nov/18/louisiana-police-deny-bobby-jindal-syria-refugees.
23. Julian Hatthem, "Obama: Shameful to Propose 'Religious Test' for Refugees," *The Hill*, November 16, 2015, https://thehill.com/policy/national-security/260260-obama-hits-bush-refugee-plan-as-not-american/.
24. B. Pfannenstiel, "Branstad Seeks to Block Syrian Refugee Resettlement in Iowa," *Des Moines Register*, November 16, 2015, https://www.desmoinesregister.com/story/news/politics/2015/11/16/branstad-urges-caution-accepting-refugees/75877326/.
25. "Means of Grace, Hope of Glory—Mary and Martha: The Relationship of Action and Contemplation," Congregational Development, July 30, 2013, http://www.congregationaldevelopment.com/means-of-grace-hope-of-glory/2013/7/30/mary-and-martha-the-relationship-of-action-and-contemplation.html.
26. Kristen Padilla, "Martha: Busy Hostess or Dragon Slayer?," *Christianity Today*, September 20, 2021, https://www.christianitytoday.com/2021/09/padilla-martha-busy-hostess-theologian-dragon-slayer/; "The Hidden Surprise in the Story of Mary and Martha," Newbreak Church, August 3, 2021, https://newbreak.church/cultural-context/.
27. Padilla, "Martha: Busy Hostess or Dragon Slayer?."
28. Martha was later canonized a saint and deemed the patron saint of cooking. Her role in dragon slaying was captured on the cover of the

1931 version of the book many people have in their homes: *The Joy of Cooking*. On this cover, Martha has a halo over her head, a purse on her right wrist, and what appears to be a broom held in her right hand, raised toward the sky, prepared to be brought down on a horned dragon supine before her. Most covers of *The Joy of Cooking*, however, have the word "Cooking" written in large red text on a white background instead of the version that commemorates Martha and the dragon. See Steven Heller, "The Daily Heller: When 'The Joy of Cooking' Slayed Dragons," *PRINT Magazine*, May 23, 2024, https://www.printmag.com/daily-heller/the-daily-heller-when-the-joy-of-cooking-slayed-dragons/.

29. Kari Lydersen, "100 Armed Agents and 143 Arrests: The ICE Raid That Traumatized a Small Ohio Town," *Guardian*, September 25, 2018, https://www.theguardian.com/us-news/2018/sep/25/ice-immigration-raid-meatpacking-plant-ohio.
30. *Toolkit: Lost in the U.S. Immigration Detention System*, Freedom for Immigrants, 2018, https://www.freedomforimmigrants.org/toolkit-lost-in-detention.
31. Nick Miroff, "After an ICE Raid, Few Americans Showed Up to Work at This Texas Meatpacking Plant," *Texas Tribune*, March 5, 2018, https://www.texastribune.org/2018/03/05/even-after-ice-raid-few-american-workers-showed-work-texas-meatpacking/.
32. Amy B. Wang, "A Couple Died in a Car Crash While Fleeing ICE Agents in California, Authorities Say," *Washington Post*, December 12, 2017, https://doi.org/10-2019/WashingtonPost/2017/12/05.
33. *Detained and Disappeared: Enforced Disappearances Perpetrated in Immigration Detention by the United States*, Freedom for Immigrants, 2021, https://static1.squarespace.com/static/5a33042eb078691c386e7bce/t/61ae943be71448138264802e/1638831165517/Detained-and-Disappeared_FFI_120621.pdf.
34. Jon Campbell, "ICE Online Detainee Locator Plagued by Problems, Attorneys Say," Sunlight Foundation, September 5, 2019, https://sunlightfoundation.com/2019/09/05/ice-online-detainee-locator-plagued-by-problems-attorneys-say/.
35. Emily Ryo and Ian Peacock, *The Landscape of Immigration Detention in the United States: Special Report*, American Immigration Council, 2018.
36. To be clear, these are not just Latino naming conventions. Many cultures have more than one last name, and millions throughout the

world spell their names with accents and tildes. The ICE Locator is incapable of processing well-established, globally acknowledged naming conventions that essentially apply to everyone in their custody.

37. While my citizen privilege means I could never be detained by ICE, I can only imagine the impossibility of finding me in the ICE Locator. When I was born, my parents named me Daniel James Lopez. But with a due date of January 7, my December 13 birthday meant I was born almost a month premature, resulting in elevated levels of bilirubin in my blood. When my dad would come home from work, he would ask my mom, "How's the bilirubin doing?," referring to the bilirubin levels turning my skin yellow. My parents then began to refer to me as Bill, even though my birth certificate, unable to predict the Latino proclivity for *apodos* based on physical features, said nothing of the sort. With access to a lawyer in my family, my parents legally changed my name to William (the formal English name for the nickname Bill), resulting in my current William Daniel-James Lopez, with a hyphen on my driver's license, no hyphen on my passport, and, as you have correctly identified on the spine of this book, the occasional disappearance of the *J* initial altogether when I sign things, including book contracts. So to find me in the ICE Locator, my first name could be William, William Daniel, William Daniel James, or William Daniel-James. My last name could thus be Daniel-James Lopez, Daniel James Lopez, James Lopez, or Lopez. If ICE had taken the time to read what I have written about them and noticed my name on the book, the "James" may not be in their database at all, resulting in yet more possible combinations of first and last names.

38. Department of State v. Muñoz, 23-334, Brief Amici Curiae of Professors and Scholars Filed, March 28, 2024, https://www.supremecourt.gov/DocketPDF/23/23-334/306216/20240328163653846_23-334%20Amicus%20Brief.pdf.

39. "How Do I Locate Someone in Immigration Detention?," December 2012, accessed March 1, 2025, https://www.ice.gov/doclib/news/library/factsheets/pdf/odls-brochure.pdf.

40. "Detained and Disappeared: New Report Documents Hundreds of Disappearances in U.S. Immigration Detention System," Freedom for Immigrants, August 30, 2021, https://www.freedomforimmigrants.org/news/2021/8/30/detained-and-disappeared-new-report

-documents-hundreds-of-disappearances-in-us-immigration-detention-system.
41. *Detained and Disappeared: Enforced Disappearances Perpetrated.*
42. "The United States Disappeared the CIA's Long-Term 'Ghost Detainees': II, Background," Human Rights Watch, October 2003, https://www.hrw.org/legacy/backgrounder/usa/us1004/4.htm.

5. Where Do You Stop Being a Teacher?

1. US Census Bureau, "RACE," Decennial Census, DEC Redistricting Data, PL 94-171, table P1, 2020, accessed March 5, 2025, https://data.census.gov/table/DECENNIALPL2020.P1?q=hamblen+county.
2. US Census Bureau, US Department of Commerce, "ACS Demographic and Housing Estimates," American Community Survey, ACS 1-Year Estimates Data Profiles, table DP05, 2023, accessed March 5, 2025, https://data.census.gov/table/ACSDP1Y2023.DP05?q=hamblen+county.
3. US Census Bureau, "ACS Demographic and Housing Estimates," American Community Survey, ACS 5-Year Estimates Data Profiles, table DP05, 2019, accessed March 5, 2025, https://data.census.gov/table/ACSDP5Y2019.DP05?q=Tennessee.
4. Hamblen County School District, Great Schools, 2020, https://www.greatschools.org/tennessee/morristown/hamblen-county-school-district/#Students.
5. Travis Dorman and Jamie Satterfield, "ICE Raids Grainger County Meatpacking Plant Amid Charges Owners Avoided $2.5M in Payroll Taxes," *Knoxville News Sentinel*, April 5, 2018, https://www.knoxnews.com/story/news/crime/2018/04/05/ice-raids-meatpacking-plant-grainger-county/490673002/.
6. For more on the willingness of educators to support Latinx students, see R. Gabriela Barajas-Gonzalez, Heliana Linares Torres, Anya Urcuyo, Elaine Salamanca, Melissa Santos, and Olga Pagán, "'You're Part of Some Hope and then You Fall into Despair': Exploring the Impact of a Restrictive Immigration Climate on Educators in Latinx Immigrant Communities," in *Advocacy and Policy Change for Undocumented Student Success*, ed. Enrique G. Murillo, Jr. and Sharon Velarde Pierce (Routledge, 2024).
7. Tim Craig, Scott Wilson, and Nick Miroff, "U.S. Defends Secretive Mississippi ICE Raids as Local, State Officials Decry Effect on

Children," *Washington Post*, August 9, 2019, https://www.washingtonpost.com/national/us-defends-secretive-miss-ice-raids-as-local-state-officials-decry-effect-on-children/2019/08/08/485d6240-ba21-11e9-b3b4-2bb69e8c4e39_story.html.

8. Julia Ainsley and Didi Martinez, "What ICE Did and Did Not Do for Kids Left Behind by Mississippi Raids," NBC News, August 9, 2019, https://www.nbcnews.com/politics/immigration/what-ice-did-did-not-do-kids-left-behind-mississippi-n1040776.

9. Notably, the reporter asked Trump about "migrant children." It is highly unlikely that these were migrant children. More likely, they are some of the millions of children with undocumented parents. These children, born in the US, are US citizens. The reporter likely meant to say "the children of migrants," but Trump was certainly not going to correct her. This blurring of lines is not abnormal and allows the public to resolve some of the guilt of the harm of these events. Whether it's only the adults who are harmed during raids or the children as well, it doesn't matter, as they are all migrants anyway, and all have homes in countries outside the US. The reality, of course, is that for many of the parents and all the children, the US is their home.

10. The school and town are both pseudonyms due to their size.

11. Here, Troy calls the company Load Trails. The company's actual name is Load Trail.

12. Jonathan Blitzer, "An ICE Raid Has Turned the Lives of Hundreds of Tennessee Kids Upside Down," *New Yorker*, April 24, 2018, https://www.newyorker.com/news/dispatch/an-icesmall-raid-has-turned-the-lives-of-hundreds-of-tennessee-kids-upside-down.

13. Zoe Carpenter, "What Happens When ICE Shows Up?," *Rolling Stone*, December 17, 2018, https://www.rollingstone.com/politics/politics-features/ice-raid-tennessee-769293/; Catherine E. Shoichet, "ICE Raided a Meatpacking Plant. More than 500 Kids Missed School the Next Day," CNN, April 12, 2018, https://www.cnn.com/2018/04/12/us/tennessee-immigration-raid-schools-impact/index.html.

14. Shoichet, "ICE Raided a Meatpacking Plant."

15. Hollie Silverman and Jason Hanna, "A Quarter of a Mississippi School District's Hispanic Students Were Absent the Day After an Immigration Raid," CNN, August 9, 2019, https://www.cnn.com/2019/08/09/us/mississippi-immigration-raids-friday/index.html.

16. J. Jacob Kirksey and Carolyn Sattin-Bajaj, "Immigration and Customs Enforcement Raids the Pillar of a Community: Student Achievement, Absenteeism, and Mobility Following a Large Worksite Enforcement Operation in North Texas," *American Behavioral Scientist*, November 8, 2023, 00027642231215992. Ahead of print.
17. Carolyn Heinrich, Mónica Hernández, and Mason Shero, "Repercussions of a Raid: Health and Education Outcomes of Children Entangled in Immigration Enforcement," *Journal of Policy Analysis and Management* 42, no. 2 (2023): 350–392.
18. Sofia Avila, "The Effect of Workplace Raids on Academic Performance: Evidence from Texas," *Sociological Science* 11 (2024): 258–296.
19. While immigration worksite raids provide a heightened example of the impacts of immigration enforcement and education, everyday immigration enforcement also harms Latino student educational performance. Thomas Dee and Mark Murphy found that if ICE collaborates with local police in a given school district, Hispanic students are more likely to leave the district. J. Jacob Kirksey and colleagues found that more deportations within 25 miles predicted a larger math achievement gap between white and Latino students. Thomas S. Dee and Mark Murphy, "Vanished Classmates: The Effects of Local Immigration Enforcement on School Enrollment," *American Educational Research Journal* 57, no. 2 (2020): 694–727; J. Jacob Kirksey, Carolyn Sattin-Bajaj, Michael A. Gottfried, Jennifer Freeman, and Christopher S. Ozuna, "Deportations Near the Schoolyard: Examining Immigration Enforcement and Racial/Ethnic Gaps in Educational Outcomes," *AERA Open* 6, no. 1 (2020): 2332858419899074.
20. Amber Phillips, "'They're Rapists.' President Trump's Campaign Launch Speech Two Years Later, Annotated," *Washington Post*, June 16, 2017, https://www.washingtonpost.com/news/the-fix/wp/2017/06/16/theyre-rapists-presidents-trump-campaign-launch-speech-two-years-later-annotated/.
21. Brad Brooks, "Victims of Anti-Latino Hate Crimes Soar in U.S.: FBI Report," Reuters, November 12, 2019, https://www.reuters.com/article/world/us/victims-of-anti-latino-hate-crimes-soar-in-us-fbi-report-idUSKBN1XM2OP/.

22. Kim Parker, Juliana Menasce Horowitz, Anna Brown, Richard Fry, D'Vera Cohn, and Ruth Igielnik, "Urban, Suburban and Rural Residents' Views on Key Social and Political Issues," Pew Research Center Social and Demographic Trends Project, Pew Research Center, May 22, 2018, https://www.pewresearch.org/social-trends/2018/05/22/urban-suburban-and-rural-residents-views-on-key-social-and-political-issues/.

6. A New Overground Railroad

1. William Daniel Lopez, Juan Gudino, Tamara Shull, Gladys Godinez, and Nicole Louise Novak, "Large-Scale Immigration Worksite Raids: Community Disaster, Community Response," *Journal of Community Practice* 32, no. 1 (2024): 86–106.
2. Sergio González, "The Sanctuary Movement," Oxford Research Encyclopedia of American History (website), June 30, 2020. See also Maria Cristina Garcia, *Seeking Refuge: Central American Migration to Mexico, the United States, and Canada* (University of California Press, 2006).
3. Sophie H. Pirie, "The Origins of a Political Trial: The Sanctuary Movement and Political Justice," *Yale Journal of Law and the Humanities* 2 (1990): 381; "The Sanctuary Movement," Southside Presbyterian Church, n.d., https://www.southsidepresbyterian.org/the-sanctuary-movement.html.
4. "Underground Railroad" is used to describe the network as well, though it's most often used to reference the movement of enslaved people during the American Civil War.
5. Gavin R. Betzelberger, "Off the Beaten Track, on the Overground Railroad: Central American Refugees and the Organizations That Helped Them," *Legacy* 11, no. 1 (2011): 3.
6. Sergio González, "The Sanctuary Movement," Oxford Research Encyclopedia of American History (website), June 30, 2020.
7. "The Origins of the Sanctuary Movement," Smithsonian Institution, July 11, 2023, https://www.si.edu/object/origins-sanctuary-movement%3Aposts_68564f448f9b1710776ed1c15201b413.
8. Kristin Elizabeth Yarris and Whitney L. Duncan, eds., *Accompaniment With Immigrant Communities: Engaged Ethnography* (University of Arizona Press, 2024).
9. L. Moore-Eissenberg, "At County Jails, Corso's Workers Tell Story of Immigration Enforcement," *Blade*, August 5, 2018, https://www

.toledoblade.com/local/2018/08/05/Corso-s-workers-tell-story-of-immigration-enforcement-in-heartland/stories/20180718253.
10. Here, I describe parents as "mothers" or "fathers," the parental identities—along with all their culturally ascribed responsibilities, like providing economically or caring for children—that I encountered while doing this work and that tend to be common in Latino immigrant families. There are other parental identities and styles of parenting not tied to biological sex.
11. Gretchen Livingston, "Facts on Unmarried Parents in the US," Social and Demographic Trends Project, Pew Research Center, April 25, 2018, https://www.pewresearch.org/social-trends/2018/04/25/the-changing-profile-of-unmarried-parents/.
12. "U.S. Citizen Children Impacted by Immigration Enforcement," American Immigration Council, June 24, 2021, https://www.americanimmigrationcouncil.org/research/us-citizen-children-impacted-immigration-enforcement.
13. Randy Capps, Heather Koball, Andrea Campetella, Krista Perreira, Sarah Hooker, and Juan M. Pedroza, *Implications of Immigration Enforcement Activities for the Well-Being of Children in Immigrant Families* (Urban Institute; Migration Policy Institute, 2015).
14. Katherine M. Collins, Nicole L. Novak, Gladys E. Godinez, Tamera L. Shull, and William D. Lopez, "The Repercussions of Large-Scale Immigration Worksite Raids on Immigrant Women: Results from Six Rural Communities," *Journal of Community Practice* 30, no. 2 (2022): 128–142.
15. Heather Marcoux, "This Separated Immigrant Mom Hasn't Been Able to Breastfeed Her Baby for 2 Weeks," *Motherly*, August 21, 2019, https://www.mother.ly/life/separated-breastfeeding-immigrant-mother-ice-raid/.
16. William D. Lopez, Nicole L. Novak, Nourel-Hoda Eidy, Tamera L. Shull, and Angela Stuesse, "Challenges to Addressing Mental Health Repercussions of Large-Scale Immigration Worksite Raids in the Rural United States," *Journal of Rural Mental Health* 47, no. 1 (2023): 59.
17. Saria Hassan, Unjali P. Gujral, Rakale C. Quarells, Elizabeth C. Rhodes, Megha K. Shah, Jane Obi, et al., "Disparities in Diabetes Prevalence and Management by Race and Ethnicity in the USA: Defining a Path Forward," *Lancet Diabetes & Endocrinology* 11, no. 7 (2023): 509–524.

18. Samantha Artiga, Latoya Hill, and Anthony Damico, "Health Coverage by Race and Ethnicity, 2010–2022," Kaiser Family Foundation, January 11, 2024, https://www.kff.org/racial-equity-and-health-policy/issue-brief/health-coverage-by-race-and-ethnicity/.
19. For more on rural "legal deserts," see Michele Statz and Paula Termuhlen, "Rural Legal Deserts Are a Critical Health Determinant," *American Journal of Public Health* 110, no. 10 (2020): 1519–1522.
20. Miriam Jordan, "ICE Came for a Tennessee Town's Immigrants. The Town Fought Back," *New York Times*, June 11, 2018, https://www.nytimes.com/interactive/2018/06/11/us/tennessee-immigration-trump.html.
21. MacKenzie Elmer, "Dozens Rally in Mount Pleasant Day After ICE Arrested 32, Mourning Families Torn Apart and Demanding Answers from Local Police," *Des Moines Register*, May 11, 2018, https://www.desmoinesregister.com/story/news/2018/05/10/mount-pleasant-immigration-raid-illegal-immigration-iowa-raid/598598002/.
22. Monte Reel, "Two Towns Forged an Unlikely Bond. Now, ICE Is Severing the Connection," *Bloomberg*, December 27, 2018, https://www.bloomberg.com/news/features/2018-12-27/two-towns-forged-an-unlikely-bond-now-ice-is-severing-the-connection.
23. Dora Capozza, Rossella Falvo, Gian A. Di Bernardo, Loris Vezzali, and Emilio P. Visintin, "Intergroup Contact as a Strategy to Improve Humanness Attributions: A Review of Studies," *TPM-Testing, Psychometrics, Methodology in Applied Psychology* 21, no. 3 (2014): 349–362.
24. Alexander P. Landry, Ram I. Orr, and Kayla Mere, "Dehumanization and Mass Violence: A Study of Mental State Language in Nazi Propaganda (1927–1945)," *PLoS One* 17, no. 11 (2022): e0274957, https://doi.org/10.1371/journal.pone.0274957.
25. James J. Weingartner, "Trophies of War: U.S. Troops and the Mutilation of Japanese War Dead, 1941–1945," *Pacific Historical Review* 61, no. 1 (1992): 53–67, https://doi.org/10.2307/3640788; Landry, Orr, and Mere, "Dehumanization and Mass Violence"; Erin Steuter and Deborah Wills, "Making the Muslim Enemy: The Social Construction of the Enemy in the War on Terror," in *The Routledge Handbook of War and Society: Iraq and Afghanistan*, ed. Steven Carlton-Ford and Morten G. Ender, pp. 257–267 (Routledge, 2010).

26. Herbert C. Kelman, "Violence Without Moral Restraint: Reflections on the Dehumanization of Victims and Victimizers," in *The Criminology of War*, ed. Ruth Jamieson, pp. 145–181 (Routledge, 2014).
27. Armando Rodríguez-Pérez and Verónica Betancor, "Infrahumanization: A Retrospective on 20 Years of Empirical Research," *Current Opinion in Behavioral Sciences* 50 (2023): 101258.
28. Scott Neuman, "During Roundtable, Trump Calls Some Unauthorized Immigrants 'Animals,'" NPR, May 1, 2018, https://www.npr.org/sections/thetwo-way/2018/05/17/611877563/during-roundtable-trump-calls-some-unauthorized-immigrants-animals.
29. Kathleen M. Palm, Melissa A. Polusny, and Victoria M. Follette, "Vicarious Traumatization: Potential Hazards and Interventions for Disaster and Trauma Workers," *Prehospital and Disaster Medicine* 19, no. 1 (2004): 73–78, https://doi.org/10.1017/S1049023X00001503.
30. Natalie McNeillie and John Rose, "Vicarious Trauma in Therapists: A Meta-Ethnographic Review," *Behavioural and Cognitive Psychotherapy* 49, no. 4 (2021): 426, 426–440, https://doi.org/10.1017/S1352465820000776; McNeillie and Rose are referencing the work of Laurie A. Pearlman and Karen W. Saakvitne, *Trauma and the Therapist: Countertransference and Vicarious Traumatization in Psychotherapy with Incest Survivors* (W. W. Norton, 1995).
31. McNeillie and Rose, "Vicarious Trauma in Therapists: A Meta-Ethnographic Review."
32. Pearl Fernandes, Niels Buus, and Paul Rhodes, "Vicarious Impacts of Working with Refugees and Asylum Seekers: An Integrative Review," *Journal of Immigrant and Refugee Studies* 22, no. 3 (2022): 483, 482–502, https://doi-org.proxy.lib.umich.edu/10.1080/15562948.2022.2049949.

7. It Was the Bed Bugs That Broke Her

1. This chapter draws from the following sources, among others cited in the text:

    Trip Gabriel, "An ICE Raid Leaves an Iowa Town Divided Along Faith Lines," *New York Times*, July 3, 2018, https://www.nytimes.com/2018/07/03/us/ice-raid-iowa-churches.html; Grace King, "Iowa WINS ?Financially Adopting? [*sic*] Teen After Dad Deported to Guatemala," September 30, 2018, https://www.southeastiowaunion.com/news/iowa-wins-financially-adopting-teen-after-dad-deported

-to-guatemala/; Hinda Seif, "'Layers of Humanity': Interview with Undocuqueer Activist Julio Salgado," *Latin Studies* 12 (2014): 300–309, https://doi.org/10.1057/lst.2014.31; Leslie Scanlon, "Immigration in Small-Town Iowa: One Church Reaches Out to the Community—the Presbyterian Outlook," *Presbyterian Outlook*, August 27, 2018, https://pres-outlook.org/2018/08/immigration-in-small-town-iowa-one-church-reaches-out-to-the-community/; Monte Reel, "Two Towns Forged an Unlikely Bond. Now, ICE Is Severing the Connection," *Bloomberg*, December 27, 2018, https://www.bloomberg.com/news/features/2018-12-27/two-towns-forged-an-unlikely-bond-now-ice-is-severing-the-connection.
2. Nicole and a third student, Naomi, were also with me when the interview began but had to leave to conduct another interview before we concluded.
3. Jeanne Batalova and Nicole Ward, "Central American Immigrants in the United States," Migration Policy Institute, August 29, 2018, https://www.migrationpolicy.org/article/central-american-immigrants-united-states.
4. "World Bank Open Data," World Bank, 2023, https://data.worldbank.org/indicator/BX.TRF.PWKR.DT.GD.ZS?end=2023&locations=GT&skipRedirection=true&start=1977&view=chart.
5. "The Dream Act: An Overview," American Immigration Council, May 8, 2024, https://www.americanimmigrationcouncil.org/research/dream-act-overview.
6. See the original DREAM Act here: DREAM Act, 107th Congress, 2nd Session, S. 1291. https://www.congress.gov/111/bills/s729/BILLS-111s729is.xml#ID266FC8B3D67046C298EEE35544419CD7.
7. "Deferred Action for Childhood Arrivals (DACA): An Overview," American Immigration Council, September 30, 2021, https://www.americanimmigrationcouncil.org/research/deferred-action-childhood-arrivals-daca-overview.
8. Barack Obama, "Remarks by the President on Immigration," Obama White House Archives, June 15, 2012, https://obamawhitehouse.archives.gov/the-press-office/2012/06/15/remarks-president-immigration.
9. Katie Reilly, "Here's What President Trump Has Said About DACA in the Past," *Time*, September 5, 2017, https://time.com/4927100/donald-trump-daca-past-statements/.

10. Nina Totenberg, "Supreme Court Rules for Dreamers, Against Trump," NPR, June 18, 2020, https://www.npr.org/2020/06/18/829858289/supreme-court-upholds-daca-in-blow-to-trump-administration.
11. Roberto G. Gonzales, *Lives in Limbo: Undocumented and Coming of Age in America* (University of California Press, 2016); see also Tom K. Wong, Greisa Martinez Rosa, and Adam Luna, "DACA Recipients' Economic and Educational Gains Continue to Grow," Center for American Progress, August 28, 2017, https://www.americanprogress.org/article/daca-recipients-economic-educational-gains-continue-grow/.
12. Hunter Walker, "Donald Trump Just Released an Epic Statement Raging Against Mexican Immigrants and 'Disease,'" *Business Insider*, July 6, 2015, https://www.businessinsider.com/donald-trumps-epic-statement-on-mexico-2015-7.
13. Ellie Quinlan Houghtaling, "Trump Goes off the Rails with Gross Rant About 'Sick' Migrants," *New Republic*, April 2, 2024, https://newrepublic.com/post/180363/trump-off-rails-gross-rant-migrants.
14. Howard Markel and Alexandra Minna Stern, "The Foreignness of Germs: The Persistent Association of Immigrants and Disease in American Society," *Milbank Quarterly* 80, no. 4 (2002): 757–788, https://doi.org/10.1111/1468-0009.00030.
15. J. Dearen and G. Burke, "Pence Ordered Borders Closed After CDC Experts Refused," AP News, October 3, 2020, https://apnews.com/article/virus-outbreak-pandemics-public-health-new-york-health-4ef0c6c5263815a26f8aa17f6ea490ae.
16. Colleen Long, "Title 42 Is Ending. Here's What It Has Done, and How US Immigration Policy Is Changing," AP News, May 12, 2023, https://apnews.com/article/immigration-biden-border-title-42-mexico-asylum-be4e0b15b27adb9bede87b9bbefb798d.
17. Leonardo Castañeda and Katie Hoeppner, "Five Things to Know About the Title 42 Immigrant Expulsion Policy," American Civil Liberties Union, March 22, 2022, https://www.aclu.org/news/immigrants-rights/five-things-to-know-about-the-title-42-immigrant-expulsion-policy.
18. Roberto R. Redfield, "Rescind the Recently Extended Order 'Suspending Introduction of Certain Persons from Countries Where a Communicable Disease Exists,'" Action Network, n.d., https://actionnetwork.org/petitions/rescind-the-recently-extended-order

-suspending-introduction-of-certain-persons-from-countries-where-a-communicable-disease-exists.

19. Deena Shanker, Michael Hirtzer, Jen Skerritt, and Lydia Mulvany, "Pork Producer Shut Down: Tyson (TSN) Closes Iowa Plant," *Bloomberg*, April 22, 2020, https://www.bloomberg.com/news/articles/2020-04-22/tyson-foods-to-indefinitely-suspend-waterloo-operations-k9bbgnr9.

20. Gosia Wozniacka, "Poor Conditions at Meatpacking Plants Have Long Put Workers at Risk. The Pandemic Makes It Much Worse," *Civil Eats*, April 17, 2020, https://civileats.com/2020/04/17/poor-conditions-at-meatpacking-plants-have-long-put-workers-at-risk-the-pandemic-makes-it-much-worse/.

21. William D. Lopez, Nolan Kline, Alana M. W. LeBrón, Nicole L. Novak, Maria-Elena De Trinidad Young, Gregg Gonsalves, et al., "Preventing the Spread of COVID-19 in Immigration Detention Centers Requires the Release of Detainees," *American Journal of Public Health* 111, no. 1 (2021): 110–115. See our Amicus Brief, O.M.G. et al. v. Chad Wolf, No. 1:20-cv-0786 J.E.B, https://niwaplibrary.wcl.american.edu/wp-content/uploads/O.M.G.-et-al-v.-Wolf-et-al.-ECF-24-Motion-for-Leave-and-Brief-of-Amici-Curiae.pdf.

22. Jason Wilson, "Leaked Emails Reveal Trump Aide Stephen Miller's White Nationalist Views," *Guardian*, November 14, 2019, https://www.theguardian.com/us-news/2019/nov/14/stephen-miller-leaked-emails-white-nationalism-trump.

23. "Donald Trump on the Role Genetics Play in Success—Video," Oprah.com, 2016, https://www.oprah.com/own-oprahshow/donald-trump-on-the-role-genetics-play-in-success-video.

24. Michael Gold, "Trump's Remarks on Migrants Illustrate His Obsession with Genes," *New York Times*, October 10, 2024, https://www.nytimes.com/2024/10/09/us/politics/trump-migrants-genes.html.

25. Seema Mehta, "Blowing the 'Racehorse Theory' Whistle," *Los Angeles Times*, 2020, https://enewspaper.latimes.com/infinity/article_share.aspx?guid=f7927a63-d5b7-4097-a9cb-0c2d910def46.

26. Ginger Gibson, "Trump Says Immigrants Are 'Poisoning the Blood of Our Country.' Biden Campaign Likens Comments to Hitler," NBC News, December 17, 2023, https://www.nbcnews.com/politics/2024-election/trump-says-immigrants-are-poisoning-blood-country-biden-campaign-liken-rcna130141.

Epilogue. A Beautiful Morning in the Heartland of the US

1. The epilogue draws data from the following sources.: Nicole L. Novak, Arline T. Geronimus, and Aresha M. Martinez-Cardoso, "Change in Birth Outcomes Among Infants Born to Latina Mothers After a Major Immigration Raid," *International Journal of Epidemiology* 46, no. 3 (2017): 839–849; J. Jacob Kirksey and Carolyn Sattin-Bajaj, "Immigration and Customs Enforcement Raids the Pillar of a Community: Student Achievement, Absenteeism, and Mobility Following a Large Worksite Enforcement Operation in North Texas," *American Behavioral Scientist* (November 28, 2023): 00027642231215992, ahead of print; Claire Wang, "Millions of Mexican Americans Were Deported in the 1930s. Are We About to Repeat This 'Ethnic Cleansing'?," *Guardian*, December 3, 2024, https://www.theguardian.com/us-news/2024/dec/03/trump-mass-deportation-plan-1930s-repatriation-program; Clarissa-Jan Lim, "Trump White House Sparks Backlash for Posting Dehumanizing 'ASMR' Deportation Video," MSNBC, February 19, 2025, https://www.msnbc.com/top-stories/latest/trump-white-house-mocks-immigrants-deported-asmr-x-elon-musk-rcna192820; Jeff Mason, Idrees Ali, and Ted Hesson, "Trump to Prepare Facility at Guantanamo for 30,000 Migrants," Reuters, January 30, 2025, https://www.reuters.com/world/us/trump-says-he-will-instruct-homeland-security-pentagon-prepare-migrant-facility-2025-01-29/; Berenice Garcia, "Texas Offers Trump More Land to Stage Deportations," *Texas Tribune*, November 26, 2024, https://www.texastribune.org/2024/11/26/texas-donald-trump-deportation-land-offer/; "Can Trump Revoke Birthright Citizenship?," BBC News, January 20, 2025, https://www.bbc.com/news/articles/c7vdnlmgyndo; "Zelaya v. Hammer," National Immigration Law Center, February 21, 2019, https://www.nilc.org/litigation/zelaya-v-hammer/; J. Holly McCall, "Settlement Finalized in 2018 Grainger County Slaughterhouse Raid," *Tennessee Lookout*, February 28, 2023, https://tennesseelookout.com/2023/02/28/settlement-finalized-in-2018-grainger-county-slaughterhouse-raid/; "Prophets of a Future Not Our Own," US Conference of Catholic Bishops, n.d., www.usccb.org. https://www.usccb.org/prayer-and-worship/prayers-and-devotions/prayers/prophets-of-a-future-not-our-own.

Index

absenteeism, 154–55
Abused: The Postville Raid (documentary), 61
academic performance, 154–55
adulthood, abrupt transition to, 97
Agriprocessors Inc. (Postville, Iowa) worksite raid: charges from, 31–33; conduct of, 30–31; detainee processing after, 31–33; helicopters used in, 61; immediate effect of, 33; legacy of, 9–10, 30; narrative of, 31, 33–34; public familiarity with, 25
airports, in "Muslim travel ban" response, 121–24
Al (Mount Pleasant interviewee), 47
Alicia (behavioral health counselor), 182
Alien Registration Number, 142
Allen (Texas) worksite raid, 11, 155
Alshawi, Mr., writ of habeas corpus on behalf of, 122–23
American Civil Liberties Union, 105, 122–23
American public. *See* public
Ana (O'Neill interviewee), 96–97
Angel Moms, 42–44, 222
Anneka (law student), 178, 194–95
apodos (nicknames), 138–39
Army National Guard, 52–53
Asian immigrants, scapegoating of, 15–16

ASMR: Illegal Aliens Deportation Flight (video), 226
asylum seekers, 167–68, 211–12
attorneys: availability of, 118, 124–25; in Muslim travel ban response, 121–24, 134; right to, 103, 117; vicarious trauma of, 195. *See also* immigration attorneys
Avila, Sofia, 155

babies. *See* children of detainees
bail. *See* immigration bond
Bean Station worksite raid. *See* Southeastern Provision worksite raid
bed bugs, 212–14
Bella. *See* Reyes, Bella
Biden, Joseph R., 9–10, 26
Bienvenidos, 163–65, 180
biological determinism, 3, 215–16, 217, 219–23
Black drivers, racial profiling of, 70–72
Blanca (reporter), 111–12
Blitzer, Jonathan, 154
bond. *See* immigration bond
Border Patrol: Latino immigrants in Texas and, 15–17; use of facility in Corso's raid, 175, 179
border separations, 101–6
Branstad, Terry, 127, 129
Brantley, James, 57

INDEX

breastfeeding, 177-78, 194
Brown Dog Gelato, 174
Brownsville, Texas, detention center at, 105
Bush, George H. W., and Sanctuary Movement, 168
Bush, George W.: immigration enforcement under, 9-10, 26; immigration reform under, 28. *See also* Agriprocessors Inc. worksite raid
Bush, Jeb, 128-29
Bush, Laura, 105
businesses, ICE impersonation of, 75-76

Camayd-Freixas, Erik, 31-33
Casa Padre (Brownsville, Texas), 105
Cathy (educator), 146-47, 153, 158
Cervantes, Lupe (Guadalupe) (team member), 181
Challenger space shuttle, 48
chaos, 22, 149
Child Protective Services (CPS), 176
children of detainees: age at time of separation, 87-88, 97, 248n8; breastfeeding and, 177-78; educational impacts on, 153-56, 259n19; fear for, on day of raid, 86; after Fresh Mark raid, 12-13; health impacts on, 86-88, 99-100, 155; information sharing with, decisions about, 48, 97-99, 148-49, 150, 152; after Midwest Precast Concrete raid, 201-5; official support for, lack of, 148-49, 258n9; placement of, after deportation of parents, 176, 200-205; after removal of father, 93; school transportation for, 150; siblings, as caretakers, 96-97, 152-53; social networks in supporting, 87, 176-77; after Southeastern Provision raid, 51-52; without families after, 201-5; in workforce, 96-97. *See also* families of detainees

churches: gatherings at, after raids, 58, 73; languages used in, 6-7; in organizing after raids, 111-15, 136-37; politics of, 113. *See also specific churches*
Cindy (church staff member), 55
Coco (film), 16-17
Collins, Katie (team member), 170, 171, 174, 181
communication, in communities: educators in, 84, 129-30; during Load Trail raid, 73-74, 77, 151-52; during Midwest Precast Concrete raid, 59-60, 83-84, 129-30; O'Neill raid and, 62-66; during Southeastern Provision raid, 150
communities: building trust with, 165, 222; connecting, after raids, 186-87; door knocking in, 64, 74, 77-79, 156-60; role in research study, 20-21, 239n40
Comprehensive Immigration Reform Act of 2007, 28
consent of public, in deportation, 21-22, 227
contraband, and racial profiling, 71-72
Corso's Flower and Garden Centers (Sandusky, Ohio) worksite raid: day of, 175-76; evolving needs after, 165; medical needs after, 179, 180-83; staging of, 174-75; in string of ICE raids, 11; transportation needs after, 166, 168-73; vicarious trauma after, 195-96; women detained during, 175-80; working conditions before, 174
COVID-19 pandemic, 211-12

INDEX

criminal narrative, about immigrants: community contact and, 7, 186; political use of, 16–17; in scapegoating, 16; in traffic stops, 71; Trump on, 41–44, 160, 209–10; white people and, belief in, 7, 41–44, 160, 186, 209–10
Cristián (pastor), 77–78, 113–14, 247n39
cross-cultural communication, 138–39
cruelty: in appeal of Trump, 39–40; public consent in, 21–22, 227; as reason for worksite raids, 22, 34–35, 162
"Cruelty Is the Point, The" (Serwer), 39–40
Cruz, Ted, 128–29
culto, 68–69
Customs and Border Protection (CBP). *See* Border Patrol

DACA (Deferred Action for Child Arrivals), 206–8, 214, 220–21
Dallas Volunteer Attorney Program, 119
Darweesh, Mr., writ of habeas corpus on behalf of, 122–23
da Silva, Ronald, 43
Deferred Action for Child Arrivals (DACA), 206–8, 214, 220–21
dehumanization, 187–88, 209
Department of Homeland Security: presidential appointment to, 26; in prosecution of detainees, 102–4
deportation: cost of, to families, 92–95; of Dreamers, 206–7; fault in, 214; in Michigan, 17–18; preparing for, 88; public consent in, 21–22, 227; in Texas, 15–17; after traffic stops, 72; after trial, 32; vs. voluntary departure, 95; white experience of, 13–14, 17–19
Des Moines Register, 185

Destiny (organizer): in finding a church, 111–15; organizational talents of, 109–10
detainees: bond for, 93–95; disappeared, 144, 226; identifying, 137–39; lawsuit brought by, 227; legal options of, 31–33; legal representation for, 117–18; length of detention, 249n14; locating, 139–44; official purpose in detention of, 102–3, 251n23; processing, 31–33, 55–58, 62, 64–65; requirements upon release of, 166, 169–73, 177–78; single mothers as, 179–80; voluntary departure as option for, 95. *See also* families of detainees
Development, Relief, and Education for Alien Minors Act (DREAM Act), 206–8
diabetes, 183
Diane (attorney), 195
Diego (Mount Pleasant interviewee), 59–60
disease. *See* infectious disease narrative
diversity hiring initiatives, as threat to white dominance, 39
Domingo-Garcia, Maria, 178
door knocking *(tocar la puerta)*: consent to enter and, 74–76; by educators, 156–60; after Sumner raids, 74, 77–79; during Swift raids, 64
DREAM Act (Development, Relief, and Education for Alien Minors Act), 206–8
Dreby, Joanna, 92
driver's licenses, 72, 91–92, 204–5
driving: removal of husbands and, effect of, 91–92; riskiness of, 69–72, 204–5, 214, 245n20. *See also* transportation
drug crimes. *See* criminal narrative

INDEX

Easter Mass, 53
economic class, in election of Trump, 37–38
economic narrative, about immigrants: political use of, 27–28; Trump on, 42
Edgar (immigrant), 200–205, 209, 212–14
Edith (Mount Pleasant interviewee): about, 2–3, 199–200; bed bugs and, 212–14; beliefs about Latino immigrants, 3, 217; decision to include, 218–24; experience with immigrants, 201–5, 209
educational impacts, after worksite raids, 153–56, 259n19
educators: community trust in, 157–58; in day-of communications, 84, 129–30; home visits by, 156–60; information sharing by, decisions about, 48, 148–49, 152; politics and, 161–62; raids compared to September 11 by, 47; response planning by, 148–53
Eidy, Nour (team member), 174, 181
Eileen (reporter), 68
Elisio (Mount Pleasant interviewee): about, 81–82; on day of raid, 83–86, 88–89, 100–101; immigration bond for, 93; survivor's guilt of, 95–96
empathy, 188–89
enforced disappearance, 144, 226
excessive use of force, 227. *See also* violence
exhaustion, 125, 189, 191

families of detainees: children supported by, 87; financial impact on, 32–33, 92–95, 203–4, 250n16; after Fresh Mark raid, 12–13, 249n12; public faces of, 134–35; after removal of husband, 91–95, 203–4, 249n14; roles of worker and driver in, 91–92; separation at US-Mexican border, 101–6; separation during Muslim travel ban, 101–6; separation during raids, 89–91; social networks in supporting, 87, 176–77; after Southeastern Provision raid, 51, 57–58. *See also* children of detainees
Father Jim. *See* Jim
fathers. *See* men, fathers, and husbands, immigrant
Fernanda (detainee), 178
food, providing: after Midwest Precast Concrete raid, 130–32, 186–87, 203–4; after Ohio raids, 165; after Southeastern Provision raid, 132, 156
force, excessive use of, 227. *See also* violence
forced sterilization, 217
Freedom for Immigrants (nonprofit), 139, 141
Fresh Mark (Salem, Ohio) worksite raid: evolving needs after, 165; food provisions after, 131; identifying detainees after, 137–38; organizing after, 13; police during, 12; in string of ICE raids, 9–10; transportation needs after, 166, 168–73; vicarious trauma after, 195–96

genetic traits of immigrants, beliefs about, 3, 215–16, 217, 219–23
Golash-Boza, Tanya, 97
Goodman, Adam, 15
Gordon (attorney), 176
government, in disaster response, 46–47

INDEX

Grand Island, Nebraska, O'Neill raid staged in, 62–66
Grand Rapids, Michigan, 210
Great Grammie, 1–2
Guantanamo Bay, 226
Gudino, Juan (team member): in decision to include Edie's story, 219–24; graduate studies of, 217; on Latino identity, 221; as participant in interview with Edie, 3, 200, 209, 218; reaction of, during interview with Edie, 203, 214, 216
Gyllenhaal, Maggie, 105

haggling, 204
Hamblen County, Tennessee, 145–46
health care. *See* medical care
heartland, defining, 235n1
heaven, requirements for entry to, 112–13
helicopters, 29, 30, 60–62, 73, 85, 155
hiding: after Fresh Mark raid, 13; after Load Trail raid, 157–58; after Southeastern Provision raid, 150, 158–60
highways of Texas, 116
Homan, Tom, 101
humanitarian disaster: natural disasters as analogies for, 45–48; recollections of, 45; as strategy for worksite raids, 34–35
Hurricane Katrina, response to, 45–46, 243n1
husbands. *See* men, fathers, and husbands, immigrant
hypervisibility: ICE Locator and, 144; Latino experience of, 7–8; of research team, 9, 21; while driving, 69–72, 245n20. *See also* invisibility

ICE (Immigration and Customs Enforcement): bond and, profit from, 250n16; children of detainees and, 149; confusion in identifying, 76, 78, 247n39; consent to enter home and, 74–76; government role of, 236n7; Latino detainees of, percentage of, 141–42; locating detainees of, 141–44; at Midwest Precast Concrete raid, 85, 248n2; in public spaces, 73–74; regional roles of, 18; ruses used by, 75–76; during staging of raids, 62–63. *See also* deportation; police
ICE Locator, 141–44, 255n36, 256n37
identity theft, as justification of raids, 29, 31–33
immigrants (general): acceptable vs. "perfect," 208; under Bush, 28–29; dehumanization of, 187–88; disease narrative about, 209–12; Dreamers, 206–8; driver's licenses and, 72, 91–92, 204–5; economy threatened by, 42; employers of, as targets, 73; good vs. bad, 43; infectious disease narrative about, 209–12; jobs threatened by, 42; narratives about, 27–28, 41–44, 209–12; outside perspectives on, 50–51; "perfect," 202–3, 204, 205–9, 221–22; scapegoating of, 15–16, 40–44; Social Security numbers and, 208; support for, 202–5; in traffic stops, 72, 245n20. *See also* criminal narrative; Latino immigrants; men, fathers, and husbands; women, mothers, and wives

INDEX

immigration attorneys: importance of, 116; ongoing need for, 183–85; in Sumner organizing, 111–12; vicarious trauma of, 195

immigration bond, 93–95, 165–66, 250n16

immigration enforcement: presidential policies on, 9–10; as racist agenda, 124; under Trump, 10, 22, 101–6. *See also* Department of Homeland Security; ICE; worksite raids; *specific locations*

immigration violations: administrative solutions for, 102–3; as criminal offense, 103–4; warrants for, 74–75, 76

immigration worksite raids. *See* worksite raids; *specific locations*

industrialization, and ICE targets, 10. *See also* worksite raids

infectious disease narrative, about immigrants, 209–12

infrahumanization, 187–88

intergroup contact, 188

International Refugee Assistance Project, 122

interviews vs. conversations, 200

invisibility: effects of, 8–9; ICE Locator and, 144; after ICE raids, 18–19; of women, in public narrative, 134–35. *See also* hiding; hypervisibility

Iowa Bridge, 82, 126–28

Iowa State Historical Building, 218

Iowa worksite raids. *See* Agriprocessors Inc. worksite raid; Midwest Precast Concrete worksite raid

Iraq, Operation Desert Storm in, 52–53

Irish immigrants, scapegoating of, 16

Isaac (pastor), 67–69, 71–74, 77, 114–15

ISIS, 128

Israelites, 79–80

jails, searching for detainees in, 140

Jay. *See* Tucker, Jay

Jim (priest), 52–58, 132, 184

Jindhal, Bobby, 128–29

Joaquín (Salem interviewee), 99–100

jobs. *See* economic narrative

John (Mount Pleasant interviewee), 60–61

Juan. *See* Gudino, Juan

Juana (Mount Pleasant interviewee): about, 81–83; on day of raid, 83–86, 89–91; on future, 106–8; on impact of detention on families, 92–95; survivor's guilt of, 95–96; volunteer work of, 186–87

Julio (team collaborator), 53–54, 146–47

Justice for our Neighbors, 109

Katrina, Hurricane, response to, 45–46, 243n1

Kimberly (organizer), 137–39, 163–65, 189–90

Kirskey, J. Jacob, 154–55

Kurdi, Alan, 127

La Migra. *See* Border Patrol

Larry (Bean Station interviewee), 50–52, 131

Latino(s): diabetes risk of, 183; naming conventions of, 141–42, 255n36; in traffic stops, 70–72, 245n20; white passing, 221

Latino immigrants: acceptable vs. "perfect," 208; Angel Moms and, 44; Border Patrol and, 15–17; children as, solo travel by,

200–201; deaths of, at US–Mexico border vs. worksites, 211–12; dehumanization of, 187–88; disappeared, 144, 226; disease narrative about, 209–12; Dreamers, 206–8; driver's licenses and, 72, 91–92, 204–5; economy threatened by, 27–28, 42; employers of, as targets, 73; good vs. bad, 43; in industrial jobs, 10; infectious disease narrative about, 209–12; jobs threatened by, 42; narratives about, 27–28, 41–44, 209–12; numbers of, actual vs. believed, 7; outside perspectives on, 50–51; as percentage of ICE detainees, 141–42; "perfect," 202–3, 204, 205–9, 221–22; political messages about, 27–28; scapegoating of, 15–16, 40–44; Social Security numbers and, 208; support for, 160–61, 202–5; in Tennessee, 145–46; in traffic stops, 72, 245n20; white beliefs about, 3, 7, 41–44, 215–16, 217, 219–23. *See also* criminal narrative; men, fathers, and husbands, immigrant; women, mothers, and wives

law enforcement. *See* ICE; police

League of United Latin American Citizens (LULAC), 82

Leah (Mount Pleasant interviewee), 47–48

legal counsel. *See* attorneys

Lesley (volunteer), 173–74, 179, 183

Leslie (educator), 146, 161

Lisa (volunteer), 167–70

Liz (nurse), 179

Load Trail (Sumner, Texas) worksite raid: attorneys in response to, 117–21; churches in response to, 113–15; community

communication during, 73–74, 77, 151–52; door knocking during, 74, 77–79; educational impacts of, 154–55; educator home visits after, 157–60; legal preparations after, 184–85; social media in response to, 111

Lofgren, Zoe, 33–34

Luke 10:38–42, 132–36

LULAC (League of United Latin American Citizens), 82

Lupe. *See* Cervantes, Lupe

lynchings, cruelty of perpetrators, 39–40

Madison, Troy (educator), 151–53, 157, 161–62

marcado ("marked"), 18–19. *See also* hiding

Marcoux, Heather, 178

Marroquín, Naomi (team member), 47–48, 264n2

Martha and Mary, story of, 132–36, 254n28

Martina (volunteer), 177

Matthew 25:35–40, 112–13

medical care: coordinating, 165; for hosted children, 202–5; immigrant women and, 179; mobile clinic for, 180–83

Mein Kampf (Hitler), 216

Melanie (attorney), 115–16

men, fathers, and husbands, immigrant: removal of, effect on families, 32–33, 91–95, 249n14; use of terms, 261n10. *See also* children of detainees; detainees; families of detainees

Mexican Consulate, 138–39

Michael Bianco, Inc., raid on, 25

Michigan: deportation system in, 17–18; US–Mexico border and, 14

Midwest: definition of, 235n1; US–Mexico border and, 14

INDEX

Midwest Precast Concrete (Mount Pleasant, Iowa) worksite raid: agencies involved in, 60–61; children after, 201–5; community-building after, 186–87; community communication during, 59–60, 83–84, 129–30; day of, 83–86, 88–91, 100–101; effects on families, 91–95, 249n14; factory interior after, 89–90, 248n2; factory interior during, 85; food provisions after, 130–31, 186–87, 203–4; helicopters used in, 60–62; media coverage of, 185–86; organizing after, 129–31; in string of ICE raids, 11; vicarious trauma after, 196–97; white managers' reactions during, 90, 249n11; working environment before, 82
military coup, worksite raids compared to, 51
military invasion, worksite raids compared to, 60
Miller, Stephen, 214–16
Mississippi Clarion Ledger, 185
Mississippi worksite raids, 11, 154, 178, 185
mobile clinic, 180–83
mojado, 13–14
Moore, John, 104
Morristown, Tennessee. *See* Southeastern Provision worksite raid
Moses, 79–80
mothers. *See* women, mothers, and wives, immigrant
Mountain View Elementary School, 145–48
Mount Pleasant worksite raid. *See* Midwest Precast Concrete worksite raid
murderers. *See* criminal narrative
Muslim travel ban, 121–24

Mutu, Constantin, 105
Mutz, Diana, 38–39

names of detainees, confusion about, 138–39, 255n36
Naomi. *See* Marroquín, Naomi
National Cattle Congress, 30–31
National Guard Armory, as detention center, 55–58
National Immigration Law Center, 227
National Museum of African American History and Culture, 39–40
natural disasters, as analogies for humanitarian disaster, 45–48
networking, in organizing, 129–30, 136
New Bedford, Massachusetts, ICE raid in, 25
news media: family separations covered by, 104–5; worksite raids covered by, 185–86
New York Times, 185
nicknames (*apodos*), 138–39
Nicole. *See* Novak, Nicole
Nielsen, Kirstjen, 26
North Texas, risks to Latinx drivers in, 69–72. *See also* Isaac (pastor); Load Trail worksite raid
North Texas Immigration Alliance, 119–25
"Not in Custody," 143
Nour. *See* Eidy, Nour
Novak, Nicole, 19–20, 110, 217, 222–23

Obama, Barack: DACA under, 206–7; immigration enforcement under, 9–10; worksite raid use and, 26
Office of Refugee Resettlement (ORR), 201
Ohio Friends in Health, 181–82

INDEX

Ohio worksite raids. *See* Corso's Flower and Garden Centers worksite raid; Fresh Mark worksite raid
O'Neill (Nebraska) worksite raid: community communication and, 62–66; staging of, 62–66; in string of ICE raids, 11; vicarious trauma after, 194–95; violence of, 194
Online Detainee Locator System (ODLS), 141–44, 255n36, 256n37
Operation Desert Storm, 52–53
Operation Streamline, 103
Operation Wagon Train, 25
Operation Wetback, 14, 226
Orchard Green, Texas, 151
organizing: attorneys in, 117–21; churches in, 111–15, 136–37; after Muslim travel ban, 121–24; networking in, 129–30; reporters in, 111; trauma experienced during, 118
ORR (Office of Refugee Resettlement), 201
Overground Railroad, 167–68

Paris, Texas, 67–69, 111–15
Paying the Price: The Impact of Immigration Raids on America's Children (Urban Institute), 63
"perfect" immigrants, 202–3, 204, 205–9, 221–22
Pharis, Marilyn, 42
"*Poderoso de Israel, El*" (song), 79–80
police: confusion in identifying, 67, 76, 78, 247n39; ICE impersonation of, 75; Load Trail raid and, 77–78; at Midwest Precast Concrete raid, 60–61, 85; at Southeastern Provision raid, 56. *See also* ICE
political impasses, 191

Port Clinton, Ohio, 174–75
post-traumatic stress disorder (PTSD), in children of detainees, 86–87
Postville worksite raid. *See* Agriprocessors Inc. worksite raid
president, in use of worksite raids, 26–27. *See also specific presidents*
prisons, searching for detainees in, 140, 142–43
processing, of detainees: facilities for, 62, 64–65; at Postville, 31–33; after Southeastern Provision raid, 55–58
PTSD (post-traumatic stress disorder), in children of detainees, 86–87
public: in deportation, consent of, 21–22, 227; fear of identity theft and, 33; lack of response of, after worksite raids, 108; voters, narratives of worksite raids for, 27–28
public health, immigrant issues in, 14

quilts, 1–3, 213

racehorse theory, 215
racial profiling: detainee lawsuit over, 227; of drivers, 69–72, 245n20; in hypervisibility, 8
Red Sea, 79–80
replacement theory, 215–16
reporters, in organizing after raids, 111–12
research study: description of, 19–20, 239n40; pseudonyms used in, 22–23; role of communities in, 20–21, 239n40
research team: hypervisibility of, 9, 21; racial makeup of, 6. *See also individual members*

INDEX

Reyes, Bella (team member), 3, 200, 203, 209, 214, 216, 219
rideshare system, after Ohio raids, 166, 169–73
role models, 196–97
ruses, used by ICE, 75–76
Ruth (volunteer), 195–96

Sal (volunteer), 170–73
Salem, Ohio, 5–6. *See also* Fresh Mark worksite raid
sanctioned massacres, 188
Sanctuary Movement, 167–68
Sanders, Trish (organizer), 125–26, 129–31, 201
Sandusky worksite raid. *See* Corso's Flower and Garden Centers worksite raid
Sara (detainee), 179–80
Sarah (educator), 159, 243n1
Sattin-Bajaj, Carolyn, 154–55
school. *See* educators
school mobility, after worksite raids, 154–55
Scott (volunteer), 167–70
self-care, 193
September 11, as analogy for worksite raids, 47–48
Serwer, Adam, 39–40
Sessions, Jeff, 101–2, 214–15
single mothers, detention of, 176–80
skin color, in Swift worksite raids, 29
Soboroff, Jacob, 105
social media: biological determinism promoted on, 216; in organizing for Sumner, 111, 113–14; in worksite raid coverage, 175
Social Security numbers, 208
social status, in election of Trump, 38–39
Sonia (nurse), 179

Southeastern Provision (Bean Station, Tennessee) worksite raid: agencies involved in, 56; children of detainees of, 51–52; community communication during, 150; conduct of, 50; detainee processing after, 56–57; detention center for, 55–58; educational impacts of, 154, 155; educator home visits after, 156–60; families of detainees of, 51, 57–58; food provisions after, 132, 156; impetus for, 49, 56–57; lawsuit over, by detainees, 227; legal preparations after, 184; media coverage of, 185; natural disasters as analogies for, 45–48, 243n1; response of educators to, 147–50; roles in organizing after, 133; in string of ICE raids, 10–11; triage after, 58; vicarious trauma after, 192–93
Southern Poverty Law Center, 227
Stacy (Bean Station interviewee), 46–47
sterilization, forced, 217
St. John's Church (Salem, Ohio), 5–6, 12–13, 137
St. Peter's Catholic Church (Morristown, Tennessee), 50, 58, 132, 225
Sumner worksite raid. *See* Load Trail worksite raid
Suriname, 50–51
Swift & Company (multistate) worksite raids, 25, 29, 63, 64
Sylvia (elementary school principal): on feeding families, 132; home visits by, 156–60; meeting with, 146; in response planning, 148–50, 152–53; on support for students, and politics, 161–62; worksite raid compared to September 11 by, 48
Syrian refugees, 126–29

INDEX

tattoos, as search parameter, 143
teachers. *See* educators
Ted (educator), 146
Tennessee worksite raid. *See* Southeastern Provision worksite raid
Texas: deportation system in, 15–17; highways of, 116; in string of ICE raids, 11. *See also* Isaac (pastor); Load Trail worksite raid
Thomas, Ginger, 104
traffic stops, 70–72, 245n20
"traffic stop-to-deportation pipeline," 72
transportation, for released detainees, 166, 169–73. *See also* driving
triage, 58, 132, 137, 195
Trinity Presbyterian Church (Mount Pleasant, Iowa), 81–83, 129–31, 186–87, 203–4
Trish. *See* Sanders, Trish
Troy. *See* Madison, Troy
Trump, Donald: candidacy announcement of, 35–37; cruelty in appeal of, 39–40; dehumanization of immigrants by, 188–89; Dreamers and, 207; executive orders embraced by, 33; immigrant narrative used by, 209–10; immigration enforcement under, 10, 22, 101–6; replacement theory in policies of, 215–16; second inauguration of, 1; white anxiety in election of, 37–40; worksite raids embraced by, 26. *See also* worksite raids; *specific locations*
Tucker, Jay (attorney), 119–25, 184–85
Tyson Foods, 211–12

unemployment benefits, inaccessibility of, 92

US–Mexico border: during COVID-19 pandemic, 211–12; in deportation system, 15–17; public discourse about, 21

vicarious trauma: of attorneys, 195; managing, 196–97; of organizers, 189–90; politics in, 191; research on, 190–91; of volunteers, 192–96
violence: dehumanization and, 188; interpersonal, raids as, 48; during O'Neill raid, 194; public consent in, 21–22; public fear of, leveraging, 44; during worksite raids, 100–101. *See also* cruelty
visibility. *See* hiding; hypervisibility; invisibility
voluntary departure, vs. cost of trial, 95
voters. *See* public

warrants, for immigration violations, 74–75, 76
"wetback," 14
white people: community building with, 186–87; criminal narrative about Latinos and, belief in, 7, 41–44, 160, 186, 209–10; deportation system and, experience of, 13–14, 17–19; distrust of, after worksite raids, 158–59; dominance of, diversity hiring initiatives as threat to, 39; dominance of, immigrants as threat to, 37–40; educators, home visits by, 156–60; in election of Trump, 37–40; genetic inferiority of Latinos and, beliefs about, 3, 215–16, 217, 219–23; infectious disease narrative and, belief in, 209–14; Latinos passing as, 221; number of Latino immigrants and,

white people (*continued*)
believed vs. actual, 7; "perfect" immigrant and, 205; reactions of, during Midwest Precast Concrete raid, 90, 249n11; in replacement theory, 215–16; in traffic stops, 70–72

wives. *See* women, mothers, and wives, immigrant

Wolf, Chad, 212

women, mothers, and wives, immigrant: detention of, 11, 175–80; financial impact on, 32, 92–95; invisibility in public narrative, 134–35; at Midwest Precast Concrete, after raid, 90–91; as "suddenly single" mothers, 92; use of terms, 261n10. *See also* children of detainees; detainees; families of detainees

workers' compensation, inaccessibility of, 92

worksite raids: in 2018 and 2019, 10–12; characteristics of, 19; children without families after, 201–5; community-building after, 186–87; cruelty as reason for, 22, 34–35, 162; as deterrent, 149, 153, 197–98; distrust of white people after, 158–59; educational impacts of, 153–56, 259n19; escaping, 140–41; historic occurrences of, 25; hospitality after, 2–3; lack of public response, 108; media coverage of, 185–86; military invasion as analogy for, 60; narratives crafted for, 27; in Postville, Iowa, 9–10; public consent in, 21–22; remoteness of, 124–25; resistance vs. compliance during, 100–101; secrecy of, 149, 258n9; uncertainty about location, 62–65; uncertainty about targets, 66–67. *See also* Fresh Mark; Midwest Precast Concrete worksite raid; organizing; *specific locations*

writs of habeas corpus, 122–23

Yvonne (Grand Island interviewee), 62–66

Zepeda, Eric, 43

"zero-tolerance" immigration policy, 101–6

Browse more books from **HOPKINS PRESS**

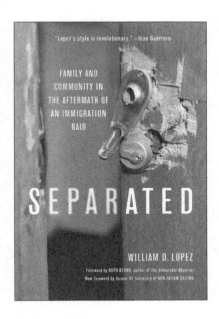
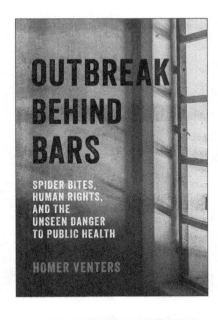

JOHNS HOPKINS UNIVERSITY PRESS

PRESS.JHU.EDU